Masr

Masr

An Egyptian Miscellany

Roger H. Guichard, Jr

WIPF & STOCK · Eugene, Oregon

MASR
An Egyptian Miscellany

Copyright © 2015 Roger H. Guichard Jr. All rights reserved. Except for brief quotations in critical publications or reviews, no part of this book may be reproduced in any manner without prior written permission from the publisher. Write: Permissions. Wipf and Stock Publishers, 199 W. 8th Ave., Suite 3, Eugene, OR 97401.

Wipf & Stock
An Imprint of Wipf and Stock Publishers
199 W. 8th Ave., Suite 3
Eugene, OR 97401

www.wipfandstock.com

ISBN 13: 978-1-4982-3107-7

Manufactured in the U.S.A.   12/21/2020

For Martha

Contents

Preface | ix
Glossary of Arabic Terms | xi

1 The Tour | 1
2 The Nineteen Eighties | 10
3 The Opera House | 22
4 The Oases | 28
5 The Flame Trees of Dokki | 49
6 Serabit el-Khadem | 52
7 Wadi Natroun | 69
8 Cairo on Foot | 75
9 David Roberts | 89
10 Malaysia | 95
11 The Meeting | 104
12 The Movies | 108
13 Al-Andalus | 113
14 Democracy in Egypt | 138
15 Budapest | 147
16 The Seminar | 160
17 Lake Nasser | 166
18 Siwa | 187
19 George Herbert Walker Bush | 198
20 Telecom 99 | 203
21 The Zabbaleen | 225
22 The City | 234

Preface

Visitors have often remarked on the celebrated light of Egypt. There is something about the soft diffusion of sunlight in the country that makes it visually special. Beginning in the early nineteenth century a combination of that light and the new, more sensitive technology of lithography conspired together to allow artists to capture with unprecedented fidelity the country's monuments, Pharaonic as well as Islamic.

But there is another way in which the word light captures the reality of Egypt. In Arabic it is said that the blood of a people is either "light" or "heavy": *damuhum khafif* or *damuhum thaqil*, an Arabic speaker will say. Where the blood of others in the region could be said to be heavy, that of the Egyptians is emphatically light and it always seems to have been that way. Here, the word serves as a proxy for "cheerful" or "humorous" or "optimistic." They have even corrupted the classical Arabic of the comparison by pronouncing the word for "heavy" as *ti'il* instead of *thaqil*, "lightening" the word by changing the weighty *qaf* of classical Arabic into the *alif* of the colloquial language. Egyptians will do things their own way and they always have.

This essential optimism has allowed them to avoid some of the darker chapters that have characterized the histories of other countries in the region. Egypt has had its share of traumas in recent years with episodes of revolution and violence, some of which are detailed in the pieces that follow. But even with the burning down of most of European Cairo by the mob in 1952, the disastrous Six-day War in 1967, the assassination of Sadat in 1981, the riot of the conscripts in 1986, massacre by Islamists in Luxor in 1992, and the recent episodes of political and social upheaval, the essential buoyancy of the Egyptian people always seems to shine through. They have endured tough times before and will survive these latest traumas as well.

Some attribute this to Egypt's cosmopolitanism and its transformation in the nineteenth and twentieth centuries by the relatively enlightened tyranny of Mohammed Ali, followed by the British and French condominium. Others see a more fundamental cause: a kind of hubris, born of Egypt's long history and pride as a country fundamentally different from, and better than, other countries. This pride has somehow survived spasms of violence and upheaval, the population growth, economic collapse, and political uncertainty that today threaten to reduce most Egyptians to the status of little more than paupers in their own land. There is a timelessness about their response and a refusal to subscribe to the most extreme solutions to their conundrums that stands out.

In the book that follows I have tried to capture some of the fundamental Egyptian buoyancy and optimism. But I didn't have to try very hard. The attitude is infectious and anyone who has lived for any length of time in the country is in danger of succumbing. The pieces, some long and some short, reflect a sometimes wry, occasionally humorous, but always affectionate view of an essentially unchanging Egypt. They were originally not written for publication, but simply to chronicle my own exposure to the country, warts and all. That exposure was for a total of ten years in the last two decades of the twentieth century, working for American consulting firms on large telecommunications projects. That may seem a limited vantage point from which to view to the country. But the explosive diffusion of technologies that connect people has given even greater scope to the Egyptians' natural garrulousness and loquacity. In the long run there may be hope in that.

Other assignments in the Middle East, Africa, and the Indian subcontinent tended to highlight, among other things, what made Egyptians different from everyone else. In some of the other places there was the possibility of actually accomplishing something that made the work there, perhaps, more rewarding. But they weren't nearly as enjoyable. It was the irrepressible good humor of Egyptians that made it so.

Incidentally, the country is known locally as *Masr*, the word derived from the Arabic triliteral root meaning "to build, settle, civilize." To most natives "Egypt," probably derived from the word "Copt" in its earlier Christian phase, is not only unknown but unpronounceable.

Glossary of Arabic Terms

Ablaq	Piebald; a style of building or decoration, consisting of horizontal bands of red stone alternating with white; sometimes painted
'Aish	Pocket bread, either *baladi* or *shami*
Al-Ahram	Literally, "The Pyramids"; name of the flagship of Cairo daily newspapers
'Amm	Literally "uncle"; often applied to older, uneducated men
'Arabiya	A vehicle, in Egypt an automobile
Bahri	Literally "riverine"; applied to one branch of the Mamluks
Bakshish	A gratuity
Baladi	Literally, "country" as in "country bumpkin"; a kind of coarse pocket bread
Bawwab	A doorkeeper or guardian
Bedu	A Bedouin
Beit	A dwelling, describing a house, apartment, or tent
Birket	A pond, of which there were once several in Cairo
Birseem	Clover, a common fodder for animals in Egypt
Burgi	Literally "of the citadel"; applied to a second branch of Mamluks
Eid al-Adha	The Greater Bairam, a feast celebrated during the Hajj
Eid al-Fitr	The Lesser Bairam, a feast celebrated at the end of Ramadan

Fellah(een)	Farmer or peasant, specifically from the Delta
Fellaha	A female *fellah*
Fool medammes	Broad beans, the staple diet of Egypt
Forn	An oven
Gallabiya	An ample gown, often wide-sleeved, worn by *fellaheen* and *sa'idis*
Goha	A simple-minded peasant, but dumb like a fox
Hara (Haret)	A neighborhood or quarter in Fatimid Cairo
Hijab	The veil covering the head and neck, not the full face-veil; common in Egypt
Iftar	Breakfast, often referring to the meal breaking the fast
Ikhwan	Literally "brothers"; often referring to the Muslim Brotherhood
Istiraha	A rest house or inn
Jebel	A mountain
Karkaday	A refreshing drink made from hibiscus and sold on the streets in Egypt
Khalig	The canal from the Nile that once formed the western boundary of Fatimid Cairo
Khamsin	Literally "fifty"; refers to wind that blows from the Western Desert in the spring in Egypt
Khatkhuda	An Ottoman military title, often assumed by Mamluks; occasionally appears in vulgar form of *kikhya*
Khawaga	A schoolmaster or pedant; a term often applied to foreigners
Kufiya	A kerchief worn by peasants, often checked black or red and white
Mamluk	Literally "owned"; refers to caste of white slaves in Egypt
Masr	The Arabic name of Egypt

Nabataean	An ancient Arab people who once occupied northern Arabia and southern Syria; known primarily for the city of Petra
Qarafa	A cemetery
Qarafatain	Dual form of the word, referring to the Northern Cemetery and Southern Cemetery in Cairo
Ra'is	Literally, a chief or head; often a ship's captain
Sa'idi	A farmer or peasant, specifically from Upper Egypt
Sha'bi	Popular, from "the people"
Shami	Literally "Syrian"; refers to white bread as opposed to *baladi*
Shari'	A street
Shebab	A youth
Shisha	A water pipe
Sufragi	A waiter or steward
Suq	A market
Ta'mia	Bean paste, generally deep-fried
Tekiyya	A Sufi hospice
Wadi	A valley
Wafd	The political party called after the delegation that Egypt tried, unsuccessfully, to send to the peace conference in 1918
Wikala	A caravanserai or rest house
Zabbal(een)	A garbage collector
Zawiya	A small, informal Muslim house of prayer

1

The Tour

"*Aiwa, ya bulbul.*" Gallal was bellowing at the cop in the dusty little crossroads. We were looking for the road to Fayoum. A literal translation of the phrase might have been "Hark, oh nightingale," but literal translations never really worked with the colloquial language in Egypt. Gallal was looking for the road to Fayoum since it was the first stop on our tour of the accounting units of Upper Egypt. Oweis would have known, since he lived in Fayoum, but he had gone ahead and would meet us at his farm. Oweis was a typical employee of the Egyptian telephone company, a midlevel civil servant for whom the job was a sinecure. His real interest was his farm. He was also one of Sami's boys.

Sami was the general manager of finance in the company, and he was riding in the front seat of the van next to the driver. That was the seat of honor, and it was the same all over the Middle East. The king was always seen riding in the front seat of his Rolls when he arrived at some state function, coverage of which constituted most of the local television fare in Saudi Arabia. It was the democratic thing to do in that most autocratic of countries, a remnant of the old Arab egalitarianism. Later, when we visited the accounting units, the managers would vacate their chairs and Sami would sit at their desks in their place.

Sami took care of his boys, dispensing the little favors that made the difference in the company world. A man could double his monthly salary by attendance at special meetings or service on special committees. The American vice president of a large technology firm, in Egypt to negotiate a contract for a computerized identification system, finally gave up when he realized that the committee evaluating the proposal had no incentive to come to a decision and so disband itself. At a higher level, interlocking directorships were a regular source of income for a well-placed man.

There was nothing wrong with what Sami did. He was just taking care of his boys. Gallal was the younger man who was seen as Sami's eventual replacement. Like most Egyptians he liked to laugh. He was also a bit of a decision maker. That was unusual enough to make him stand out. The short-term replacement for Sami, and the man who actually replaced him when he retired a year later, was Mousa. That was a little surprising since Mousa was a Copt. But, to the company's credit, they promoted him and he was widely recognized, even by the Muslims, as one of their best general managers. Beneath the surface calm, of course, the old tensions still simmered. It was the kind of deep-seated animosity that could break out in another *Zawiyat al-Hamra*. There, a Christian tending plants in the Cairo neighborhood of that name reportedly spilled water on a Muslim on the balcony below, or maybe it was the other way around. Some said it really had to do with rival plans to build a mosque or church in the area. At any rate, by the time they restored order the Kalashnikovs had come out and many were dead.

A question about the incident illustrated the importance of context in learning a language. The word *zawiya* could be found in Hans Wehr's *A Dictionary of Modern Written Arabic*, the best Arabic–English dictionary in the market, and there was a learned discussion of the term in Brill's *Encyclopedia of Islam*, with the information that it originally applied to a monk's cell and was later associated with Sufism. But nothing equaled the immediacy of asking the Egyptian chief accountant what it meant and learning that it was now a small, informal mosque where you could just pop in for a prayer, so to speak, and that they were scattered all over Cairo. Colloquial Egyptian Arabic was littered with words you learned only by using them. The *aiwa* of Gallal's salutation was actually *ay wallahi*, or "yes, by God," and was the normal conversational word for "yes," minus any consideration of God. We had learned *na'am* for "yes" in classical Arabic but in Egypt it was used politely and was the equivalent of "I beg your pardon?" There was an even more rustic "yes" in colloquial Egyptian: *aaaaaaah*. It defied any etymology.

Mousa had not come with us on this trip since someone had to mind the store in Sami's absence. In fact, with one exception, we were all Muslims in the van. I was the *khawaga*, the foreigner or teacher or tax collector under whose yoke Egyptians had groaned for millennia. It was Sami's word, and it bespoke a kind of good-natured tolerance. But the "*ya khawaga*" with which he usually greeted me—preceded by the vocative particle that is still a living part of Arabic—always had a little edge to it. I was not one of them and the word was a constant reminder of the difference. All of our conversations were, of course, in Arabic.

Another one of Sami's boys was Mahmoud. He was seated in the back of the van. A spare, tightlipped little man with a pencil-thin mustache who smoked cigarettes in an ivory holder, he looked like a classic silent-movie villain. In five years working with the company I never discovered what, if anything, he did, except to assent with alacrity to whatever Sami said. He always called Sami *ya basha* or *ya bey*, the Turkish honorifics still widely used in Egypt. Also with us in the van was Abdel Rahman, another one of Sami's boys, and another one whose duties were difficult to define. Like all of them he was friendly but in a reserved sort of way. The last of our complement was the driver, *amm* Qabeel. *Amm* was Arabic for "uncle" and was used affectionately with older, uneducated men. Qabeel was the Arabic name for Cain (Habeel was Abel). But even though he was only a driver, *amm* Qabeel participated in our discussions and was accepted as a full-fledged member of the group. He was also, arguably, its most important member.

The road to Upper Egypt was the standard two-lane track that ran alongside the Nile through every village between Cairo and the Sudanese border at Wadi Halfa. Over it passed the commerce of Egypt, from carts pulled by horses, bullocks, and donkeys to the omnipresent Peugeot 504 station wagons and American Mack trucks loaded with tons of sheet steel. They often came together and the accidents were horrific. The hulks lay by the side of the road, some of them hardly recognizable as having been vehicles at all. *Amm* Qabeel was the man who kept us out of trouble, and in the two weeks on the trip we had many near misses. The van was a medium sized Toyota and none of us wore seat belts. *Amm* Qabeel and Sami were in the front seat with nothing between them and their maker but an inexpensive copy of the Qur'an. The rest of us were only marginally better off. But, thanks to *amm* Qabeel, we returned in one piece. He later had an accident in Cairo and broke both femurs. When I left Egypt he was walking painfully with two canes, but his irrepressible good humor was still intact. "*Ya amm* Guichard," he would shout across the parking lot, waving one of the canes at me.

I was in Egypt on that October morning because I worked for Arthur D. Little and ADL was the prime contractor on a huge USAID-funded telecommunications project. Egypt had one of the lowest penetration rates in the world and it could take as long as thirteen years to get a telephone. The sector was a natural for aid, especially since there was a direct correlation between the efficiency of the telecommunications system and the level of foreign direct investment in a country. In the 1970s representatives of international companies in Egypt had to fly to Cyprus on the weekends to make telephone calls. It was crazy. The project had first been proposed in the middle of the decade by that ultimate fixer, Adnan Khashoggi, and somehow

Bruno Kreisky, the prime minister of Austria, had become involved. But it really took off after Camp David in 1979 and the beginning of the large-scale American involvement in Egypt.

Everyone else was there too. The Europeans were interested and had put together a consortium of Siemens Germany, Siemens Austria, and Thomson CSF of France. No one could understand why a little player like Austria was involved, although it may have been the Kreisky connection. The European aid was tied to their national suppliers, like everyone else's. But it was also tied to the terms of the American aid, and the Europeans had to offer a combination of grants and soft loans that brought the overall interest rate below an agreed-upon figure. And they had to meet the American switch price. That was a sore point because AT&T came in low on the switches, assuming they could make up the difference on the network or outside plant. But they lost the outside plant contract to Ford Aerospace and the switch prices were locked in. The Japanese were also there, financing smaller projects in the Canal Zone, the funds coming from their Overseas Economic Cooperation Fund. The Swedish manufacturer, L. M. Ericsson, had been in Egypt long before the others and was doing its best to keep the business alive, although their local manufacturing facility was badly out of date.

Those were the big players. But there were also the World Bank, the British, the Italians, and even the Finns. The whole world seemed to be lined up to lend money to the Egyptians. It was the kind of attention that led inevitably to corruption, and we later learned that one of the undersecretaries in the ministry had been caught in a sting accepting a bribe from the Ericsson representative. The latter was a tall Egyptian known when I was there as the two-meter Copt. After they caught him they found a satchel full of money in the chicken coop in the undersecretary's yard. But I think this was an exception and most involved did not succumb to the temptation. The project was also very interesting from a financial point of view and there were few things I didn't see in five years on the job.

One of those things was *not*, however, the development of an efficient, commercially-oriented telephone company. The Arab Republic of Egypt Telecommunications Organization, or ARETO, was a medium-sized company by our standards. But it had a huge workforce with a ratio of employees to lines in service about ten times our own. Like other public-sector entities in Egypt it was a government employer of last resort and was growing with every graduating class from Cairo University or 'Ain Shams. ADL's responsibility was to help ARETO write the technical specifications for the American portion of the project, assist with contract award, and oversee the installation of the switches and outside plant. For the supervisory work there was a subcontractor, Continental Telephone, an Atlanta-based operating company. The project eventually amounted to about $250 million in soft loans and grants to finance switches in Cairo and Alexandria, with the cable networks to connect them to each other and to the European switches and networks.

But there was another part of the project, and that was where we came in. With the privatization emphasis of the Reagan years just beginning, USAID had attached covenants to the loans and grants requiring ARETO to wean itself of inefficient practices and excess employees. There was hardly an area of their operations that didn't need improvement: they were poorly organized, poorly managed, and hardly planned at all. The sequence seemed to be decide, implement, *then* plan. Their accounting systems were like something out of Dickens. In an early report they were described as "primitive" and this caused an uproar, the translation of the word into Arabic suggesting a relation to prehistoric man. We smoothed their ruffled feathers by steering them away from the "crude" or "little evolved" meanings of the word, and towards the one that spoke of "original, primary." But prehistoric was not far from the truth. The books of account were two meters wide, with a meter each for the debits and the credits. Every unimportant detail was recorded, but the really useful information, like the type of equipment, was not. The inventory systems were chaotic and the stock—when they could find it—was old and most of it obsolete. In short, USAID had determined that ARETO would become a modern company managed on private-sector principles. Arthur D. Little was the instrument by which this transformation would take place.

In retrospect it seems obvious that we were bound to fail, if only because we had no power to enforce compliance. Not only was ARETO an employer of last resort, but telephone service was considered the subsidized right of every Egyptian. Everyone with a telephone had 1,500 free calls a year, and it didn't matter whether the call was for a minute or an hour. And on the infrequent occasions when people were connected they talked for hours. It was useless to argue that the average Egyptian didn't *have* a telephone, and that the subsidy was largely nonexistent. The telephone density in Egypt in 1979 was about one per hundred as compared with seventy per hundred in the United States. But the Minister of Communications, who was to be the most durable member of the government over the next fifteen years, would not keep his job by bowing to the demands of a foreign aid agency. USAID held the whip hand, in this case the power of the purse. But it was responsible, simultaneously, to move the money through the pipeline and ensure compliance with the conditions precedent. The two were mutually exclusive, and the result was predictable. The money flowed and ADL rather than ARETO, was generally blamed for the shortfalls.

The Egyptians have been around for a while and they knew that eventually they would outlast us. In the end, they got their switches and networks and we made sure they accounted for them properly. We increased their knowledge of international finance and often acted as their spokesman in dealings with foreign lenders. But we did not make them a commercially-viable entity. We were a management appendage to an equipment contract. At 10 percent of the equipment price, we were about average for these projects. Shortly after we arrived ARETO became ARENTO, the Arab Republic of Egypt *National* Telecommunications Organization, the change brought about by an act of the Peoples' Assembly. It was supposed to free them from government interference. But it was largely cosmetic and consisted of inserting the word *qawmia* into their Arabic title. It flowed through to the English acronym.

The first stop on the tour was at Oweis's "farm" where we would spend the night. It wasn't really a farm but a walled compound that included a two-story house with a small orchard in the back. There were several trees in the orchard, including a grapefruit, and I had casually remarked that I liked grapefruit. So Oweis had gotten up early the next morning and picked some of the fruit. But none of the Egyptians, including Oweis, knew how to eat it. I told them to halve it with a knife. They did and tried the flesh, but made terrible faces. So I said that some people sweetened it with sugar. But even with a liberal application of the national drug of Egypt, they pronounced the grapefruit inedible.

We were off by mid-morning and traveled unhurriedly. The next city on our itinerary was Beni Suef and we arrived early in the afternoon. We paid a visit to the accounting unit where a little business was conducted by Sami, sitting in the manager's chair. When we arrived at a unit the manager would usually be on the phone, talking on one or more of the several variously-colored instruments arranged on his desk like bowling trophies. A mark of status was to talk on as many as you could at the same time. After this work, or what passed for work, we would generally retire to the ARENTO *istiraha*, or rest house, where we took our ease. The sight of grown men, senior executives at that, padding around the common room in their pajamas at three o'clock in the afternoon was hardly the image of ARENTO we were trying to cultivate. We drank tea and talked about anything and everything: America, Egypt, business, the weather, Islam, Christianity.

The mornings were typically spent on the road and we had lunch along the way. It cost next to nothing. A loaf of whole-grain *baladi* bread—not the bland *shami* version—with the halves filled with *fool medammes*, or Egyptian broad beans, cost about twenty piasters, or fifteen cents. It was enough in the way of carbohydrates and protein to sustain a man for the day. Add a little white cheese, pickles and *ta'amia,* or deep-fried bean paste, and it was more than enough. In the evening we went to dinner, either at a restaurant or one of the telecommunications engineers' clubs where the food was plentiful and filling. Dinner was a display of the extraordinary ability of the average Egyptian to eat. The per capita consumption of wheat in Egypt is the highest in the world, and they can put it away like no people I have seen. The meal would begin with a cubic foot of macaroni, hewn in great chunks out of a general mass like blocks from the limestone quarries of Turah. This would be followed by rice, potatoes and meat. It was accompanied by the same *baladi* loaves we had for lunch. After the meal there was more tea at the *istiraha*. We generally turned in early.

It became obvious early in the trip that I lacked lounging attire for the long afternoons. When we left I was wearing Levi's, Sami having observed that he noticed that the *youth* in America wore jeans. So, after dinner on the second evening we all went to the *suq* where we selected my *gallabiya.* Like everything else with this group it was a communal decision with each one offering his opinion on the correct pattern and color. We eventually selected a very *sa'idi*, or Upper Egyptian, striped garment with wide sleeves. I still have it.

And so the days went, punctuated by the timeless rhythms of Egypt. There is a photo of us throwing stones at dates in the trees somewhere south of Beni Suef. When they were ripe the dates came in great clusters, attached to the tree by fibrous orange-colored stems as thick as a man's wrist. There were many varieties and they appeared in the markets in Egypt in the harvest season in mounds of yellow, orange, and red. Bought green, that is, red, yellow, or orange, they ripened quickly and if they were kept uncovered fruit flies soon filled the house. They could also be bought at any time of the year in a thick sugary mass. In Upper Egypt they were spread on mats to dry and later appeared in the market as desiccated, unappetizing-looking lumps. But moistened with a little water or saliva they were edible. The stems were laid on the road and the weight of passing vehicles separated the individual fibers so that they could be worked into mats.

We moved steadily south, first to el-Miniya, then Mellawi and then Assiut. At each financial unit we would repeat the experience of Beni Suef, Sami occupying the manager's chair and fielding questions from the local staff. Most of the discussions concerned the current account, which each unit maintained with headquarters. Assiut, an Islamist stronghold, was also heavily Christian and the two phenomena were perhaps related. But these Muslim gentlemen made sure that I saw all the Christian sights, from the spare and clean monasteries cut into the limestone cliffs a thousand feet above the Nile Valley, to the Lillian Trasher orphanage in the city itself. Lillian Trasher was a lady from Indiana who founded a Christian orphanage in 1911, and it was still going strong. Someone later said it was the largest orphanage in the world. A man by the name of Girgis—that Christian name *par excellence* in Egypt—showed us around. Here was the dormitory, there were the workshops and over there was the dining hall. He was conducting the tour in Arabic but broke into occasional pidgin English: the food was served cafeteria style, "*ya'ani*, help yourself." The statement and the man and the setting were all Egyptian, through and through.

From Assiut we moved on through Sohag and Qena to Luxor. Qena was memorable for the only eunuch I ever saw, a Copt who worked for ARENTO. He was tall and lean with wide hips, narrow shoulders, and long slender hands. His beardless face was very plastic and capable of a wide range of expression. Eunuchs had a long history among the Arabs and Turks, and the Byzantines before them, often occupying very powerful positions. They could be unnaturally cruel and despotic.

Luxor represented a kind of halfway station on the trip. It had been a week of entertaining conversation, interesting sights, and an extended view into the everyday lives of the executives we worked with. But I was ready for a beer and the company of my own kind. At first, they were suspicious. Why did I want to leave them? And what was there to see in Luxor? It was all I could do to keep one of them coming along as a chaperone. I made a short visit to the Luxor museum, since I had already seen it. Then I went where I really wanted to go, which was to the Etap Hotel for a beer. There was the usual collection of Europeans in the outside bar and the Stellas—brewed in Egypt under license from Amstel Corporation—were tall and cold. Aswan peanuts were famous throughout Egypt, and I ate plate after plate. When I returned to the *istiraha* after dark they were outraged, like the parents of some wayward teenager. Where had I been and what had I been doing? No one checked my breath (the thought of alcohol would never have crossed their minds) but they were clearly concerned. I turned in, having stored away enough in the way of forbidden fruit to last for the rest of the trip. We left the Etap and the Europeans and the Stellas behind the next morning, on our way to Edfu and then Aswan.

Aswan was a part of Nubia and the head of the accounting unit was dark. It was not the brown of Egyptians like Sadat, but black like a ripe eggplant. There was something different about the city, more than the heat and the languor and the cataracts. The whitewash on the exchange building seemed whiter and the people seemed darker than anywhere farther north. It was Africa in a way that the rest of Egypt was not. We made the obligatory tour of the High Dam, of the monument to the Egyptians and Russians who had built it, and there was pride in the breasts of these particular Egyptians at the accomplishment. Forgotten for the moment was the fact that it proved to be a mixed blessing, increasing the salinity of the soil, raising the water table, and the incidence of Bilharzia. The year-round supply of irrigation water meant that farmers spent several hours a day thigh-deep in the medium where the parasite thrived.

After a brief meeting with the accountants in Aswan our tour was complete. We had showed the flag in Upper Egypt, met all the accountants, occupied their desks briefly, conducted a little business, and were now ready to depart. We were probably 600 miles and three days from Cairo. But if the journey down to Upper Egypt had been a marathon, the return was a sprint. We made only one detour, to the *suq* at Akhmim, famous for its cotton fabrics. Otherwise we drove in long unbroken stages, often into the night. *Amm* Qabeel earned his pittance on this part of the trip. I don't think anyone was paid a per diem, so there was no reason to delay. Later, in Pakistan, accountants would stop for tea in Attock at the confluence of the Indus and the Kabul, since it allowed an extra hour of the day to slip by, and an extra quarter of the allowance.

Surprisingly, we didn't get on each other's nerves. There were continual discussions and they often became wild and disorderly, with everyone shouting at once. We settled into an odd rhythm, with each of us responsible for a little ditty in Arabic. Mine was "*salamtu li'na*," or "may His peace be upon us." Sami's was "*hafazak Ullah*," or "God keep you." We all waited patiently for our cues, and when Sami ended the litany with the final "*hafazak Ullah*," we all burst out laughing.

Two weeks after we had set out we arrived in Ma'adi, the suburb south of Cairo where the *khawagas* lived. We were all tired and soiled and, without a decent shower in any of the *istirahas*, we were caked with fine dust. I invited them in, which was the Egyptian thing to do. But they were just as anxious as I to be at home and they declined. That was fortunate because I don't think I could have taken another afternoon of tea and polite conversation. I was ready for anther Stella.

2

The Nineteen Eighties

The decade of the eighties was a dramatic time to be in Egypt. First, there was the assassination of Sadat in October of 1981, coming as much of a shock to the expatriate community in Cairo as to the rest of the world. Sadat had become the darling of Washington and Hollywood after the peace treaty with Israel, more popular by far in the United States than in his own country. But beneath the surface sophistication, the tailored suits and Gucci shoes that, by comparison, made Jimmy Carter look like the peanut farmer that he was, in his heart of hearts Sadat himself was a *fellah*, an Egyptian farmer from Mit abul Kom in the Delta.

In many respects he was a remarkable and courageous man and it could be said that he was martyred for his beliefs. He was certainly gutsy and the expulsion of the Russians in 1972 was an impulsive and—on the face of it—irrational act, typical of the man. There he was, in the unpopular period of no war and no peace, under mounting domestic pressure to act, and the Soviets seemed the key to his military option. They were everywhere and during the war of attrition Russian technicians manned SAM batteries and Russian pilots flew combat missions over the canal. Yet, on July 5th of that year Sadat announced that the Soviet military mission was terminated: the advisors were to leave and all equipment was to become the property of Egypt.

Within a month twenty thousand Russians were gone. To the surprise of everyone—most notably the Israelis—the Egyptians held their own in the October War that followed just over a year later. The Russians, for other reasons, were not missed. They were arrogant and kept to themselves, two things the Egyptians never liked, and they were notoriously tight-fisted. Russians would buy individual oranges in the *suq*, to the amusement and contempt of Egyptians who never bought anything except by the kilo. After the collapse of the Soviet Union, however, they were back. The apartment building in Zamalek was full of Russians, teenaged boys with New York Yankee ball caps worn backwards, and girls featuring green fingernail polish. Their parents worked for *Aeroflot,* which now offered direct flights between Cairo and Chicago. And this time they seemed to have money, judging by the cars they drove.

If leadership in the region has since passed into the hands of calculating midgets, Sadat was an impulsive giant. But beneath the popular figure seen in the West there were serious problems brewing. He was unable to prevent corruption in his own family and, like many men whose power and repute grow too quickly he couldn't, or wouldn't, tolerate contradictory views. He became imperious and unyielding, too fond of talking about his friend Jimmy and his friend Henry and too ready to lock up anyone who disagreed with him. When he died he was already a spent force. The opening to Israel stands as his greatest achievement, but it is fortunate for his reputation that he exited the scene before a combination of hubris and indifference tarnished it irreparably.

American commentators observed that Egypt changed after the assassination. But that showed that they didn't understand the country, either before or afterwards. Yes, Sadat embodied a hope for the future, for the end to the millennia-old "Arab-Israeli dispute." We referred to it as if it were something out of Genesis, a hoary conundrum older than time. Both the Egyptians and the Jews *had* been around for a while. But this particular problem was a twentieth-century political problem created by twentieth-century political people. And such were the forces arrayed against a solution that it would surely be the twenty-first century before it was resolved. The hope that Sadat embodied probably had more to do with America than with Egypt or Israel. It seemed part of that old-time religion with its biblical resonance and there even seemed a tie to the civil-rights movement in the United States, to "Let my people go" and "We shall overcome".

It was no accident that an evangelical American president was the moving force behind Camp David. But if religion lay behind this step toward reconciliation, it would later play a more controversial role in our approach to the Middle East. Forces were gathering in both the United States and Israel—in a kind of unholy holy alliance—that would fly from the Christianity of Jimmy Carter to the fire and brimstone of the Old Testament. Sinai was one thing, but the Land of Israel was another thing entirely. It was God's land, and any concession in the interests of peace would be visited with damnation if not worse. And then there was always Armageddon to look forward to, although in the end only the Christians would be saved. Presumably there was still time for the Jews, and the Israelis, to see the error of their ways.

The Egyptians had enough of war, now that they recovered their self-respect with the crossing of the canal in 1973. But there was no groundswell of support in Egypt for this particular peace. When the Israelis complained that all the old bureaucratic strictures against full diplomatic relations had not been removed at the stroke of a pen they revealed their naiveté. Popular Egyptian hostility to Israel was deep and abiding, both matter-of-fact and fantastic. There was the historic enmity between the two religions, exacerbated by twentieth-century political developments. Early in the century the Zionists had insinuated themselves into the good graces of the hated British and gained their backing in an enterprise that resulted in the virtual dispossession of the occupants of Arab Palestine. But the Egyptian attitude was accompanied by prejudices, old and new, that gave it the tincture of unreality. The popularity of the televised production of that crude forgery, *The Protocols of the Elders of Zion*, shown during Ramadan, was evidence of Egyptian susceptibility to western demagogy on the issue. But how would they know it was a forgery? It made sense and, anyway, the ability of the average Egyptian to separate fact from fiction in a product of the West (the *Protocols* was a creation of the Czarist secret police) was impossible given a chasm of language and perspective.

Under the circumstances, a cold peace was probably the best that could be expected and it seemed unlikely that real accommodation with Israel would come any time soon, Camp David or no Camp David. To a greater degree than in other Arab countries, Jews in Egypt had been accepted over the years, becoming prominent in society and commerce before political Zionism made further assimilation impossible. The *nakba*, or catastrophe, in 1948 marked the end of that relative tolerance. And the old Qur'anic strictures (in the A. Yusuf Ali translation), stemming from the hostility of the Jews of Medina to the Prophet and his new dispensation, were there to fill the void when it all came apart:

> v. 64. The Jews say: "God's hand is tied up." Be *their* hands
> Tied up and be they accursed for the (blasphemy) they utter.
> Nay, both His hands are widely outstretched:
> He giveth and spendeth (of His bounty) as He pleaseth.
> But the revelation that cometh to thee from God
> Increaseth in most of them their obstinate rebellion and blasphemy.
> Amongst them we have placed enmity
> And hatred until the Day of Judgment.
> Every time they kindle the fire of war, God doth extinguish it;
> But they (ever) strive to do mischief on earth.

And God loveth not those who do mischief.

To the Egyptian Muslim there was nothing prejudicial about the passage, just the truth as it appeared in God's holy book. And the Israelis ignored the part of Camp David that dealt with the Palestinians. That was the insurance policy Sadat attached to his solo performance, the link to his Arab constituency, the concession he managed to wring from Begin (not that Begin had the slightest intention of honoring it) and the key to a wider peace. In the end it wasn't enough to save him.

When the assassination took place in Nasr City that October morning we all hustled back to Ma'adi and hunkered down. The embassy reactivated the warden system that had fallen into abeyance and we had a few meetings before it fell by the wayside again. When we returned to work a week later I spoke with the chief accountant, searching for what I hoped would be adequate words to express my sympathy for Egypt's loss. But he only snorted "for what"!? He was not an unfeeling man and later tearfully broke the news of the Challenger disaster to me. But Sadat's death didn't mean much to him or to the average Egyptian. While it was a sad ending for the man—and the story had all the elements of a Greek tragedy—it was not felt to be a national calamity for Egypt.

The most immediate impact of Camp David, other than opening the tap of American economic and military aid, was the return to Egypt of the Sinai Peninsula. It was never clear why the Israelis gave it back while clinging tenaciously to a place like the Gaza Strip. Northern Sinai is a barren waste but the south contains one of the most dramatic landscapes on the planet, partly because of its biblical associations. That seemed to be even more reason for the Israelis to keep it. And strategically it had been the closing of the Straits of Tiran by Nasser that was the proximate cause of war in 1967. You didn't have to subscribe to the popular view of the Israelis as supermen to acknowledge the guts and improvisation of their performance in the conflict that followed. It was long before America had armed them to the teeth and they hurtled down the east coast of Sinai in requisitioned bread trucks. They carefully bated the trap into which Nasser, already bogged down in the morass of the Yemen, obligingly stepped, which gave the lie to the notion that it was a just war. But the Egyptians surrendered without much of a fight, although it was hard to fight without air cover in a place like the Sinai. The Israelis surrounded the outmaneuvered *fellaheen*, killed some in cold blood, took the shoes of the rest and invited them to walk back to Cairo. Many didn't make it.

In the sixteen years the Israelis held Sinai they conducted archeological research in the historic sites, built a few hotels, and managed the coral reefs that contained some of the most spectacular collections of marine life on the planet. One of the fears about the treaty was that an ecological disaster would follow the return of the reefs to the Egyptians. But it was the Israelis who left behind an environmental mess—mounds of trash—when they pulled out, purposely, according to the Egyptians. They were a tough little people and could be nasty when they wanted, so the charge would not have been out of character. I didn't know if the allegation was true but we certainly saw the trash.

We visited Sinai shortly after the turnover in April of 1983. It was a ten-hour drive from Cairo to St. Catherine's Monastery in the central massif in the south of the peninsula. The initial part of the trip was to Suez on the canal, just over an hour away. The tunnel under the canal, built by the Japanese, had just been opened and at first we went through in convoy, waiting for enough cars to make up a party before being escorted to the other side by an army vehicle. Later, cars were permitted to go through individually as they arrived. That was before a problem appeared with the concrete used in the structure, and it was back to the old convoy system.

After the canal we turned south and the scenery improved, but it still had a sameness that made the drive monotonous. *Aiyun Musa*, or Moses's Wells, sounded more interesting than they looked, an area of brackish water surrounded by untended palm trees. Palms can look like the epitome of desolation if the lower branches are not removed on a regular basis. In the United States we were used to the sight of untrimmed palms, with their skirt of gray leaves fringing the tree. Here, it indicated abandonment. A palm required a great deal of attention, from a kind of "bundling" of the stamen and pistil in the mating season to the wrapping of clusters of young fruit in plastic bags as they matured. Those two staples of Arab husbandry, the date palm and the camel, both required human assistance to reproduce effectively. Like the palms, camels were not very good at it.

Further south were the *Hamam Faraoun*, or "Pharaoh's Baths," celebrated since antiquity for their healing properties. But they had an unpleasant sulfurous odor and the area was full of trash. As the roads in Sinai improved increasing numbers of Egyptians came to the beaches on the eastern shore of the Gulf. They were better than those nearer the canal. They were nothing like the magnificent white-sand beaches on the Mediterranean coast, declared off-limits by the military for reasons of security. Those represented a gold mine and half the population of northern Europe would come if the beaches were developed. However here you had to be careful because of mines. Several children had recently been killed while playing with devices they found on the beach.

Most of Egypt's four billion barrels of proven reserves of oil were in the Gulf of Suez, and the platforms accompanied us as we moved south. That made the Israeli willingness to relinquish the peninsula even more puzzling. Many were flaring gas and they constituted a kind of beacon at night. Occasionally, large tankers moved offshore. But the canal would not take the really big ones, in spite of regular contracts with the Japanese to widen and deepen it. The tankers went around the Cape if they were going to Europe or North America.

Abu Rudeis—called Burdeis by the Egyptians—always marked a stage. Until then foreigners were not permitted to leave the coastal road. Inland were the turquoise mines and the Pharaonic temple of *Serabit el-Khadem*, first seen by a European, Carsten Niebuhr, in 1762. It was originally a 4th-dynasty complex with many intact upright steles. But in 1983 everything off the beaten path in Sinai was off-limits to travelers because of the danger of mines. Prepared Israeli positions snaked over the hills in many parts of the peninsula and it wasn't until years later that we saw *Serabit*.

Also to the east were pilgrim routes into Sinai and the *Wadi el-Mokatteb*, or "valley of inscriptions." European scholars had heard of the existence of these undeciphered writings and there had been considerable interest in them when they were first reported early in the eighteenth century as possible precursors of the square Hebrew script, learned by the Children of Israel during their wanderings in the wilderness. But they were later found to be just names in Nabataean or other precursors of Arabic, scratched on exposed surfaces by generations of pilgrims going to the holy places in the south of the peninsula. The south had been holy long before the coming of Islam.

At Abu Rudeis we turned inland and began a hundred kilometer dash to the southeast before the landscape began to become more interesting. The flat gave way to an area of horizontal sandstone, laid down in sedimentary layers over millennia and then washed away, leaving a few yellow pillars that had escaped the force of the inundations. They stood, very dramatic in their nakedness, a clear signpost of the process that had taken place: how a valley had once been clear, then filled with soft sedimentary material, then scoured once again, cleansed of all but these sentinels. Up to the sandstone, the trip was a marathon to be endured. But now our patience was rewarded. The colors began to change from the dull yellow-browns that characterized the coast. There were wild flowers in the spring and, as we came at different times of the year, the stones in the *wadis* were rearranged, evidence of the force that water still exerted in these desert areas where there was nothing to hold it back. Now, there was reddish soil mixed with the yellow. Little pink lizards scuttled away on our approach.

Wadi Feran was the portal to Sinai proper. It was more interesting than what had gone before, but even the extensive palm groves were no preparation for what was to come. It was only when you looked *up*, from the familiar palms and the Bedouins and the goats, that the massif of southern Sinai appeared, barren monoliths behind the village of Feran that rose to nearly 10,000 feet. These were not mountains preceded by foothills or plains. There was nothing gradual about them. Their color changed with the time of day. At dawn, they were gray and then dun-colored at noon. In the setting sun they turned first pink then fiery red. The colors were also different because there were different elements, including a grey-green material laid down between layers of granite, now exposed again after millions of years of weathering. With the uplifting and folding it had turned ninety degrees from its original axis. It was harder than the granite and, when the other was eroded, it remained and now made its serpentine way along granite ridges, looking like the armored plate on the spine of a dinosaur. Occasionally, grains of golden sand would collect together against a ridge, and the resulting mass would be softly rippled by the wind.

Everywhere, the land was exposed in its nakedness. The granite, soft and friable, was weathered by wind-blown particles of sand. Over the years they would make a hollow, then enlarge it, scouring deeper and deeper into the rock. The cliffs were full of these cavities and it gave them the look of giant flaked pastries. Further on, great alluvial fans poured down either side of the mountains to the center where the road ran, ridiculous in its presumption. The car was like a ship in the immensity of the ocean, a tiny speck if anyone cared to look. No, Sinai was a special place. Only here did the landscape match the biblical story. Geologically everything seemed to conspire together to make it a setting worthy of Genesis or Exodus.

The monastery of St. Catherine's was generally the destination on the first day. With prior arrangements in Cairo it was possible to stay at the monastery itself. But it was not particularly comfortable—the rooms were notorious for their bedbugs—and we knew few who did. We stayed at a hotel near the airport, about five miles down the valley from the monastery. It had been built by the Israelis and was already suffering from the terminal neglect of the Egyptian Hotels Corporation. But it had been poorly constructed to begin with and the joinery was suspect, with windows that didn't open and doors that didn't shut. Our first visit had been at Christmas and it was freezing outside. Snow was on the ground and there was no hot water in the taps. A Kerosene heater was supposed to remedy the cold, but it emitted such noxious fumes that we turned it off. But one of the party still took her customary morning—but this time bitterly cold—shower.

The common dining room, with European-style meals served three times a day, was always interesting for a clientele that often consisted of tour groups. The meals were the usual tough steak or chicken with large, irregularly-shaped French-fried potatoes, but the rolls were good, like Egyptian *shami* loaves but whole-wheat. The hotel would also pack a box lunch for those climbing the mountain. By the time we left Egypt in the middle of the decade, a Swiss corporation was building a new hotel in *Wadi Raha*, a mile from the monastery. It was on the site where Sadat had a favorite rest house, built in an area that was supposedly off-limits to development. That was another problem with Sadat. He seemed to have rest houses all over the country.

The next morning the drive to the monastery was always a reminder of why we came. The mountains were sheer granite and there was almost nothing but the monoliths, rising dramatically out of the flat. There were a few trees in the monastery garden and a couple of cypresses at the Basin of Elijah halfway to the top of the mountain. But for the most part there was only granite. Like Feran, it was grey in the morning, dun-colored at noon, and crimson at sundown. After that it was pitch black and the immensity of the place dwarfed us and the monastery, whose few twinkling lights made it seem even more remote and fragile here in the wilderness.

Built by the Byzantine empress Helena in the fourth century as a fortified refuge for the religious of Sinai, the monastery became a regular pilgrimage site thereafter. There had been improvements since but the rough quadrangle and nine-foot thick walls were as they had been for nearly two millennia. With the coming of Islam, the authorities had approached the victorious Arabs and tradition has it that the Prophet himself signed a document granting the monastery official protection. Others—Mamluks, Ottomans, and the Napoleonic French—followed suit.

Mount Sinai, if by that was meant the mountain behind the monastery, appeared on the map at 2,285 meters, or 7,395 feet. Surprisingly, it was not the highest peak in the vicinity and the great cone of Mt. St. Catherine was nearby, a thousand feet higher and separated by a narrow valley. But what made Sinai so dramatic was that it rose almost sheer from the level of the valley below. There were two ways to the top. The first, a gradual path ran from behind the monastery to the Basin of Elijah where it joined the second, a set of over 3,700 steps laboriously wrested out of the granite by the monks and leading almost straight up the face of the massif. The view of sunrise from the top was supposed to be spectacular and, on an early visit, I virtually ran for an hour and a-half in the inky blackness to the summit. Then the sun came up, looking like every sunrise I had ever seen. I was wearing a heavy Irish fishermen's sweater and I sat and panted while the wind blew bitterly cold through the coarse weave of the sweater.

But if the sunrise was unremarkable the rest of the view from the top was not and it repaid the effort. To the east was the Gulf of Aqaba and beyond, the coast of Midian and Saudi Arabia. North of that were the towns of Aqaba and Eilat. To the west, lay the mountains on the far side of the Gulf of Suez. And everywhere, rippled like waves, were the stupendous granite peaks that made up the southern part of the peninsula. A mosque and chapel had been built at the summit but in the early morning they were locked and empty. The whistling of the wind and the scratching of the little rodents who were the permanent denizens of the place were the only sounds that disturbed the silence. They would come out of their burrows in the rock after the initial alarm of an arrival, and resume the process of gathering the food they carried away for storage. It was a moment to be savored.

The way down was always at a more leisurely pace. There would be time to look for petroglyphs and Nabataean graffiti on the flat near the chapel of Elijah. On the steps we would meet people making their painstaking way to the top, from serious mountaineers in serious boots to Belgian nuns wearing sturdy street oxfords, more suitable to the classroom than the mountains, fortifying each other with cries of "*courage, courage.*" Once I met a group of Egyptian teenagers—probably Copts— carrying boom-boxes and literally dancing their way to the top in their disco shoes. It wasn't much of a mountaineering problem, but the setting was spectacular and the climb was worth the effort, over and over again. Biblical scholars speculated as to whether the area was large enough to accommodate the hosts of the Children of Israel for the giving of the Law—more than 600,000, not including women and children, according to Exodus. Their conclusions were mixed. In the late twentieth century a regular stream of Christian pilgrims—Europeans, Africans, and Asians—would make their way to the top of the mountain. The nearby "People of the Book"—Muslims and Jews—seemed indifferent to its attractions.

At the bottom there would be time to explore the monastery grounds or the church itself. At the car park the Bedouins offered a few things for sale, but they weren't of the manufactured sort, being large naturally-occurring crystals of amethyst, or delicate fern-like formations in the rock, or little packets of wild oregano. A tomato sauce made with the oregano of Sinai always seemed to taste better, but it was probably just the thought that made it so. I particularly remembered climbing the mountain in a light falling snow and, later the same day, snorkeling at Sharm el-Sheikh without a wetsuit.

On our first trip the roads were primitive and we had four flat tires, two at a time, twice. But we were with another party and waited for several hours under the stars for the other car to make the run into Feran and back with the tires. It was followed by a wild drive through half the night, over roads that had been partially washed away, to Sharm el-Sheikh. The morning revealed an ugly yellow-brown landscape outside the hotel window and a flat leaden expanse of water. It was the only hotel in town and had also been built by the Israelis. The area was festooned with barbed wire and there were piles of empty beer bottles everywhere with labels in Hebrew.

But the scene under the water more than compensated for the trash. The reef had not been fished out the way it had been further south and from the moment you entered the tepid soup it teemed with life. There were Moorish Idols, Groupers, Parrotfish, Imperial Angelfish, Harlequin Tuskfish and Long Nosed Butterfly fish. They swam singly and in schools, in water from the depth of a foot to the deeper water at the end of the reef, a hundred yards out. The sand was gray and the fish provided all the color on the flat. But the water gradually changed to light blue, and then it was royal blue as the reef dropped off, precipitously, to the depths below.

It was very sudden, like gliding off a cliff face and, even with buoyancy of the water there was a momentary fear of falling. It might have taken your breath away had there been any breath to spare under the snorkel. The perspective at once changed from horizontal to vertical. Where the fish had once been all around us, they were now below and there were big fish down there. Divers would weight themselves and go down among them. Diving later became a passion of expatriates in Cairo and people came from all over the world to dive off Sinai. In terms of underwater life Sharm el-Sheikh was supposed to be on a par with the Great Barrier Reef.

But even after the mountains and the reefs, the Sinai had still more to offer. The east coast was dotted with little settlements, typically on the tip of an alluvial fan that poured out from a break in the mountain barrier. Dahab and Nuweiba' were not as spectacular for diving as Sharm el-Sheikh, but they were much prettier. Near Nuweiba', there was an old Turkish fort and farther north an island that had been held by Crusaders. At the northern end of the Gulf of Aqaba there was a view of Egypt, Israel, Jordan, and Saudi Arabia where they all came together. Yachts and schooners sailed down the Gulf, their masts prominent against the Saudi coast, and they anchored in the evening off the settlements.

The track from St. Catherine's to the east coast was at first unimproved and for most vehicles it was necessary to retreat to the west before rounding the tip of the peninsula at Ras Mohammed. But later the Egyptians pushed a road through and it was a spectacular drive. The solid granite of the massif near the monastery soon gave way to sandstone and it was weathered in interesting colors and shapes, looking like a southern extension of Wadi Rum in Jordan.

Sinai was always an escape, from Cairo and the pressures of population and crowding to spaciousness and silence. But it was more than just the quiet: it was a journey away from heat and the river to the high desert; from torpor and monotonous yellow sand to a place where geological forces had transformed the landscape into every color and shape imaginable. We went as often as we could, sometimes on a long weekend driving for two days just to spend a third among the massifs.

In the middle of the decade came another domestic Egyptian tremor, the riot of the conscripts, and another period under curfew for foreigners. Like elsewhere in the developing-world the army was involved in nearly every enterprise in the country, from dairy farming to the manufacture of arms. But beneath the privileged officer class lay a huge mass of conscripts, many of them illiterate. They were paid a pittance and while they were not subject to the same abuse as in, say, the Russian army, still military service was not popular with the average *fellah* or *sa'idi*. So when their term of conscription was unilaterally increased in January of 1986 their frustrations reached a boiling point and they poured out of the camps, located on the Alexandria road just beyond Giza.

They vented their rage on institutions that catered to two symbols of oppression, westerners and wealthy Arabs. A few miles down the road were the five-star hotels that increasingly dotted the landscape around the pyramids and further on, occupying both sides of Pyramids Road, lay the nightclubs favored by Gulf Arabs. The conscripts first trashed the Movenpick, killing a few Europeans in the process, before reaching the Mena House Oberoi. There, they torched all the cars in the parking lot and assaulted the main entrance before moving on to the clubs. I was staying at the Mena House at the time, on my way to an assignment in Saudi Arabia, but had been at dinner downtown that night. On the way back at midnight the Pyramids Road was blocked, although detours by a series of side streets brought me to within half a-mile of the hotel. But the scene ahead was one of chaos, with burning buildings, overturned cars, and milling crowds illuminated by the fires. A policeman said "if you go any farther they will kill you." So I retreated and spent the next several days in the city under curfew with a friend. When I reached the Mena House a week later I found the luggage, oriental carpets, and camera in the room untouched. A desk clerk had the presence of mind to throw the power switch when the doors at the main entrance were smashed and the rioters, put off by the dark, moved on to the neon lights and blaze of the nightclubs.

The incident was a reminder that beneath the veneer of its American orientation, cooperation in the peace process, and verbal commitment to democracy and market reforms, Egypt was a miserably poor country. There was no guarantee that more of the same was going to fundamentally alter the equation. The structural problems were too great, the poor too numerous, and the military and commercial elites too entrenched for anything dramatic to change. What was surprising was that there weren't more outbreaks like that of the conscripts. With occasional exceptions the Egyptian people were long-suffering, unfailingly polite, and welcoming to strangers. But there was a limit to their patience. It was said that if there were free elections in Egypt, the ruling National Democratic Party would finish a poor third to the Muslim Brotherhood and the New Wafd. But short of a violent upheaval, it seemed unlikely that the Brothers or the Wafd would be given a chance to rule.

3

The Opera House

Many Egyptians considered the country an oasis of European culture in the great desert of the Arab World. There was even a question as to whether Egyptians were Arabs at all. Some didn't think so. They had been so dominated by foreigners over the last two millennia that the population today was a mixture of alien influences grafted onto the original Pharaonic stock: Persians, Greeks, Romans, Berbers, Arabs, Kurds, Armenians, Turks, Jews, Circassians, Georgians, Italians, French, and British had all left their mark. The Arabs may have been the least of them. This was mainly true of Cairo and Alexandria, although the famously green eyes of Mansura were said to be a legacy of the French of the Napoleonic period. The most recent influences were British and French. Beginning with the dynasty of Mohammed Ali they increasingly set the cultural tone of the country. Well-to-do Egyptians sent their sons to British schools where they studied English and their daughters to convent schools where they learned French.

The height of European influence in Egypt was probably reached under the Khedive Isma'il who built the Suez Canal and, in so doing, mortgaged the country to the European bondholders. It was the pressure of the bondholders that led to the intervention in 1882 and the British and French condominium. One of the most egregious of the Europeanizing Isma'il's excesses was the building of an opera house in what came to be known as Opera Square. It sat near the Ezbekiya Gardens and the equestrian statue of Ibrahim Pasha. The old Shepheard's Hotel was nearby and, beyond it, Clot Bey Street and the red-light district that was relatively sedate during the Second World War until the arrival of the Australians. Now, prostitutes were a distant memory and the original Shepheard's was long gone, burned down during the riots of 1952. The Ezbekiya Gardens, originally developed by Mohammed Ali as a promenade for the Europeans, were gone as well.

THE OPERA HOUSE   23

The old opera house, a Victorian wooden pile, burned down under mysterious circumstances in 1971. It had lasted just a hundred years. Before the fire it was the scene of carriages arriving with great pashas and their ladies. Verdi's *Aida* premiered there. There was now a new opera house and it included a small museum devoted to the old. One of the exibits was a receipt for the telegram "*que S.A. le Khedive adressa a Verdi pour le feliciter au lendemain de la Grande Premeire.*" It had been sent by the British Indian Submarine Telegraph Company, Ltd. on Christmas Day, 1871. A tour of the museum exhibits was a retrospective on the Cairo of the late nineteenth and early twentieth century.

There were a few of the original costumes, although almost everything had been consumed by the flames. A scale model of the original structure detailed its outlines and photographs showed visiting troupes, dancers, prima donnas, and grandees. The great melon-shaped head of Georges Abyad was prominent in the photographs. He seemed to have been a kind of impresario, the Diaghilev of Egypt. The Arabic transliteration of his name was not Girgis—that most Christian of Egyptian names—but Georges in the French style, using the odd *jeem* with three dots. He looked Armenian. The diameter of his head began at about nine inches in the region of the jaw. By the time it had reached the brows it was six inches and gradually gave away to almost nothing. The back of his head was utterly flat, a characteristic of the Armenians noticed by Herodotus.

Another great head was that of Abdel Rahman Sidqy, who was the director of the company during the 1940s and '50s. In the photographs of the visit of the *Comedie Francaise* there was still an occasional fez in evidence. There were also photos of Nasser and his pal, Salah Salem, after whom the airport road was named, and other members of the Revolutionary Command Council. Surprisingly, the old programs revealed as many Muslim names as Christian: there seemed to be an Ahmed 'Alaam for every Daulit Abyad. There were programs from the great performances, *L'Embuscade* on the 13th of April 1910 and *Le Dedale* on Fbruary 21st, 1919. The British may have run the country but the Egyptians looked to the French for their culture. After the fire in 1971 there was still a Cairo Opera Company, but the performances were held in the Gumhuriya Theater across the river in Imbaba. It just wasn't the same thing.

The Japanese, of all people, came to the rescue. The tied loans of their Overseas Economic Cooperation Fund had financed mobile telephone exchanges and microwave networks in the early 1980s. But in the middle of the decade they offered to finance a new opera house with a grant of $45 million. Construction began in May of 1985 and was completed in March 1988. It was inaugurated on October 10th of that year, appropriately, with a performance of *Aida*. President Mubarak was there along with the *glitterati* of Cairo. The new complex included two halls, the main hall with a seating capacity of 1,200 and the small hall that seated 500, as well as workshops, art galleries, museum, and a music library.

At 45,000 square meters the cost worked out to a thousand dollars per meter. The main hall was done in brick red and the stage had a maximum proscenium width of sixteen meters. It was equipped with twenty-three motorized battens and four manual, counter-weighted battens. Lighting was provided by a Pacolis memory light-control board with 243 circuits, including sixty in the auditorium. The sound system consisted of a twenty-four-channel mixer with two open-reel tape decks, two cassette decks and a DAT recorder. The text of the operas was flashed in electronic Arabic on a panel high above the stage. Occasionally I found myself consulting the panel, the written Arabic being more understandable than the sung Italian.

The above details were provided by Moustafa Reda, the opera house's director of public relations, a Ministry of Culture employee, at a meeting in his office next to the main hall. As usual in Egypt he wanted to know *who* I was and *why* I wanted to know about the opera house. When I told him that I was a consultant in a sister ministry, I became "*ya sa'at el mustashar*," or "oh eminent adviser," and he pulled out all the stops, so to speak. He sent his deputy with me into the bowels of this very public-sector organization to find a brochure with the requisite background "informations." The brochure also contained a list of the affiliated performing companies, among them the Cairo Symphony Orchestra, the Cairo Opera Company, and the Cairo Ballet. They were all very good and there was liberal programming of Arabic music and theater scattered among the European warhorses.

But it was the European performances that stood out. The Bolshoi appeared in November of 1995. They were not a touring group with the same name like some surrogate Harlem Globetrotters, but the *real* Bolshoi, and they were spectacular. Then in December there was Yehudi Menuhin and the Lithuanian State Opera Orchestra with a performance of Handel's *Messiah*. Later there was *Aida* by the Cairo Opera Company, and it was good theater with the familiar choruses. The props were certainly authentic. The 1996–97 season offered a varied fare, from "Masterpieces of American Movie Music" to pieces by heavyweights like Dvorak, Mendelssohn, Bruckner, Brahms, and Mozart. There would also be the *Nutcracker* and *Swan Lake* performed by the Bolshoi, and the operas *The Barber of Seville* and *The Masked Ball*. The most expensive ticket for most performances was twenty-five pounds, or about $7.50. It really was a cultural oasis.

There was also the "Great Symphonies" series by the Cairo Symphony Orchestra. In November the second of the series showcased the works of

Beethoven, J. Francais, and Ravel. The orchestra for the Beethoven was sixty-five strong, fifty-one strings and fourteen others, mainly woodwinds. The audience was only about twice that number. There were perhaps a dozen Egyptians and as many women among the musicians. The rest looked like European males. The conductor was a Bulgarian from Varna, known as Stalin in the bad old days. During the country's brief flirtation with the Eastern Bloc, Egyptian public-sector employees went on package holidays to Varna, there to cling to its pebbly Black Sea beach.

There were lesser ensembles as well, given in the small hall behind the main opera house. One, scheduled for the evening of October 27, 1996, was *del Quartetto Telemann* from Milan. It was advertised as a quartet. But a spokesman appeared onstage with news of a change. After a polite smattering of applause, he bowed awkwardly before announcing in excellent, if slightly wooden, English that the bassoonist had met with an accident in Milan and would not be present. They would instead be a trio. This meant a change in the program. The trio sonatas would remain but some of the other sonatas and concertos would be modified. The instruments were described in oddly archaic English: *"flute, oboie, and pianoforte."* All of the new pieces seemed to consist of four movements: *allegro, adagio, allegro, adagio.* By the time he finished describing them we all knew the sequence by heart. He then disappeared.

A few minutes later the trio took the stage, each deferring to the others in a courtly little dance before they took their seats and busied themselves with the housekeeping chores incumbent on musicians preparing for a concert. The oboist moved his chair and music stand a foot forward before moving them back to where they had been. Then he blew through the reed and examined it, first one end and then the other. He was gray-haired with a mustache and looked like Adolpho Celli, one of the early James Bond villains.

The flautist was a tall, thin man with a long equine face. He sat, first wrapping one leg around the other and then his long, almost beautiful fingers around his instrument. With a noticeable bob of his upper body he played a scale and then the same scale in reverse. He then sat back, obviously satisfied with what he had heard. He seemed the most animated of the three and regularly communed, as it were, with the audience. At one point when we missed our cue, he let us all know with a wink that applause was appropriate. The pianist arranged himself, then the height of the bench, then himself again, before the height of the bench again. Then he struck a note for the others to tune by. All were in a kind of uniform, gray suits and dark neckties.

Finally, on a silent signal, they ended their chores and became alert, like bird dogs on point. With a more pronounced bob from the flautist, they launched into a sonata by Telemann. Now, all notice of their physical idiosyncrasies vanished in the brilliant sound that came from the instruments. Each was a soloist in his own right. The difference in sound between a live musical performance and a good CD is hardly noticeable. In fact, the sound on a CD is often better. But there was still something about the immediacy of the concert that made it special. It was the real thing, with the possibility of error, although we detected none.

The presence of the audience was another difference. In Cairo they were a mixture of Egyptians and foreigners. They came in a variety of dress, unlike the main hall where the men had to wear neckties. And they were a variety of types. There were the odd Americans who wore permanent beatific smiles as if this concert was the highlight of their day or week, or maybe even their lives. The Italians looked slightly dissipated, as only Italians can. Most of the Egyptians were young and there were several girls wearing that characteristic Cairo combination: *hijab*, or Islamic wimple, and Levi's. Several Japanese sat in the back, obviously savoring the sense that it was they who were responsible for the performance in the first place.

The first part of the concert ended with a wink from the flautist and we adjourned to the coffee bar. There, he worked the audience like a politician. After the intermission we reassembled and the spokesman shuffled out to announce the new program. All the pieces were, of course, in four movements: *allegro, adagio, allegro, adagio*. The program ended with a trio by Vivaldi and the applause was thunderous. This time, we didn't need a wink.

After the concert I walked home. At eleven o'clock the evening was cool and Cairo was probably the safest major city in the world. The walk took me by al-Gala Square and the woman selling corn on the cob from a brazier. Her tiny daughter slept on the cart beside her, amid the discarded husks and corn silk. Then I turned down High Dam Street, past unfinished apartment blocks. Landlords built apartments as the money became available, and this meant starts and stops in the building program. Some used inferior materials and built many floors beyond those allowed in the permit. The collapsed eleven-story building in Heliopolis earlier in the month had five illegal floors, and bearing walls had been removed on the ground floor to accommodate a bank.

On Boulis Hanna Pasha Street the *bawwabs* had awakened from their daily slumber and sat chewing the fat. The guards at the Algerian embassy were also awake, cradling their Uzis in their laps. Boulis Hanna became Hassan Ramadan Street beyond the headquarters of the New Wafd. They were excavating for local telephone cable along the length of the street and by day *sa'idis* would bury it in a shallow grave. In the Dokki *suq* the shops were closed. The butcher was not splitting a calf's foot for madam, the carpenter putting the finishing touches on an armoire, or boys tapping dents out of fenders. The fat *fellaha* who sold greens had gone home, undoubtedly to practice spousal abuse on her husband. An occasional mongoose streaked across the street before disappearing into a vestibule.

On Mossadeq Street, tomcats with chewed ears and ruffled fur sat waiting for their next conquest. The contrast with the *Concerto di Musiche Barocche* could not have been greater. But that was what made Cairo such a special place.

4

The Oases

It would be a great loop, a total of about 1,500 miles and we would drive back up the valley of the Nile. From the map it looked relatively straightforward: southwest from Cairo to Bahriyah, the same to Farafra, southeast to Dakhla, then east to Kharga, and slightly north of east to the river at Luxor. But the guidebook cautioned that the oases were primitive, accommodations were Spartan, and "a trip through Egypt's western oases is only for the toughened traveler." It added ominously that smart travelers went well equipped as "the country between the oases is as unfriendly today as when King Cambyses lost an entire army somewhere between Kharga and Siwa."

We had wanted to see the oases for years and we spent the previous weekend listing what we would need before assembling it all. There were inner tubes, jumper cables, an extra distributor cap, spark plugs, a spare fan belt, water for the radiator, tools, and extra coolant. And that was just for the car, which had been serviced the week before. There was also water for us, bedding, food, utensils, film for the camera, guidebook, and a first-aid kit with Martha's considerable pharmacopoeia.

And more water for us. I thought we should probably take two cases of mineral water but knew that Martha would double what I recommended. So I said one and we eventually settled on three. The water was the heaviest part of the load: thirty-six bottles at one and a-half liters each meant nearly 120 pounds of water and several times on the trip it all seemed to wind up in the front seat with us, thankfully still in its bottles. We tried to combat-load everything—last in first out—but that broke down over the five days.

Actually, the analogy with war was appropriate. Our main concerns were tires and gas. The guidebooks had the same cautionary tale about traveling in the Sinai and we had done that many times. On the first trip there we had two flat tires at the same time, twice. But we were traveling with another party and had been able to stay with the car while the tires were repaired. This time we would be alone, the distances were much greater, and flat tires could be a major problem. Then, there was gas. We had spent several extra days in the Karakorams in Pakistan because of the lack of gas and we and couldn't afford a repeat of the experience. Our schedule was tight. We always filled the tank when we found gas and in the event it was available in all the oases, so we needn't have worried.

The trip began inauspiciously. The night before we left I was slicing vegetables for a salad with a sharp knife and cut through the tip of my left thumb as cleanly as if it had been a tomato. It may have needed stitches, but there was no time for that and, anyway, the Feast had just begun and everyone would be celebrating. So Martha took out her dressings and bandaged the wound. This was annoying and I imagined the cut becoming infected in the middle of the desert or trying to change a tire with only one opposed thumb. Our first ritual on arrival at the destination each day was to change the dressing and it healed quickly and cleanly and we had no flat tires. By the end of the trip the thumb worked almost as well as before.

The desert in Egypt had always appeared drab and monotonous. We had been in the Eastern Desert, close to the mountains that flank the Red Sea, and it had been more interesting than the area around Cairo. Southern Sinai was a place all to itself, with more geological variation than any other area of its size on the planet. But for the most part the Egyptian desert seemed uninteresting. The stretch from Cairo to Suez was not only boring but ugly and the Wadi Natroun was not a perceptible valley at all, but a series of depressions where hydrostatic pressure had pushed water close to the surface. There was agriculture around the monasteries in Natroun, but the green seemed to have been wrested through sheer hard work from the desert and it was not particularly lush or pretty. It was nothing like the Nefud in Saudi Arabia, where delicate pink dunes marched away to the horizon, or the great sweeping panoramas of rippled dunes in the Sahara.

We left on a morning in mid-February, the first day of the Ramadan feast, the *Eid el-Fitr*, and planned to make Bahriyah by the early afternoon. Outside Cairo, south of the road past Sixth October City, it all looked depressingly the same. Sixth October was one of those satellite cities built to attract industry and people away from the overpopulated Nile Valley. But there had been little success, so tied were Egyptians to the familiar. Several months before we had been there to visit the Egyptian German Telecommunications Industries (EGTI), a joint venture between ARENTO and Siemens to assemble digital switches. It seemed like a good idea: import substitution, a possible export market, and job creation. But the Egyptian switches were more expensive than those made in Germany, largely because of import duty on the components, so there was no export market, and the factory employed only 300, mainly women with the requisite fine motor-movement. Only half-a-dozen of the 300 lived in Sixth October City. For the others their greatest problem was the daily commute from Cairo.

There were no signs to the oases and it took several attempts before we found what the sun told us was the road to the southwest. Except in patches it hadn't been maintained in years and the prospect of debris, piles of asphalt, old tire casings, and sun glare was not inviting. But this was no time for second thoughts and we hurtled off into the unknown. The road improved after a few miles and slowly the speedometer crept up to eighty mph. There were no laser guns on the Bahriyah road and no police to cite us for speeding. But the other side of the coin was that there was no one here *at all* and I never really lost my fear of a breakdown. And the road was treacherous, new pavement suddenly returning to the old with a sickening screech of tires and a jolt as we hit the bad surface. It happened several times on the trip and it was then that the 120 pounds of water, sitting in boxes on the flat surface of the Blazer, joined us with everything else in the front seat. The weight pushed the seats forward and we sat pinioned against the dashboard until we could stop and repack the bed of the car. It was a hard lesson and I never really learned it.

We were technically in the Libyan Desert, the eastward extension of the Sahara. But we probably would see no *ergs* or *fejjs* or *regs,* characteristics of the great desert to the west. The Sahara was *the* desert, of which all others were just pale imitations. Europeans had driven south for years to see its wonders until a Tuareg revolt in Chad and Niger had effectively closed it to foreigners. In Niger we had been confined to the savannah and the Sahel, the areas closest to the river, and if permission to go north was given it was only with a military escort. Timbuktu had been closed. But there were influences of the Sahara system even here in Egypt. If nothing else, there was the *khamsin*, the wind that for fifty days in the spring blew from the desert and occasionally closed the Cairo airport. It was interesting that the fifty (*khamsin* in Arabic) days were traditionally those between Easter and Pentecost. Easter was both a solar and a lunar phenomenon, occurring on the first Sunday after the first full moon after the vernal equinox. So the *khamsin* theoretically oscillated back and forth in the spring, unlike the Moslem feasts that marched resolutely through the solar year. But I doubt that the winds kept to the schedule.

The oases on the fringe of the Libyan Desert had been not only refuges for Christians and other nonconformists but also avenues for trade and invasion. Some of the Libyans of the later dynasties had come that way and there were a few Pharaonic ruins in the oases. Had Burckhardt fulfilled his assignment from the Association for Promoting the Discovery of the Interior Parts of Africa in 1812 and joined the caravan from Cairo to Timbuktu, he probably would have gone through at least one of the oases. Instead, he went south to Nubia and wound up in the Hejaz where he contracted the dysentery that would eventually kill him. He was buried outside the *Bab en-Nasr* in Cairo and the Swiss embassy had recently restored his tomb.

It was easy to reflect on these bits of history because there was nothing about the present that was particularly interesting. Low mesas and a few cinder cones appeared, and a railroad accompanied us reassuringly on our left. But otherwise, for several hours, there was only the same dreary landscape. Then, there was just the hint of a difference and the flat appeared to give way to something below. Sure enough, we reached the edge of a kind of plateau and there, a thousand feet beneath in the distance spread Bahriyah. It was not the kind of thing that took your breath away, nothing like the escarpment dropping from Ta'if to the coast or even the road down from Riyadh. But it was a difference with some green, which increased as we descended to the flat.

A few minutes later we reached our first police check post. Fifty-gallon drums blocked the road and the policeman wearing a rough olive-drab uniform—not the black we were used to—shuffled out to the car from his striped box. The formula was to be repeated many times over the next five days and it always went according to script:

Misah el-kheir (good afternoon)

Misah en-nour (and good afternoon to you)

Kul sana wa inta tayib (many happy returns of the day)

Wa inta bi saha wa salama (and the same to you)

Inta agnabi wa la ay? (are you foreigners?)

Ihna Amricaan" (we're Americans).

We had an American car but local Giza plates and that and the Arabic always threw them. Later, in the valley, we would be quizzed about our nationality.

Inta Almani? (are you German?)

La'a (no)

Firinsawi? (French?)

La'a

Biritani? (British?)

La'a

Taliani? (Italian?)

La'a

Espani? (Spanish?)

La'a

Beljiki? (Belgian?)

La'a

Hollandi? (Dutch?)

La a"

We could have saved them the trouble but it was interesting to see who was in Upper Egypt. Most often we were asked if we were German. Only at the end did they guess American.

Bahriyah

The first order of business was a place to stay. It was only two-thirty in the afternoon but we wanted to unburden the car and ourselves and see the sights. The guidebook said that accommodations in Bahriyah were dismal but that the best was the government rest house at the iron mines, forty kilometers north of *al-Bawiti* and the heart of the oasis. So we drove down a long avenue lined with tamarisks and eucalyptus to what looked like the entrance to a village. It was not the mines themselves but the relatively modern town where the iron workers were housed. A guard directed us to the school where we would find "professor Mahmoud" who would show us the facilities. He was not there but arrived after about ten minutes and we drove back through the cluster of poorly-maintained medium-rises to the rest house. Mahmoud was not particularly friendly and looked Russian, down to his synthetic warm-up outfit. He looked like he was on his way to a track meet.

At the rest house the room was very large, actually two rooms, with a kitchen and bathroom. The bathroom was standard Egyptian issue and none of the faucets looked like they had been used recently, or maybe worked at all. Everything was stained a dirty red-brown, a product of the iron content of the water. We asked Mahmoud how much it was for a night and he said "*bil balash,*" or "for nothing," then quickly added twenty-five pounds, or about eight dollars. It would do in a pinch and we agreed that we would see what there was in the oasis proper. Half an-hour later we were in *al-Bawiti*. There was obviously water near the surface and in the distance we could see palms, but this was not the oasis of desert travelers' dreams. There were no inviting pools of water and the main street was the typical Egyptian rural squalor: litter everywhere—chicken-feathers, paper, and plastic bags—along with rheumy-eyed children and skulking dogs. To be fair, it was the first day of the Feast and everyone was in new clothes, the little girls looking particularly festive in their brightly-colored dresses.

We found gas at the second station in town. The attendant thought that there might also be gas in Farafra, our next stop. The main hotel in town was the Alpenblick and after the usual back-and-forth we found it on a little rise overlooking an odd, beehive-like saint's tomb. It was a neat, white-domed complex and there were several 4x4s with customs plates parked in front. The man at the desk said there was one double-room left at thirty-five pounds for the night and we took it in spite of the fact that there was no bath. There were common toilets and showers at the end of the little alcove, both stained the same red-brown color of the iron mines. The toilet seats were still intact but neither of the toilets flushed. The man at the desk said the water had to be turned on. He took me back and showed me the valves before flushing each one triumphantly. Of such little victories is travel made.

With us we had Ahmed Fakhry's *The Oases of Egypt, Volume 2, Bahriyah and Farafra*, from our first period in Egypt. It had cost seven and a-half pounds then but, in a week of searching, I couldn't find volume three, covering Dakhla and Kharga. Ahmed Fakhry had been the world's leading expert on the oases before his death in 1973, and his books were as much labors of love as scholarly guides to the antiquities and history of the area. Here, *al-Bawiti* had been one of the two principal towns since ancient times. But there wasn't much evidence of the early dynastic periods. The principal remains were the tomb of Amenhotep, governor of Bahriyah in the second half of the 18th dynasty (1550–1307 BC), and the tomb of Bannentiu from the 26th dynasty (664–525 BC). There were also Greek and Roman ruins but we weren't serious Egyptologists and didn't have much time, so we decided to limit ourselves to these two.

We had met a young kid, Ayman, at the gas station and he showed up later at the Alpenblick. He said he would show us the ruins but we first had to get permission from the Antiquities Department. We thought we could just find them and have a look, but he insisted it was more complicated than that. So he joined us and we drove through the dusty little streets to the director's house. The director looked like he might be a problem, with flashing eyes and a typical Sunni beard, unkempt with the mustaches clipped. But he was very polite and understanding. We had come all the way from America to see the sights and even though it was the Feast—we were interrupting his celebration and the sites were technically closed—he would give us special permission to see them. He had a little twinkle in his eye and I could see that he really didn't believe my story about America. Maybe it was the fact that the conversation was in Arabic. He refused money and told us—in no uncertain terms—not to pay anyone else. That didn't include Ayman who was with us. So we made our way across town to find Yasser, a young inspector in the department. We sat outside while Ayman explained the plan but Yasser wanted to hear it from the director himself. So we made a place for Yasser and went back to the first house. After another discussion with the director we went to the Antiquities Department where Yasser got the keys. Then we went to the tomb of Bannentiu, where access was through a six-meter shaft into a dusty mound.

The key to the padlock in the metal grating covering the shaft didn't work at first but, with typical Egyptian ingenuity, the guard poured a little water into the lock, tapped gently, and it opened on the second try. The shaft was straight down and entrance to the tomb was through a three-foot square opening at the bottom. We squeezed through the passage and emerged in the dim light into a labyrinth of Pharaonic scenes. The colors looked like they had been applied the day before.

It quickly became obvious that Yasser knew his stuff. He was a graduate of Cairo University in fine arts and was putting his knowledge to work. In Egypt the newspapers were full of announcements of "opportunities for work" and "flats for young people" and subsidized "agricultural land" for the *shebab*, or youth. It was a serious problem in the country. Lucky graduates, after a poor grounding in their major subject, taught by underpaid professors and using out-of-date textbooks, might find a job in the public sector. Others did not and a job, dowry for marriage, and furnishings for a flat were beyond the means of all but a few of the *shebab*. Most jobs had little to do with their academic preparation, such as it was. At least Yasser was working in his chosen field but I was sure his salary was a pittance.

One of the guards held a lamp on a long extension cord while Yasser led us on a tour of the tomb. There was a main chamber about eight meters square with four pillars symmetrically placed, and three smaller inner chambers. The ceiling was about six feet high and I walked with a constant stoop. To the right of the entrance of the main chamber was a representation of the ithyphallic god Amonre' Harakhti—notable here for his anatomical correctness and the fact that he was known as Min everywhere else—in addition to other gods: Anubis, Wepwawet, Horus, Apis, Nefertum, and Khonsu. There were also scenes on the north, east and west walls and on the ceiling of this, as well as the inner burial chamber. Representations of the Journey of the Sun and the Journey of the Moon lay on the wall opposite the main entrance, flanking the opening to the burial chamber. The colors—vivid reds, yellows, and oranges—were still bright. The tomb had been robbed in antiquity and reused in Roman times but there seemed to have been little damage, at least to the scenes on the walls. Yasser told us that the director said photographs were not permitted and he was strict about the prohibition. Clearly, the director was not a man to be trifled with.

Back on the surface the guards offered us tea while our eyes adjusted to the light. Next was the tomb of Amenhotep on the other side of town, through the police checkpoint and on the road to Farafra. The policemen asked for a *tasriyah*, or a pass, but accepted our passports instead and we drove to the vicinity of a hillock where there was a ruined chamber, now open to the elements, with several pillars in the middle. There was just the hint of paint on the plaster that covered the pillars. There were a few badly-weathered hieroglyphs and it looked like the interesting ones were probably below the surface of the sand that filled the body of the tomb. There wasn't much to photograph and Yasser would not permit one, even here in the open. So we made a quick tour of the site, climbing over the ruins looking for something of interest until it seemed like time to go. We drove back through the check-point and dropped Yasser at his house. We took his address to send him a photo of himself, which he at last permitted. He wouldn't accept money.

Then, Ayman asked if we wanted to see the mineral hot-springs. So we drove back toward the iron mines, stopping at a little ethnographic museum where someone had gone to considerable pains to fashion typical scenes of oasis life. The drive was through the palm groves we had seen earlier in the day and out into the desert where herds of camels were grazing. The "springs" themselves were a masonry tank fed by a large pipe. By now it was five o'clock and the sun was about to set so we headed back to the Alpenblick, where we arrived fifteen minutes later. The name was either German or Swiss. The man at the desk didn't know but had a postcard of both countries under the glass for either eventuality. After we told Ayman that we couldn't help him with a visa for the United States, he gratefully accepted ten pounds and disappeared.

There was a little open-air cafe on the hotel grounds and we sat, Martha with a Pepsi and I with a Scotch, until the cold drove us inside. The clientele was mixed, a party of Frenchmen, two American families who had driven down from Alexandria, and several Japanese. For dinner the man at the desk recommended the Bayumi restaurant that, he said, had a good selection and was very clean. It was down the hill and across the square and we were, naturally, the only ones there at six o'clock. My first sit-down dinner in Cairo had been at midnight. There was no chicken but only meat, gray and fibrous and floating in a tepid broth of canned peas in tomato sauce, and rice with vermicelli. I ate my meat and Martha's and we paid the bill—ten pounds each—which was too much. But this was, after all, the Feast. Back in the room we settled down for the night. We deployed the mosquito machine and arranged the bedding. Martha slept in a sleeping bag with our own sheets. I slept fully clothed on the bed. The night was cold and miserable and we were up long before dawn. We had our own coffee maker and a few dates and figs for breakfast. But we had made it to Bahriyah. One oasis down and three to go.

To Farafra

The system of which the oases were a part swept in a long, nearly thousand-kilometer arc from Bahriyah to Kharga and then to the Nile at Luxor. We had intercepted it here in Bahriyah where the relatively flat uninteresting desert had given way to an escarpment and descent into a low-lying pocket of fertility. The fertile areas were periodic but the escarpment seemed to be a constant, and from the map, it looked like it would accompany us all the way to Kharga. Elevations ranged from 316 meters at the iron mines to 747 meters midway between Dakhla and Kharga. The lowest appeared to be twenty-seven meters on the other side of Farafra.

As we left the police check-post from the day before the scenery already held some promise. Farafra was only 183 kilometers, or just over 100 miles, distant and the road passed through first the Black Desert and then the White Desert. This looked like it might be an interesting drive. But suddenly, after half an-hour, the road turned bad. It had not been good when we left Bahriyah but now the pavement appeared only in places. It was fortunate that we met no other cars because that allowed us to use the entire surface, and we slowed enough to navigate the areas where the pavement was intact. But then the paved surface ended completely and a dirt track stretched away into the distance. It was actually pretty, the surface a kind of golden brown with streaks of red. But it was very uneven and threatened to shake loose every nut and bolt in the car.

Suddenly, new pavement appeared again and the reason appeared with it: a microwave tower in a compound to our left, with signs of habitation. This was reassuring in case of a breakdown. Then, just as suddenly, the new road ended and we were back on the old pavement of our departure from Bahriyah. We were probably in the area called the Black Desert because cinder cones, little black pimples, now appeared on either side of the road. The sand was covered with what looked like black gravel. It was like the drive from Medina toward Mecca, only not so striking. Then we passed through a little area of green, palm trees and a settlement away to our left, and we made a note of the mileage in case of a breakdown.

The scenery continued to vary, with good road followed by bad, the prevailing colors black, brown, and red. Then we entered an area of drifts, beautifully rippled, of fine golden sand. Several miles later we came over the crest of a dune and there, a quarter of a-mile ahead of us, by the side of the road was a red car with four little figures clustered around it. As soon as they saw us they all began to wave at once. As we slowed we saw that they were Japanese. Martha said that they were four who had been turned away from the Alpenblick the afternoon before. We stopped and it was obvious what had happened: they hadn't found accommodations in Bahriyah, had driven until dark and decided to camp by the side of the road. So they had pulled the car onto the shoulder and spent the night. The remains of a fire still smoldered next to the car.

The problem was that the shoulder was made up of the fine golden sand that we had been admiring for the last ten miles. Tracks showed that they had driven about twenty yards through it until the car stuck. It was a new Mazda, with a low suspension and was now buried up to the lug nuts. They couldn't get it out. This much all seemed clear, although we had to assume a great deal because they spoke no Arabic and very little English. Then it struck us as utterly incongruous, these four Japanese, looking like students and, even after a night by the side of the road, neat as pins, driving a new red sedan, speaking nothing of the local language and stranded in the middle of the Western Desert.

They were bright and cheery and exquisitely polite, but I saw from their looks that they lusted after the rear-end of our car. But we didn't have a rope or chain and neither did they, and the S-10 Blazer was not a heavy car to begin with. With this realization they appeared crestfallen. They had already tried to back the car out, placing broken pieces of pavement under the driving wheel, but that hadn't worked. If they had been bigger, the four of them could probably have picked the car up and carried it out. It was only about ten yards from the road but, unfortunately, sitting parallel to it so they would somehow have to turn while they were backing out. The problem wasn't insoluble. But we couldn't help them.

What we could do was to alert the next settlement or police check-post that they were stuck and send someone back for them. There was a reason for these check-posts and the police always seemed to know—as we would later discover—where the foreigners were. The Japanese piped up cheerily that this was fine and they would wait for a heavier truck. They had plenty of water and the weather was cool. So they thanked us profusely for I don't know what, and we drove on. I felt a little guilty that we couldn't do more but resolved to add a heavy rope or chain to Martha's list for next time.

After about fifteen miles we came to another microwave station, looking identical to the others we had seen, down to the door slightly ajar in the little hut just inside the gate. The guard was in the back, a hundred yards from the gate and he came out carrying a glass of tea that, with the perfunctory politeness of Egypt, he offered to us. We explained that were *arba' yabanieen fi'l arabiya hamra'*—four Japanese in a red car—fifteen miles behind us and stuck in the sand. Unfortunately, he didn't have a vehicle and the telephone only connected with Bahriyah. So we asked him to contact Bahriyah with the same information. He expected a truck later in the morning and I asked him to send it back. The weathered logo on the gate seemed to be ARENTO's but when I asked him if he worked for the telephone company he said no and offered nothing further. So we assumed that the microwave system was probably military, but we later learned that all their networks were buried fiber-optic cable. So it probably had been ARENTO's after all.

The road improved after the microwave station and it appeared to be clear sailing into Farafra. The White Desert had succeeded the Black and it now appeared to be all around us: interesting formations, badly weathered by erosion, all dusted with sand like confectioners sugar. It was beautiful. Then Farafra loomed in the distance without a perceptible sense of depression. At the check-post we wished the policeman a happy Feast and told him about the Japanese. The little town was dusty and there didn't seem to be much in the way of agriculture.

But there was gas. It was only ten thirty in the morning and we still had almost a full tank. But we took what we could on principle and pressed on. The map was not clear and showed the distance from Farafra to Kharga as about 500 kilometers, or just over 300 miles. But Dakhla appeared to be a little over half way there. At our current rate that would be another four hours. It depended on the road and the guide book, treating the oases in the reverse order, spoke of the "deteriorating" road from Dakhla to Farafra. It had been published in 1991 so it remained to be seen if there had been repairs. But the road was good for most of the way and it became the most monotonous of the legs. This was dangerous because there were significant little depressions and twice we repeated our experience of the day before with the water. Each time we had to stop and repack the car. At one point the landscape became utterly featureless, as uninteresting as the ocean on an overcast day, with nothing in any direction as far as the eye could see. About sixty miles from Farafra we reached the crest of a kind of plateau, below which the desert stretched away in an expanse of gold, graduating as it rose into a light pink. The colors were beautiful, but so delicate and diffuse that I didn't even attempt a photograph.

Beyond the plateau the road made an odd hairpin turn, returning on itself for mile after monotonous mile. Then, mirages began to appear and it was amazing how real they looked. There, nestled among the dunes, were sheets of standing water like those we would later see in Dakhla. But as soon as we approached more closely they disappeared. After another hour we met a motorcycle, the first vehicle we had seen since we left Farafra. Later we met two cars. About sixty miles from Dakhla drifts of rippled, golden sand began to cover parts of the road and we had to slow to negotiate them safely. Then the bad road appeared again and at two forty we bumped our way into Mut, the first of the little towns in the oasis.

Dakhla

It was easily the prettiest of the oases we had seen, with the vivid greens of wheat and blue-green silhouettes of palm trees set against pink cliffs to the northeast. There were real pools of standing water, the first water we had seen since the palm groves of Bahriyah, but much more extensive. Everywhere were what we came to recognize as typical Dakhla donkey carts, fitted with automobile tires and driven by men in Panama hats. So we decided to spend the night in Dakhla. That meant finding a place to stay and we stopped at the first hotel we saw, the *Mubarrez*. When the man at the desk learned that we were Americans, he told us that an anthropology professor from the University of Kentucky had spent eight months here staying with him and his family, and he had later visited her in Lexington. Americans, he said with obvious sincerity, were *karim giddan, giddan, giddan, giddan*. It was nice to know that we were hospitable, an attribute so important in the Arab World.

We were offered a choice of rooms, one on the sunny and the other on the shady side of the hotel. Both were marginal, the bathrooms discolored with the same red-brown of Bahriyah and the furniture the usual barely-functional particleboard with the cheap veneer peeling off in places. But the linen looked clean, if not pressed, and we took the room on the sunny side at twenty-five pounds for the night. There were a few other guests in the hotel including what looked like an older Indian couple driving a Jeep Cherokee. There must have been others because the next morning there was an empty bottle of Jack Daniels on the table in the little common room. Or maybe the man at the desk had acquired the taste during his visit to Lexington. We unloaded the car and set out to see the sights of Dakhla.

There was a Roman temple at *Deir el Hagar* and two Hellenic tombs nearby. Both were about twenty-five miles away on the same road by which had entered the oasis. So we rattled back to the turnoff where a sign in English and Arabic announced the temple. It was a mile into the desert and had been neatly restored by an Italian archaeologist. There was a large walled compound and inside, the temple proper. An entrance pylon dating from the first century AD led to a long courtyard, beyond which sat walls in fairly good preservation with hieroglyphs, some still in their original colors. Outside the temple, but still in the compound, were several hundred large pieces of sandstone, all numbered and awaiting their place in the restored edifice.

We didn't find the Hellenic tombs. Anyway, it was late and we bumped our way back to the hotel, for a third time over the badly-pitted road. The sunset from the little balcony of the hotel was a fiery yellow and orange, and then a new crescent moon—it was the second day of the Feast—and a single star appeared together in the pale blue sky, alone and very dramatic in combination. Dinner was a baked chicken with salad, rice and vermicelli. We had read somewhere about the *aish*, or bread, of the oases but in the three days we saw only the *baladi* of the Nile valley. We were asleep early, I in the bed but Martha on top in the same sleeping bag and sheet arrangement of the first night.

To Kharga and Luxor

On the morning of the twenty-second we decided to press on to Luxor. We bought gas in Mut, the attendant fumbling with a combination of screwdriver and nozzle. The gas tanks of American cars had small orifices covered by a hinged membrane, designed to prevent fumes escaping into the atmosphere. So filling the tank was a long process, pushing down the membrane with a screwdriver and pumping at the same time. A lot of the gas wound up on the ground. The man at the hotel said that there was a new road going directly from Kharga to the bend of the Nile, eliminating a long leg to the south.

At least, that is what we hoped. But it was not to be. After several hours through featureless desert the outskirts of Kharga announced themselves by mounds of rubbish. The guidebook said that Kharga was the administrative capital of the oases and it was full of drab concrete-block buildings. It appeared uninteresting and we slowed only long enough to ask directions out of town. The policeman at the check-point told us only that Luxor was "more than ninety kilometers" away.

But it was an interesting stretch, if only for the names. We turned south, passing first through the little town of Sana', followed by Kuwait, Palestine, and then Jidda before reaching the turnoff to Luxor which, according to the sign, was 245 kilometers, or about 150 miles, away to the north of east. So this was not a new road at all, but the old one shown on the map. Then the miles fell away but not nearly fast enough because the road was bad, sometimes consisting of little more than a dirt track. We imagined ourselves on a high plateau with the Nile Valley away and below us to the east. It *looked* like a plateau, utterly featureless and monotonous except when we had the sickening realization that we were taking a bad part of the road too fast and could shortly expect the water in the front seat with us. The drive was nerve-wracking, not only because of the road but also because we didn't see another vehicle for the nearly four hours it took to reach the Nile valley.

But about twenty miles from Luxor, the scenery changed and drifts of fine golden sand began to appear again. As we began the descent the cliffs became interesting and the road improved. Then the river, lined with palms, appeared and we were soon back in a familiar Egyptian scene. We drove into the sown that encircled the town. Maybe it was the contrast with the desert we had just passed through, but everything here appeared small and ordinary, even Deir el-Bahri, Hatshepsut's mortuary temple that to Martha had always been the most noble prospect in Egypt. It was still where we had seen it twelve years before, nestled in a draw above the little village. But now there were souvenir shops lining the long avenue leading up to the striking, almost classical, façade and it sat at the end of the avenue looking like a K-Mart. Martha was furious. However we reminded ourselves that we were tourists like everyone else and resolved to get on with our sight-seeing.

In our previous visits to Luxor there had been too little time to see everything. This time, we wanted to see the Ramasseum and Deir el-Bahri again before we crossed the river and looked for a hotel. I was still having trouble with distances. Within a half-mile radius there were the Colossi of Memnon, the Ramesseum, Medinet Habu, and Deir el-Bahri. I remembered or imagined great distances. Here everything seemed crowded together.

But the Ramesseum repaid the price of admission and we wandered in the early afternoon light through the stunning ruins. The chariots and Hittite figures on the first and second pylons were fine, but most striking was the huge head of Ramses II, lying on its left ear. It was called Ozymandius by Diodorus, and by Shelly after him:

> I met a traveler from an antique land Who said two vast and trunkless legs of stone Stand in the desert. Near them on the sand,
> Halfsunk, a shattered visage lies . . .

For once, no description seemed too romantic for the setting. The complex called for repose and, after hurtling for days through the desert we succumbed, sitting and taking in the scene.

Afterwards, we made a brief pilgrimage to Deir el-Bahri. Inside, the cluttered surroundings were forgotten. Then we found the car ferry and waited in the line to cross the river. We were fourteenth in line and the ferry took about that many, depending on the size of the vehicles. But Egyptians had a habit of ignoring lines and, sure enough, a couple of men drove to the front where, after the usual bellowing and gesticulating, they were admitted ahead of everyone else. But in the end we all made the boat. After we had disentangled ourselves from the free-for-all on the other side, we drove to the old Winter Palace where we were determined to shake the dust and sand from our feet.

It was cavernous and nice in a Victorian kind of way, but they were fully booked. So the reservations manager offered to help and began calling other hotels. He started with five-stars and then moved down the list. By the time he found a room we were in the three-star category. I could hear the conversations as he talked with each of his counterparts. He told them we were looking for a room for a night and would pay cash. Cash, it turned out, was always more than the published rate.

The hotel was the New Amelios not far from Luxor temple. We were tired and the unctuous manager showed us the room only after a tour of the swimming pool and the disco on the seventh floor. But the room was very clean and modern and we took it. The manager and I then adjourned to his office where we negotiated a price of fifty dollars. The published rate was thirty-five pounds, or about eight dollars, but we were in no position to argue. They had a buffet that evening and should he put us down for two? But I thanked him very much and said we had other plans. We wanted to have dinner at the Winter Palace and then maybe see the famous sound and light show at Karnak.

Instead, dinner was in the coffee shop of the New Winter Palace, which connected with the old through an arcade. The main dining room had been reserved that night for a black-tie affair. The maître d', if such there is in a coffee shop, was harried and inefficient and there was only one waiter, who told us he had been there since seven o'clock that morning. The food was edible. Sound and light was a disappointment. There seemed to be thousands of us, mainly Japanese, wandering through the great temple, and at thirty-three pounds a ticket, it was easy to see how revenues from tourism were returning to their old levels. First the lights went out and then English-accented voices, male and female, boomed at us from several directions. We eventually made our way to the reflecting pool, above which we sat in a kind of grandstand and were subjected to a fifteen-minute harangue on the Egyptians, Alexander, Caesar, and the Romans. It was disjointed and I am not sure that if I heard it a hundred times I would have understood what they were talking about. Back at the New Amelios we fell into bed. This time Martha slept between the sheets.

Middle Egypt and Home

I was up early the next morning for a look around Luxor Temple. The large horse population in the town provided an idea of what pollution must have been like in the nineteenth century. The temple was almost deserted at seven thirty and it was very pleasant wandering through the maze of pylons and pillars. Afterwards we paid the bill and drove back to the ferry landing for the return trip across the river. We planned to go up the west bank, past Qena to el-Balyana where the road turned off to Abydos, our next stop. We weren't sure of the agricultural road, but it was Friday and there didn't appear to be much traffic. So we made better time than on all but the best stretches between the oases. The fields lining the river were a vivid green, contrasting sharply with the cliffs to the west. They were planted primarily in *birseem* and sugar cane.

In fact, it was the harvest season just then and a variety of vehicles and animals— bicycles, donkeys, camels, tractors, and carts—carried bundles of cane along the road. There was even a little narrow-gauge railroad that took the cane from the fields to the collection points. Wagons overflowing with sugar cane sat on sidings by the side of the road for most of the way to Qena. Noticeable also was the number of old taxicabs. We had seen 1950s Chrysler products in the Delta ten years before. But here, there was an even greater variety. There were late 1940s Fords—we even saw a couple of woodies—early 1950s Chevrolets, Dodges, and DeSotos. Most often the gasoline engines had been replaced with diesel and they belched black smoke. It was a typical Upper Egyptian rural scene. The little villages were squalid, but the fields were beautiful and everywhere people were busy with the harvest.

But this was not going to be an uneventful drive up the Nile Valley. Our first hint of trouble came at the police checkpoint outside Qena. We had mistakenly turned east toward the city when we were waved down by a young man in civilian clothes holding a walkie-talkie. This was different from the olive-drab uniformed police we had dealt with until then. He directed us to a parked Toyota Landcruiser where four men sat, all in civilian clothes and all carrying sidearms or Kalashnikovs. One in the back seat was asleep. There was a great deal of talk on the radio and then one of the men told us that there were problems to the north and the road was closed. This was unexpected and I protested, saying that we had come all the way through the Western Desert to see Abydos and didn't understand why we couldn't go on. He said he was sorry but we could go only as far as Dendera, three kilometers farther up the road. We were still about eighty kilometers, or fifty miles, from Abydos.

This didn't sound right and I persisted, speaking now in Arabic. For some reason this seemed to have an effect because there was another few minutes of static on the radio and then he said that we could go to Abydos after all. But we had to be careful because they were working on the road. It still sounded odd but he would say no more. When he asked what we would do next, I said that we would probably spend the night in Sohag. It all seemed mysterious, but less so when we arrived in Abydos and found that we were expected.

We decided to see Dendera as long as we were in the area and were glad we did. The massive mud-brick enclosure wall looked like it had been designed by Le Corbusier, the facade sagging along its hundreds of feet in regular undulating curves. Inside, the main temple, dating from the second century BC, was the largest and most elaborate of its day. These Ptolemaic copies of New Kingdom themes were stunning, although purists tended to dismiss them as latecomers and hybrids. Later, the Copts or Muslims—or maybe both—had defaced them and there wasn't an intact Hathor in the hypostyle hall.

At Abydos the temples of Seti I and Ramses II sat above the little town. Below, there was an outdoor restaurant, gift shop, and garden. We stopped for a soft drink before exploring the temples. The temple of Seti I contained white limestone reliefs, the finest in Egypt, and we wandered in the soft light of the interior, admitted through clerestory windows high on the walls. A hallway leading to the Osireion contained a king list with scores of cartouches and we were able to identify a few. Outside, the Osireion was closed due to ground water but the guard, with a wink, told us we could see it when the crowds, such as they were, had thinned. They were all Egyptians. But the Osireion looked less interesting than the temple of Ramses II and we walked the quarter of a-mile to the northwest to see it. Parts had been roofed over and that was a relief, as the sun was hot and the glare considerable. It was like being at Saqqara.

Back at the restaurant we had visitors. A major in civilian clothes was waiting for us, as was his boss, a colonel also in mufti. The colonel introduced his son, Ahmed, a boy of about ten, and we chatted and gave him a pen from America. The major carried a radio and wore aviator sunglasses. Like cops everywhere, he was a little full of himself. In these countries what we feared we was not the ill-will of the police but rather their capriciousness. When we got up to leave the colonel asked us if we wouldn't like to wait a little while longer. It was clear that this wasn't an invitation, but an order. It would be just five minutes, he said. There wasn't a problem, of course, but they just wanted to be on the safe side. It was a kind of *tahmin* or *ihtiyatiyat*, insurance or contingency. The colonel understood that we wanted to go to Sohag that night where, he said, we should stay at the Merit Amon Hotel. We could, of course, stay in Abydos but there was nothing like the Merit Amon here. He rolled his eyes as if to suggest that it was the finest hotel in Middle Egypt.

There had been a great deal of crackling on the radio and the words "*arabiya baida*" were repeated several times. So It seemed that we were waiting for a white car to accompany us to Sohag. The car arrived a quarter of an-hour later, a white Toyota pick-up with a fat uniformed officer in the front and several armed men in the back. We were to follow them. So we thanked the major and colonel for their hospitality and followed the Toyota out of town, staring down the muzzles of casually-held Kalashnikovs. At the checkpoint we waited behind a truck mounted with a light machine-gun before we hurtled off to the north. The driver went very fast and several times nearly lost us. We quickly covered the thirty miles to Sohag. There was no problem at the checkpoints. About five miles from the city the driver waved us ahead. The fat officer was asleep in the front seat. Just outside the town, they took the lead again and led us across a bridge to the east bank of the river. The Merit Amon was another seedy provincial hotel with peeling wallpaper and barely functional bathrooms. The man at the desk was businesslike but his eyes were not friendly. There was no disco, no pool and no bar. When I asked about a Stella he hissed that alcohol was *haram*, forbidden. He spoke civilly to us but shouted at the staff, always a bad sign.

Dinner was in the dining room and at what time would we like it served? We agreed on six o'clock. In the room we settled down to our enforced hospitality. There was nothing to see in the city, and we would have to ask the police before going anywhere. Dinner was salad, chicken, and rice with vermicelli. We were the only ones in the cavernous dining room. The waiter was a friendly little man and our immediate assumption was that he was a Copt. This was not a happy place. We would soon learn why.

There had been a recent article in the *Financial Times* announcing the retreat of terrorism in Upper Egypt:

> Assiut, the provincial capital of Upper Egypt, no longer lives up to its reputation as a hotbed for dangerous Islamic militants. A mixture of iron-fist security operations, increased money for

development, and attractive investment incentives are working to transform the town from a terrorist base to a revitalized center for commerce and industry.

Development and investment seemed to be the keys to the transformation. The area had been neglected since Nasser's time, odd since Nasser himself was a *sa'idi* from Assuit. Poverty, lack of opportunity, and neglect by Cairo had made it a fertile breeding-ground for Islamists. Actually, the problems had begun well before the rise of militant Islam. Taxis in the 1970s had to travel in convoy in the governorate as insurance against highway robbery. But with the latest upsurge in violence, the large Coptic community had been particularly targeted.

I remembered Assiut from the early 1980s when I had traveled there with an audit team from ARENTO. We had been six Muslims and one *khawaga* but they had shown me all the Christian sights, including monasteries in the hills and the Lillian Trasher orphanage, founded early in the century by a Methodist lady from Indiana. Our Egyptian friends now talked about how everyone—Muslims, Copts, and Jews—used to get along, and they lamented the passing of the culture of tolerance. The *Financial Times* article went on to add that the area was ready to welcome back tourists. However, trouble was never far away and the problems seemed to have moved north to Malawi and el-Minya. This was the official line, and the article had been cited in the *Al-Ahram Weekly,* the English-language newspaper that was the best thing to happen to Egyptian journalism since the 1980's. But nobody in Egypt believed it. What we didn't know in our seedy hotel room in Sohag was that there had been a great deal of bloodshed just south of Assiut in the past few days and the authorities were on maximum alert.

The problems began on February 14th with the killing by police in the Sohag governorate of two senior members of *al-Gama'a al-Islamiya.* The violence had escalated and a couple of days later two policemen were ambushed and killed north of the city. On February 19th—the eve of the Feast—militants from one family killed seven members of another family in al-Badari, about twenty miles south of Assiut and security forces had arrested many people. Then, the next day two Copts were killed in the village of Tasa. Finally, on the night of the twenty-first, while we were in Dakhla, gunmen had entered the Coptic village of Ezbet al-Aqbat and killed eight more. They had gone into houses in the village claiming that they were police. But they were looking for men to kill, although two of the dead were Muslims.

The Copts in the village were terrified, afraid to leave their homes and work in the fields. They were poor farmers and had no arms. After the funerals the village priest, Father Samuel William, rejected the idea of self-defense, saying that it was best left to the police. All these things happened on the east bank of the river and were later reported in government newspapers, the Arabic *Al-Ahram* on February 28 and the *Al-Ahram Weekly* for February 29–March 6. But there was a darker side. According to other sources, the Copts *were* armed and were simply biding their time. Later, in the office two Muslims and a Copt discussed the events among themselves. All feared the outbreak of civil war.

Had we known these things we might have behaved differently. I thought that the precautions were routine, since incidents in Upper Egypt had such an immediate, and negative, impact on tourism. Revenues in 1994/95 were $2.3 billion, up 20 percent from the previous year and Egypt had begun to climb out of the trough of 1992 and Luxor when terrorism had taken a heavy toll. We had obviously emerged from the security envelope at Dendera, and were now in the real Middle Egypt. The odd thing was that the security forces had let us go on. Their manner was clumsy. Instead of telling us what the problem was, or even that there was a problem, they patronized us and told transparent falsehoods. The road from Qena to Abydos was fine, and it was not under repair. It was a case-study in how not to deal with westerners.

The night at the hotel was odd. When I went out to the car for the mosquito machine and a bottle of water, the policemen followed. Our questions about the little amusement park next to the hotel went unanswered. Later, we heard people in the hall outside the room and there was that phrase *arabiya baida'* —the white car—again. Just after midnight and again later in the night there were bursts of semiautomatic gunfire somewhere in the city. In Pakistan it would probably have been a wedding, but here we didn't know.

The next morning we told the desk clerk we would leave at eight o'clock, as we had told the police the day before. In the hotel with us were two policemen, one man in black and the other in olive-drab. They had slept in the reception area and the man in black was on the phone as soon as we told him our plans. After breakfast we chatted with them while we waited. Each had five children and they were simple men, indifferent to the political problems that swirled around us here. But we were their charges and Makheet, the man in black, became visibly agitated as eight o'clock approached. The white car still hadn't come and now he became livid on the phone. We had said we were leaving at eight, and he had even confirmed that again, by phone, at six thirty that morning. Where was the car? By eight fifteen it still hadn't come and Ahmed, the policeman in olive drab and the man at the desk from the day before simply said to go. So we left.

We re-crossed the bridge to the west side of the river and the traffic policemen were helpful as we looked for the agricultural road. Finally we saw a sign to Assiut and headed north, our own masters again. But the reprieve was short-lived. At a checkpoint a few miles outside of town the policeman compared our license plate with the number written on the fleshy part of his hand just below the thumb and waved us over. This time there was no margin for error. We waited and formed up in convoy, one Toyota full of troops ahead of us and two behind. We drove very fast and they used the siren when there was traffic. People must have been used to it because, unlike our experience in Cairo, they immediately made way. We covered the seventy miles to Assiut in just over an hour and hurtled through the city at speed. It looked interesting, by far the cleanest city we had seen on the trip, and there were many graceful buildings, unlike the ugly concrete boxes that characterized much of modern Egypt.

We crossed the river and, on the other side of town, the lead Toyota motioned us in the direction of the desert road to Cairo. Then, they disappeared. We thought at the time it was an odd way to protect us: we were clearly advertised and anyone who wanted could simply have followed the convoy until the police left. It was puzzling, although the desert road was well to the east of the agricultural area and we saw nothing but sand for the rest of the day. We passed to the east of Malawi and el-Minya, and the police must have assumed that we had enough sense to stay where we were. There were undoubtedly checkpoints to ensure that we did. At Beni Suef they were waiting for the *ithnain Amricaan* and the policeman gave us a friendly "*Hamdilla salama*" when we arrived. It was the equivalent of "welcome" or "nice to see you" or "glad you made it," or maybe all three at the same time. The 220 miles to Cairo passed without incident, the last fifty seeming to take as long as all the rest put together.

In retrospect, we accomplished everything we wanted on the trip. We saw the oases, the Ramasseum, and Abydos and there had been no mechanical problems. We thought the most difficult part would be the desert and we breathed a sigh of relief when we reached the Nile Valley. But it had been the other way around. The security situation remained a mystery. Why were we permitted to go north at all? Why did they let us leave Sohag alone? We thought briefly of going to Akhmim, famous for its cotton fabrics, and that would have taken us to the eastern road and through el-Badari and 'Azbet el-Aqbat. Could the security forces really afford to provide all expatriates a personal escort through Middle Egypt? But we were glad that we hadn't asked beforehand, that being the surest way to doing nothing. It was always easier to ask for forgiveness rather than permission.

5

The Flame Trees of Dokki

Cairo could never be called a beautiful city. There were views—for example, from one of the minarets of *El-Muyeid Sheikh* towards the Azhar, or the cluster of buildings near *Al-Nasr Mohammed Qalawun*—that were glimpses of what it had been in its medieval heyday, the city of a thousand minarets. But Cairo was not beautiful in the same way that Paris was beautiful. During the day in the summer it could be hot, muggy, and dust-laden. But, like many cities in the Middle East, it could also be spectacular at night when the dust had settled and the breeze came up. Then, the lights were reflected off the water, the restaurant boats made their deliberate way between Zamalek and Rhoda, and the city came alive. Families could be seen taking the air at midnight, long after children in the United States had been put to bed. In the summer they gathered so thickly on the bridges over the Nile that they spilled over into the roadway. The traffic, always chaotic, was even more confused with lanes blocked by parked cars and strolling couples.

But there was a time during the day, from early May through early June when, from the right vantage point, the city could actually be called pretty. Looking southeast up Sad el-'Ali Street to the Nile from the eighteenth-floor terrace of a building in Dokki, the white high-rises, the canopy of trees, and the green of the water made for a rare scene. Because during this brief period the trees were in bloom and there were clusters of pinks, blues, yellows, and reds. Especially the reds. They were not just a single red, but a graduated series of hues like a good Tekke Turkoman carpet, from light brick-red through orange to a deep scarlet, not the lurid vermillions of the Pakistani copies.

The flowering trees in Cairo were identifiable by their colors: yellow Acacias, pink-flowered Orchids, light-blue Jacarandas, and red Flamboyants, or Flame Trees. Only the Acacia was native to Egypt. The Acacias were huge, the tallest fifty to sixty feet high with trunks four feet in diameter at the base. They lined Tahrir Street on the stretch outside the Opera House.

The flowers were drooping clusters of yellow, fist-sized in diameter, and ten inches long

The Orchids would have been identical to the Acacia if leaf structure were the only criterion. But instead of being tall they were low and spreading with a canopy maybe thirty feet in diameter. They bloomed from the middle of June to early September and were visible long after the flowers had dropped from the Flame Trees. The blossoms—pink petals grouped in ten-inch clusters—competed with the yellows and blues long after the reds were gone. The Jacaranda, a Brazilian import, bloomed first, briefly giving the neighborhood a gossamer covering of violet or light blue as seen from a vantage point above. Even though they bloomed earliest they lasted the longest, and violet blossoms were still visible in September.

But it was the Flame Trees that dominated the city. They were so much a part of Cairo that they almost defined it. The Flame Tree had an Arabic name—some said *ranf* and others *masleekh*—but no one really knew them by either of these names. They were concentrated on the west bank of the river in Dokki and Giza, and reached as far north as Agouza and Imbaba. They carpeted Zamalek as well, and a late-spring view was one of vivid splashes of red and orange all the way to the northern tip of the island. They blossomed in such profusion that the weight of the petals was often enough to bring branches crashing down, often in the middle of the night. They were also shallow-rooted and occasionally an entire tree would fall, crushing parked cars whose owners should probably have known better. The flower itself was a complex of reds and yellows, the corolla irregular with the stamens ten inches long. In some trees, depending on the sex, they were sparser. But in others they were so heavily clustered that there was hardly any green visible. By the middle of June the flowers were dropping, and the ground around the trees would be blood red. Reading a description of deciduous trees, of the seeds and seedlings, was a reminder of the reproductive function of flowers: there were swelling organs and cap-like sheaths, slit-like apertures and hard, slimy tips, endosperm and root hairs.

Summer evenings at the Marriott in Zamalek witnessed another display of reproductive color: the Gulf promenade, with Saudis, Kuwaitis, Qataris, Emiratis, and Bahrainis passing in review. They were clustered at tables in the outdoor restaurant, drinking fruit punch, or walking arm-in-arm through the gardens. Some wore the white thobe of the peninsula, but most had changed into western dress. The thobe was more flattering as it concealed more than it revealed. There seemed to be few mesomorphs among the Gulfies, and they were either unnaturally fat or unnaturally thin. There were supposed to be prostitutes working the crowds, but I never saw anyone at the Marriott who looked like a hooker. Maybe I was just naive.

Black and silver were the favored hues. It was if they were all Oakland Raiders' fans. There were black Levi's hoisted up around prodigious haunches, secured by black belts with silver buckles. And black shirts with silver stripes, silver shirts with black stripes, plain black shirts, plain silver shirts, and pointed black shoes with silver taps. As the groups passed one another there was an audible sound as they exchanged kisses. Groups of overweight children—they developed the tendency early—dashed among the tables with little control exercised by the adults.

But it was only the men who made the promenade. The women were seated, or were in their rooms, or in the beauty parlor where they were notoriously imperious and demanding. To say that they had more money than good sense would be to utter the average Egyptian's, half-century-long complaint. But it was hard to be sympathetic with the Egyptians. They were just as arrogant when they were on top, raised—as they all were—to believe they were the cream not only of the Arab world but of the world in general.

In 1960 the per capita GDP of Egypt had been the same as that of South Korea. Today it was one tenth of South Korea's and the gap was growing. In the Far East, the political culture was developing in the wake of the economic success. Egypt remained a backwater, the government dominated by the military and a privileged commercial elite. In the 1990s the Egyptians thought they learned the lesson of the Asian collapse: since there was no massive outflow of short-term capital from Egypt, they had been doing the right thing all along. The problem was there that was no outflow because there had been no inflow of capital, short-term or otherwise. Egypt was simply not a very friendly place to do business and it would not attract investment until it was. Meanwhile, the Egyptians talked endlessly about the superiority of their human resources. Other people had gotten on with it. Until the situation changed the Gulf promenade would continue and produce the same gnashing of Egyptian teeth.

6

Serabit el-Khadem

It would be our fourth attempt to locate the site. Serabit el-Khadem was the 4th-dynasty temple complex originally built by the Pharaoh Sneferu as a place of worship for the workers at the turquoise mines of Wadi Maghara in the Sinai peninsula. It had been unknown to Europe until discovered by Carsten Niebuhr in 1762. Niebuhr was looking for the *Jebel Mokatteb*, or the "Written Mountain," which European scholars believed might contain clues to the development of the square Hebrew script, purportedly left by the Children of Israel during their wanderings in the wilderness. It was an example of the conflation of biblical and Egyptian history characteristic of Western thinking before the deciphering of the hieroglyphs. In fact, there would be no mention of the biblical story of the Exodus in Pharaonic records when they were finally brought to light. And what Niebuhr found had nothing to do with the Children of Israel, although Flinders Petrie would later excavate the site and find evidence of a script with an affinity to the writing systems of people to the north.

We had often been up and down the western seaboard of Sinai since its return from the Israelis in 1983, although much of the peninsula had been off-limits. There was still the danger of mines and the Egyptian authorities always found "no" the easiest answer to any attempt to stray off the beaten path. But the interior of the peninsula was now open and there was finally a chance to see the temple. It would also be another opportunity to visit St. Catherine's monastery. We had seen it many times over the years, but its attractions—the spectacular setting in the granite fastness and the complex itself with its fourth-century walls—never seemed to pale.

So I left Cairo before dawn and hoped to reach Abu Zeneima about eight thirty. Abu Zeneima was on the west coast of Sinai, seventy-five miles south of Suez, and the nearest town to Serabit. This time I was alone but would take a Bedouin with me to show the way. Surely I would find someone there who knew the place. Martha and I had looked unsuccessfully for Serabit in the spring, twice from the north and once from the Wadi el-Mokatteb in the south. The first time we followed what, from the map, looked like the way, inland over bad roads south of Abu Zeneima, until we found a paved road. But that carried us too far south and we eventually emerged on the coast, just north of Abu Rudeis. On the second attempt, from the south, we found the Wadi el-Mokatteb where it should have been, a few miles over a dirt track from the Wadi Feran, fifty miles west of the monastery. There were several 4x4s parked by cliffs, and a group of Germans pouring over the rocks that lined the *wadi*, off and on, for several hundred yards.

They asked if we wanted to follow them to Serabit, but we hadn't had time to see the inscriptions and so we declined. We probably should have accepted the offer and I had a momentary pang as they sped away, trailing plumes of dust. But, at least we saw the petroglyphs of camels and gazelles, mounted men, and scores of names in the pre-Arabic Nabataean script. Later, as we moved north, there was only a confusing series of tracks. We were going northeast, as the map said we should, until we came to a lone Bedouin in a tent who told us to go back the way we had come. That was fatal, and we eventually picked up the broad Wadi Sidr that deposited us on the coast again, this time just south of Abu Rudeis.

The third time, from the north, we took a wrong track inland and after about a mile bogged down in the sand. We walked to a quarry a couple of miles to the south and a group of Bedouins came back with us in a Toyota and eased us out. I had dug under the wheels and placed pieces of scrap metal and cardboard—all that I could find—for traction. Martha gunned the engine while I lifted and pushed. But that only dug us in deeper. The Bedouins sized up the situation, stroked their chins knowledgeably, and set to work. They rocked the car back and forth, filling in the sand that I had so painstakingly excavated. Then one of them put it in second gear, they all pushed and the car moved, slowly at first, and then quickly out of the depression. They said the Israelis had taught them how to drive in the sand.

This time, I was taking no chances. I had gone to the Egyptian Exploration Society for directions before leaving Cairo. They had sponsored a trip to Serabit the year before and should know the way. The girl in the office said that although the route in the map was clear, it was best to have a guide. And it was essential to have a four-wheel-drive vehicle to reach the site. Even then, they had become stuck many times. But the quote they had just received from a local agency for a 4x4 with driver worked out to about $500 for the day, half as much as an original David Roberts lithograph of the site, and I decided to try one more time on my own. So, just before nine o'clock I stopped in Abu Zeneima at a little cafe, and sure enough, there were several men seated outside who said they knew the way to Serabit. One of them, Nur, said he had been there many times. When I asked him if the Blazer *tinfa'a*, or could make it, he said yes, the roads were fine. We eventually settled on a price of thirty pounds (or about nine dollars) for the trip out and back. This time there would be no detours.

As we set out several Bedouins waiting by the side of the road asked if the could go with us. But I was loaded for several days in the Sinai and could fit only one more, so we took Mahmoud who lived not far from the site. We went south for about three miles to the road we had taken in the spring and turned inland. It had once been paved but was now badly rutted. Eventually the last trace of pavement disappeared and we were completely in Nur's hands. When we came to a fork in the tracks that crisscrossed the area, he indicated with a wave which one to take. It was no wonder we had been lost. It looked simple on the map: go inland for twenty miles to the second turnoff, and then go south. After three miles you were at Serabit. The reality was far more complicated and I realized that I probably couldn't find it again unaided.

It was the last day of Ramadan but neither Nur nor Mahmoud was fasting. They shared a pack of *Cleopatra* cigarettes until it was gone. After an hour, we reached a group of tents that were Mahmoud's *beit* and he *nazala,* or "got down." By now all semblance of a road had disappeared, and there were only tracks, reassuring evidence at least that other vehicles had recently passed that way. I still hadn't seen any 4x4s, only a few small Toyota trucks. So maybe Nur was right about the Blazer. He was sixteen years old, he said, and had never been to school. His teeth were discolored like those of all the Sinai Bedouins, a brown line appearing halfway up the incisors when he smiled. He belonged to the *Beni Leghat* and with a sweep of his hand said that all of this land belonged to the *Leghat*.

Inland the road had, at first, been sandy. Then we went through an area of chalky limestone, with many little hills. But now we were in a broad sandy plain, covered with scrub. The going was rough but passable. When we reached the crest of a rise we almost slid down a long embankment covered with fine golden sand. It was clear that we were not going to come back *up* that bank, but Nur said not to worry since there was another way out. His Arabic was understandable, except that he sometimes swallowed his words like the Saudis. But when he was trying to explain something unfamiliar he became excited and the words came tumbling out. This soon followed. Because we were now in a wadi bed and I mistakenly took us through loose sand, not on the firmer surface on the side. For the first time the car stuck.

We got out and Nur began clearing the loose sand away under the rear tires. That didn't work and then he suggested we let some air out of the tires.

I had them checked the night before and they all carried thirty psi. He used the blunt end of a wooden matchstick and let what I later found was about ten pounds out of each tire. At that point a Toyota came by and two *Bedu* interested themselves in our predicament. One looked to be about fifty, with his front teeth missing. The other was much younger and he immediately sized up the situation. He took off his overcoat, tucked his pants legs into his socks and set to work.

He took the rubber mat from the floor on the driver's side, placed it under the driving wheel and added a little dried brush. Then he matter-of-factly took the keys from me, started the car and slowly eased out of the declivity, first backing then moving forward with a rush onto the firmer surface. The Toyota disappeared. But the younger man, Mohammed, stayed and suggested that he drive, since he was a professional driver and knew how to deal with the sand. He knew all about Serabit, having worked at the site, and would show me around. Nur now sat, eclipsed, in the back seat.

So on we went with, Mohammed driving, across the wadi bed and up a hill before dropping into the next wadi. He was short and slight and his feet barely reached the pedals. But he seemed to know how to drive in these conditions, swinging his arms and the wheel from side to side as we went through areas of heavy sand. The key seemed to be to build up speed and not stop. But when the going became heavy, he slowed and never used first gear. That only spun the tires and dug the hole deeper. We bounced up to the crest of a second ridge swinging over tracks, or more frequently, through fresh sand, and down the other side. Then, there were patches of rough pebbles and although these made the going easier, they shook the car violently. Every nut and bolt that had survived our trip to the oases in the Western Desert the year before now threatened to come loose.

We should now have been in the vicinity of the temple, and I asked Mohammed to point out Serabit when he saw it. But he only grunted. I was looking for something prominent, a mesa with a steep ascent to the flat, but every time we saw something that met that description, we passed it by. Finally, after half an hour we drew up into the long finger of a wadi that came to an end near a cliff below which sat several acacias and a corrugated tin shed. Mohammed turned the car around and stopped. We had arrived.

Nur carried a bottle of water and Mohammed carried my English translation of Niebuhr's *Travels in Arabia* with the plates of the site. *He* was fasting, he said, with a disgusted gesture in Nur's direction. He said that it would take an hour and a-half up to the site and an hour back. It was now ten thirty so that meant we would be back at the car at about two o'clock, allowing for time to look around the temple. As we began the ascent a crude sign in Arabic identifying the site as Serabit appeared at the base of the cliff.

A long trail snaked across the face of the hill before reaching a steep part in beautifully weathered sandstone. There were whorls of red and cream and beige like Petra and the eddying wind had carved holes in the soft surface. In a few places there were new concrete steps and pieces of reinforcing bar as handholds.

Mohammed said the Bedouins had made the improvements and that *aganib ketir*—many foreigners—came to see the temple. But we didn't see anyone else that day, either on the way in or out. Halfway up we reached a kind of resting place and it was clear that, for thousands of years, others had done just as we did. We sat and caught out breath beneath inscriptions in the soft red sandstone. There were crude petroglyphs of gazelles and oryx and, much older, Egyptian hieroglyphs, remarkably well preserved. There were also several representations of boats, looking like the solar boat at Giza, but with steeper prows and sterns. If the original workers at the site came directly across the Gulf of Suez from Upper Egypt, as some of Petrie's workers did in 1904, they would have come by boat.

After twenty minutes we reached the top of the cliff face, before setting off on a long, overland trek, rising then falling over a series of plateaus. Nur was wearing sandals and Mohammed black penny-loafers, still with his pant legs tucked into his socks. I was glad for the soft crepe soles on my desert boots since they made the rocky surfaces easier to grip. We trooped along the ridges in Indian file, each of the Bedouins occasionally dropping back to share a confidence and then forging ahead again. Mohammed said Nur really didn't know anything about *Serabit* except where it was, which all the *Beni Leghat* knew. But *he* had worked at the site and I was lucky he had come along.

On the way back I paced off the distance from the temple to the cliff face. It was just over two thousand paces, or about two kilometers. No wonder the place was so hard to find and why no European had found it before Niebuhr. There was nothing on the floor of the wadi to suggest the existence of the temple. And Niebuhr probably found it by accident, there being no Jebel Mokatteb, only a Wadi Mokatteb. But if the foreigners wanted a mountain the *Leghat* would give them one, and Serabit was that mountain. It was also easy to see why Niebuhr thought it was a cemetery. As we came to the end of the long series of ridges and caught a glimpse of the site in the distance, the still-upright steles gave it the look of a country churchyard.

Up closer there were other steles, fallen over and so badly weathered that any inscriptions they may have contained were gone. Below us and to the left was a little declivity with some evidence of water and a few desert bushes, as well as a barely-legible sign in Hebrew, Arabic, and English identifying the site. But at the temple proper the upright steles were still remarkably intact. Most prominently, Niebuhr's Plate XLV I knew from Petrie to be the stele of Hor-ur-Ra from the 12th dynasty. Mohammed and Nur were both interested in the Niebuhr plate and together we matched the individual hieroglyphs in the plate with those on the stele. The photograph in Petrie's *Researches in Sinai* shows many of the figures in the stele to be indistinct, but most of those we saw were sharp and clear.

The stele in Niebuhr's Plate XLVI was also there. There were other details recognizable from a reading of Petrie: the ablution basins, the recesses for hinges in the floor, the broken statues of the goddess. Much had been taken away, either to the Egyptian Museum or the British Museum in the ninety years since Petrie worked the site. He was able to read its long history from nothing more than these brown stones. They all spoke to him, not just those with hieroglyphs. But Petrie was a phenomenon. We wandered through the temple, over the successive additions in the building program until we reached the original structure, the sacred cave.

The cave was marked with a sign that said "No enterey" but we entered anyway. The ceiling, supported by a single square pillar, was falling and a steel plate over a threaded two-inch column had recently been added. It was just high enough that we could stand. Inside, the hieroglyphs on the walls were sharp, not having been subjected to the same weathering as those on some of the steles. Outside, the desert spread out below. Mohammed said it all belonged to the *Leghat*. It was they, he said, who had worked at the site and he himself had carried rock to make a kind of sitting area to the right of the entrance. He also said it was they who had plastered over the missing parts of some of the steles.

It was now just after noon, but in early February the temperature would not reach much above sixty degrees Fahrenheit. So I sat outside in the warm sun and reviewed in my mind the successive additions to the temple as described by Petrie. Then we left. On the way down, Nur dropped back to tell me that Mohammed really didn't know what he was talking about and that he wasn't a good man anyway. He kept motioning to his right hand as if there were something wrong with it or, more probably, with Mohammed's. But he seemed the less experienced of the two and by the time we reached the bottom he had gone through most of the bottle of Baraka. Neither Mohammed nor I had drunk.

Niebuhr had made that same ascent on September 11, 1762. He doubted that he would find what he was looking for. If it was ancient inscriptions that were the purported precursors of Hebrew, his reservations were well founded. What he had stumbled on was an Egyptian temple, although it had strong Semitic characteristics. He hoped that the site might be of interest to scholars and that one day it might be excavated. These hopes were to be fulfilled, as news of the discovery led to a regular stream of visitors of the hardier sort in the next two centuries. David Roberts saw the site in February of 1839, although his lithograph *Temple on Gebel Garabe* displays so little of his customary detail that one wonders if was really *Serabit* that he saw. Edward Robinson visited the site a month later and published his impressions in his *Biblical Researches in Palestine, Mount Sinai and Arabia Petrea.*

The definitive work on the site would come with the arrival of Flinders Petrie in December of 1904. Petrie was realizing a long-held ambition to explore the area in Sinai where the Egyptians mined turquoise. He concentrated first in the Wadi Maghara where the mines were located, finding evidence there of workings as early as the 3rd dynasty and the Old Kingdom. But in early January the party moved on to a second mining area close to Serabit. Here the workings were mostly of the Middle and New Kingdoms and the workers had erected a place of worship for the deities of the area. This was Niebuhr's "cemetery." Petrie's work kept him there for nearly three months. He took two bases and by means of triangulation of the hilltops and the use of a prismatic compass, drew plans of the contours of the ravines around the site.

Of the temple itself he identified the earliest part to be the sacred cave, dating from the 4th-dynasty reign of Sneferu. Inside the cave he found evidence of work under several Middle Kingdom pharaohs of the 11th and 12th dynasties, from 2040 to 1787 BC. Finding an extensive bed of ashes around the cave, he dug deeper and found fragments of pottery, his revolutionary clue to dates. As to the meaning of the ashes, Petrie deduced that Lepsius's earlier speculation about a smelting works was incorrect. In the first place, fuel for the fires was nowhere to be found on the plateau and would have to have been carried, laboriously, up from the valley floor. And what had previously been taken for slag was also wrong, due to Lepsius's ignorance of mineralogy. This was no foundry. Instead, the ashes were probably the remains of fires that had a religious purpose: this was a place of worship, characteristic not of Egypt but of Palestine, where incense and sacrifices were burned in high places. His reasoning is generally accepted today.

The "great goddess" was the Egyptian cow goddess Hathor, in her incarnation as the "Mistress of Turquoise," the mining of which was the purpose of the expeditions. The remainder of the puzzle then unfolded. A period of neglect coincided with the 2nd Intermediate Period (1640–1532 BC) before New Kingdom expeditions were again sent to Sinai. The shrine was repaired and extended in a series of additions that snaked away from the cave in a west, then west-by-south direction. Hatshepsut was the greatest builder, with her co-ruler, her nephew Thutmosis III (1479–1458 BC).

From this period dates the most imposing part of the complex, the Hathor *Hanafiyeh*, with its four pillars of Hathor standing around the central basin.

From the period of Hatshepsut also dates the cave-shrine of Sopdu, the god of the eastern desert, next to that of Hathor. Ramesses II (1290–1224 BC) rebuilt the sanctuary without removing all traces of previous builders, his usual practice, and Ramesses IV altered it. To the west of the court leading into the shrine Petrie identified no less than fourteen separate structures—pylons, ablution chambers, and other rooms—added at different times and ending with a final room built by Sety I. Later Pharaohs altered but did not add to the extent of the complex and the 240 feet from the sacred cave to the chamber of Sety I defined the temple whose broad outlines remained today.

In the highly-developed bureaucracy of Pharaonic Egypt the mining expeditions were organized under a single high official. The size of the expeditions varied greatly, from several hundred in the reign of Amenemhat III to several thousand in the reign of Ramesses IV. Foreigners were also employed, most often as guides and hostages for the good behavior of the local tribes. Steles carved from the local sandstone recorded the details of the expeditions, and others listed the names of the pharaohs in whose reign the expeditions took place. Workmen occasionally scratched their names on the margins of the steles before they left. These scratchings were noticed by Petrie and led to his most important discovery at the site: evidence of a new and unknown script. It would later come to be known as "proto-Sinaitic," and would represent an important link in the development of the writing systems of the Near East.

The company packed up their squeezes and cartons of artifacts and left for Suez, arriving in early March, 1905. There was more to the temple than the major structures and steles, and Petrie collected trays and offering cones, stone and glazed vases, bangles, and beads for the museums in Cairo and London. Aesthetically, his most valuable find was the beautiful little head of Queen Ty that is displayed today in the Egyptian Museum, listed as exhibit 144. It is tiny, the fragment measuring no more than three inches high by two inches wide and two inches long. In addition to the statue of Ty, there are six blocks cut or blasted out of cliff faces at Maghara, including one with a clear cartouche of Sneferu. And in the north wing of the museum there is a display of six panels with fragments of the proto-Sinaitic script. They are identified only in Arabic and are poorly lighted and displayed.

After Petrie, the site was worked by others who focused mainly on the proto-Sinaitic scripts in the vicinity of the mines, and not on the temple itself. In February of 1977 a team from the Tel Aviv University Institute of Archaeology conducted a week-long expedition to the mines and announced the discovery of "a long-lost inscription of Thutmosis IV." But the meager results only demonstrated that, after Petrie, very little was left for others but to correct minor errors or complete slight gaps in his work.

The car was where we left it, looking very small among the acacias in the wadi below. According to Petrie, the terrain was made up of a tertiary basalt flow over an iron bed on a sandstone base, which was itself laid down over metamorphic and earlier rocks. But the whole system had been uplifted and shifted and the sandstone in many places had been sheared off by years of water flow in the many wadis that now constituted ravines. All this made driving an adventure, over soft sand, alluvial deposits, and occasional black *harras*. Mohammed said that if we went back to his *beit* he would re-inflate the tires. So we bumped back the way we had come, from Wadi Umm Aghraf where we had parked through what looked like Wadi Bateh. But it was difficult orienting myself. The compass was useless in the car, always showing due north, until I realized it was pointing at the engine block.

At the *beit*, a concrete-block shell with several clapboard outbuildings, we arrived to a welcome from a band of ragged little barefoot boys, sprinting by the side of the car until we came to a stop. They stared up at me with wild black eyes until the boldest demanded a *qalum*—a pen—and then *monaye*. The man with no teeth and the Toyota were there, and the adults sent the boys away to find the pump. But it was only a bicycle pump and by the time they finished with one rear tire it had less air than when they began. I later found it had only eighteen psi, hot. A tire would generally increase when hot from driving so the actual reading was lower. The recommended pressure was thirty-five psi, cold.

I had seen Serabit and now thought about going back through Wadi el--Mokatteb to the south. It led to Wadi Feiran and the road to St. Catherine's, my next stop. Everyone said it was easy and much shorter than going back north to Abu Zeneima. However, that left the question of how Nur would get back to the town, where he had work. But for an extra ten pounds he agreed to make his own way back and fifteen minutes later we left him near a rough track where he would find a ride. Then we returned the way we had come, this time far from any visible tracks until we came to the head of the plateau and plunged down the other side.

Mohammed was still sitting too far back and at the bottom I suggested we stop and move up the seat. Now, he sat well forward with the wheel in both hands, still swinging with his whole body as we went through areas of heavy sand. He drove reasonably well, but had trouble with the emergency brake and couldn't start on a hill. We would coast down backward before he could start again, and several times he had trouble with the clutch and brake. When I asked if he really knew how to drive he bared his teeth and said that is what he *was*, a driver. Nur didn't know anything. You had to have *mokh*—brains—and *khobar*—experience—to do what he did.

He was twenty, he said, and had been to school for six years. A red checked *kufiya* was pulled tightly around his head, out of which protruded his slightly prognathous profile. Afterwards, we settled into a kind of odd rhythm, speeding up when the going was smooth and then slowing as we went through the bad parts. In one stretch of what looked like firm sand we stopped so that I could take a photograph. But even though we seemed to be sitting well up out of the sand we stuck and it took five minutes to free the car. We eased forward in second gear, chattering violently, and I wondered if there would be a clutch or gear-box left when we reached Wadi Mokatteb. Then as the car picked up speed we were off again.

After about an hour I noticed what Nur must have been trying to tell me: Mohammed had only three fingers on his right hand. It wasn't as if one had been amputated. It just wasn't there. It appeared that a middle finger had been removed, and everything pulled together. I asked him about it and he muttered something about an accident. He was cradling the wheel in an odd, three-fingered grip, still swinging and speeding up, then slowing down. But he never seemed to get the gears right. After an hour I asked him where Wadi Mokatteb was and he said it was *kaman taht shwaiya*, or just a little farther on. After another half-hour I asked the same question and got the same answer, with a look that said "keep your shirt on, we'll get there."

Other than noting from the sun that we were going in a generally southerly direction, I had no idea where we were. The map showed that it was only about twenty-seven kilometers as the crow flies from Serabit to Wadi Feiran, but we were taking anything but a straight line. I later looked at the 1:1,000,000 Survey of Egypt map, and a route "passable for light cars" seemed to be the one we had taken: about six kilometers due east from Serabit was the *Ramlet Himeiyir* or "sandy tract with bushes" and then a track southeast in Niebuhr's Wadi Khamila for about the same distance before turning to the south and then southwest in Wadi Seih to a place where, after about twenty winding kilometers, the latter joined the Wadi Sidr. From there it went east of south through the Wadi Mokatteb to the intersection with Wadi Feran.

Meanwhile, we bumped on. We entered a wide valley that looked like the Wadi Sidr of our attempt in the spring. And then I had a sudden foreboding. I hadn't even thought about gas, but this nosing through wadis for hours on under-inflated tires must have eaten it up. From my vantage point on the passenger side the needle looked like it was on empty. I told Mohammed we needed gas and he said fine, it was available nearby. After another few minutes he left the middle of the wadi and headed toward the entrance to a small ravine. Another Bedouin came out from a little shack and Mohammed asked if he had gas. He nodded and we bumped up the ravine, now on a track that was covered with pebbles and irregularly shaped rocks. At the head was a little encampment under some thorn trees and a tin shack with a padlock on the door. Mohammed backed and turned the car, stalling it several times in the process. He said he would deal with the Bedouin, Mahmoud, and how much gas did we want?

I thought twenty liters was enough and gave him twenty pounds. Mahmoud followed us on foot and arrived a few minutes later. He opened the shack and took out a five-gallon tin. Then he filled it with gas, siphoning from a five-hundred gallon drum. Finally, Mohammed held the tin on his shoulder and Mahmoud sucked on the hose until the gas flowed. The car quickly drank the twenty liters. The twenty pounds was about the same price we would have paid in Cairo. I finally had enough of Mohammed's driving and said I would take the wheel. He bared his teeth. But to show that he was still in charge he said that Nur didn't know anything. If I had been with *him* I wouldn't have known where to get gas. You had to have *mokh* and *khobar* to be in this business. I said so what, Nur was history. He bared his teeth again.

We made our way back to the main track, and half-an-hour later we were in an area that I recognized near Wadi Mokatteb. But we were too far west, and so we headed overland, careening crazily through scrub and swinging to avoid the boulders strewn over the flood plain. It was the roughest part of the trip and the car shuddered violently as we dropped off little precipices into dry stream-beds and then up the other side, before setting off through more brush and loose sand. Finally we reached what we were looking for: a sign in English and Arabic announcing Wadi Mokatteb, placed there by the Egyptian Antiquities Organization.

We had seen it in the spring, and I had taken several rolls of film of the scripts and crude petroglyphs of gazelles, camels, and ostriches. But the area now seemed insignificant after the sights of the last several hours. It was almost as if you would miss it if you blinked. What the Europeans in Cairo, and Copenhagen, hoped in 1762 was that the "writings" were in the Hebrew script, learned by the Children of Israel during their wanderings in the wilderness. But these were just names of travelers on their way to the religious shrines in the south, probably Nabataean and dated from the early Christian era, a period fifteen-hundred years after the purported events in the Bible.

So we didn't stop but pushed on to the road through Wadi Feran. A few minutes later we came up over an outcropping of what looked like limestone and there was the road, just as we had last seen it before turning north that spring. After another 500 yards of scrub, sand, and rocks, we pulled up on the smooth asphalt surface. After the rattling of the last seven hours, the feeling was almost sensual. Mohammed had spotted a Toyota to the west of us as we came out and he asked me to speed up until we had pulled ahead. Sure enough, the Toyota emerged onto the road and came in our direction. In the highly-developed communism of the desert Mohammed's red-checked *kufiya* was all it took to stop the Toyota. He negotiated briefly with the driver, climbed in the bed of the truck and, with a final wave of that three-fingered hand, he was gone.

So, we had done it. Instead of the $500 with a rented 4x4, it had cost all of about fifty dollars, with gas and equal payments to Nur and Mohammed. The twelve dollars that each of them earned was probably too much, and there were those who would say I was shamelessly spoiling the Beni Leghat. But, in Mohammed's case, by the time he got back to his *beit* it would have been a full day's work. It remained to be seen if the car hadn't suffered permanent damage. Reassuringly, it purred along at seventy mph without a troubling sound. At less than twenty psi the tires seemed to be one with the pavement and even the annoying little rattles that I noticed before Abu Zeneima were gone.

At four thirty the sun was low in the west, and the granite walls around Feran glowed red as I drove toward St. Catherine's. I knew from our trip in the spring that it was exactly fifty miles to the monastery from the turnoff to the Wadi Mokatteb. Driving was such a pleasure on this smooth surface that, as the miles slipped by, I almost hoped it wouldn't end. We had left the main road south of Abu Zeneima that morning at about nine fifteen, and spent most of the day on rough tracks with the windows rolled down. The inside of the car was covered with fine white grit, and my hair was so matted that I couldn't pass a comb through it. By the time the road turned, imperceptibly, first south and then west on the final approach to the plain of Raha, I was ready for a shower and a hot meal.

I probably should have known better. I arrived at the hotel just as they were breaking the fast and the reception area was closed and locked. When I returned half an-hour later it was open and a room was available. But even though the water heater made encouraging sounds, the thermometer didn't register and the water ran bitterly cold. So I asked reception to check the water heater. A *fellah* arrived a few minutes later and confirmed that the heater was working. Not for the first time that day I was advised to be patient. But an hour later the water was still cold. So my shower would have to wait for the next morning when it ran so hot that it scalded me when I shaved.

That evening, the dining room was unheated and it was nearly freezing inside. There was a large central fireplace, the chimney above it covered with wrought-iron designs surmounted by a steer's head, blackened with soot. But for some reason they didn't light a fire on this, one of the coldest days of the year. *Al-Ahram* listed a recent low at *Katarin* as two degrees Celsius, or about thirty-six degrees Fahrenheit, but it felt much colder that night. Like most poorly insulated buildings, it was probably colder inside than out. The waiters hustled back and forth with uncharacteristic alacrity. They were probably just trying to keep warm. The rest of us, the usual collection of half-board guests, sat huddled with our hands pressed between our thighs. A child wailed in its misery, what we all felt like doing. The first course was a soup, but that was followed by a large, crisp—and very cold—salad. The effort to chew the main course, two thin, tough filets, at least kept me warm.

The next morning after a shower it was almost as cold at breakfast, although a few tables received radiant heat from the rising sun. Then, it was off to see the sights. After the activity of the day before I was not feeling heroic. And I had climbed the mountain so many times that I didn't feel the need to hurtle, yet gain, up that path. Besides, the last time the traffic had been so heavy that we had to stand aside to let the crowds pass on the steepest part of the ascent. So I decided to have a look at the monastery, which I hadn't seen in years.

At the entrance a monk said that it would open at nine o'clock, through the little door on the northeast side. Inside, a steady stream of visitors circulated by, first, the "burning bush," then into the basilica, then out the way we had come. Everything else on the monastery grounds was closed. The burning bush was a *Rubus Sanctus,* a Central Asian plant that appears elsewhere in the environs of Jebel Musa. It filled a stone planter box and for what must be the most famous bush in the world, there was no one to enforce the prohibition against carrying a piece of it away. In the basilica, through the eleventh-century Fatimid doors, there was first the small narthex with its displays of icons and a sampling of manuscripts kept in the library. There were Persian, Amharic, Arabic, Greek, and Syriac texts.

In the church itself, through the sixth-century Byzantine doors, there were the familiar icons lining the walls, silver candelabra, the altar, and the hard wooden seats. Everything beyond the nave was roped off. A monk was posted in a side aisle to ensure that no one stepped over the line. But he seemed glued to the spot and I later saw that he was standing in front of an electric heater. That seemed an un-monastic thing to be doing but maybe they didn't make monks like they used to. Outside, the bookshop was closed. The proprietor hadn't shown up. Then it was out the little door again.

It was an abbreviated tour, unlike a previous visit when we had wandered for several hours over the grounds. In fact, the monastery was under unprecedented pressure and everyone seemed to be at fault. Joseph Hobbs's *Mount Sinai* was an excellent history of this sacred spot, but it didn't paint a very flattering picture of the Greek religious or encouraging view of the future. The monks were misfits or saints, pious, greedy, hostile, generous, unpleasant, credulous, stupid, or devoted, depending on who you read. They were uninterested in the surroundings, spoke no Arabic, and had done nothing over the centuries to bring the message of Jesus Christ to the peninsula. Or, they were simple ascetics, and their disinterest was the best evidence of their otherworldliness. The Bedouins, descendants of the original stock of two hundred families brought as serfs from Wallachia, Bosnia, and Anatolia to serve the monastery, were devoted, dirty, extortionate, greedy, hardworking, mendacious, and rapacious, all at the same time.

The Egyptian government, always suspicious of this outpost of Greek Orthodoxy on their territory, were uninterested in, if not actively hostile to, the Christian character of the monastery and the surrounding sites. They were remote riverine bean-eaters, bureaucrats whose only interest was in the hard currency that the sites, a kind of Sinaitic Disney World, would bring in. The hotel in Wadi Raha, although it made an attempt to integrate itself into the surroundings, was built in disregard of the centuries-old prohibition against building on sacred ground. It was run with a particularly Egyptian well-intentioned inefficiency. The only hope was that in their ineptitude they couldn't do more damage. But there had been plans to build an elevated tramway from the middle of Raha to the summit of Ras Safsaafa, alternately trumpeted and denied by the bureaucrats in Cairo. Who knew what the future would bring?

It was the Israelis, as usual, who were to blame. Their occupation from 1967 to 1983 had replaced Egyptian neglect. But it had fundamentally changed the peninsula, bringing the Sinai out of its isolation and introducing large-scale tourism with its train of service-related jobs and day wages for the Bedouins. The Egyptians saw that the Israelis had taken an interest in the Sinai and they were determined to learn from the experience. There was even an office of the *mukhabarat*—the secret police—in the little town of Katerin to monitor the comings and goings of the Bedouins. They were supposed to be still loyal to the Israelis. Next time around there would be no vacuum into which an outside power could step.

But it was really *us*, the visitors, who were the greatest threat. We were pious pilgrims, credulous fundamentalist Christians, amateur historians of the peninsula, agnostics, scoffers at the Bible story, nature-lovers, hikers, backpackers, hippies, or just tourists. The monks, for all of their ill-tempered complaints about the plague that had descended on them in their desert fastness, could at least close their doors and keep us at bay. They already had, in a sense, with their now-truncated tours of the monastery.

But there was no closing the door to the mountain, and up and down we went in a steady stream. There were Germans, Filipinos, Koreans, French, Hungarians, British, Russian nuns, Americans, Dutch, Nigerians, Ghanaians, Japanese, elderly Belgian ladies, and Vietnamese. The Bedouins had seen us coming and now brought their camels to a kind of camel-park behind the monastery. They also couched them on the path just short of the Basin of Elijah. There had always been refreshment stands along the way, but now they were on the top, next to the chapel. They were typically Bedouin, shacks made of tin, clapboard, cardboard, or plywood, from which they hawked water, juice, biscuits, and trinkets. At the top the prices were double those at the bottom.

In the high season they needed a traffic cop to regulate the flow. They really couldn't all fit on the top at the same time. But up they still came, pilgrims or travelers or tourists who wanted to see sunrise from the summit. They joined the backpackers, now crawling out of the lairs where they had spent the night. They all left their signature, bits of toilet paper behind every rock, not to mention biscuit wrappings, tin cans, empty Baraka bottles, and other trash. Every year the Multinational Force and Observers (MFO) helped to clean up the mess, but they introduced their own brand of irreverence into the stillness, the aggressive, obscenity-laced banter of American soldiers with white-sidewalls, looking like they had just stepped out the weight-room: "Man, you'd fuck up a wet dream." There was probably nothing else to do in their isolated outposts except pump iron. And their sexual frustrations were understandable. But their words still came as a shock, as much as anything epitomizing the difference of these foreigners in the Muslim East, where sex was still for the purpose of procreation not recreation. At least, they represented an efficient military force, not those hopeless, sleepy Egyptians manning the checkpoints. Or, for that matter, the vaunted Israeli Defense Forces, the IDF, the citizen army to the north, reduced for the last twenty years to sniping at teenagers and harassing old women.

The Bedouins, lounging with their grumbling animals in the camel park filled the valley with the sounds of their raucous exchanges. They were Egyptian at least in their tone, a constant bellowing. In an attempt to escape from the crowd—ultimately foolish since I was no different from anyone else—I climbed to the Chapel of St. Theodore of Tyre and St. Theodore the Recruit. It was on the ridge to the southeast of the monastery, a thousand feet above the valley floor. From the top there was a good view of the monastery and the plain of Raha. In the cavernous valley below, with its special acoustics, people could be heard long before they could be seen as specks on a trail. We were, all of us, a plague on the landscape.

On the way back to the hotel the willows and poplars in the monastery garden were silvery in their leafless state and the almond trees were blossoming. The impression was striking in this waste of granite and sand. In the afternoon I walked a couple of miles across the plain of Raha toward the Naguib el-Hawwa where earlier visitors had mounted the pass and caught their first, breathtaking glimpse of the sacred mountain and the plain where the Children of Israel had gathered. Robinson had been particularly impressed:

> Here the interior and loftier peaks of the Sinai began to open upon us—black, rugged, desolate summits; and as we advanced, the dark and frowning front of Sinai itself began to appear . . . I had never seen a spot more wild and desolate . . . Reaching the top of the ascent or watershed, a fine broad plain lay before us . . . terminated at the distance of more than a mile by the bold and awful front of Horeb, rising perpendicularly in frowning majesty, from twelve to fifteen hundred feet in height. It was a scene of solemn grandeur, wholly unexpected, and such as we had never seen; and the associations which at the moment rushed upon our minds, were almost overwhelming.

But even this vista had been spoiled. The microwave tower with its guy wires interrupted the view and the Katarin garbage dump was the first thing a traveler coming from that direction would see today. The abandoned chicken farm was a picture of desolation and a generator ran noisily throughout the day. The back of the hotel with its outbuildings, full of trash and discarded furniture, filled the foreground. I waited for the sun to drop behind the valley wall to witness a repeat of the crimsons of the evening before. But it went down like someone had turned out the lights. This time there were no pyrotechnics. Then, suddenly, it became very cold.

Dinner was a repeat of the night before. The steer's head above the fireplace stared down mockingly at us, although there were only two of us this time, until an African family arrived as I left. I was wearing thermal underwear, Levi's, a wool shirt, a heavy woolen sweater, and a jacket, but I was still cold. I quickly finished the little half-chicken and hustled back to my suite where at least there was a heater.

The next morning it seemed to be ten degrees warmer. At breakfast I sat at a table with an elderly Hungarian couple. He was doddering with a cane, a little paste-on mustache like Walter Cronkite's, and wore a beret. His English was passable but she spoke to me only in German: was I *Englander* or *Americaner*? They were from Budapest and something struck me as very European about them as they ate, working to manipulate the little bits of bread and cheese with their noisy imperfect dentures. It was like every interview I had ever seen of eastern-European musical icons, gnarled like old oaks or cured like wine gone slightly to vinegar, sucking through their teeth while they reminisced about days gone by.

I left for the coast after breakfast, intending to spend the night at Nuweiba' or maybe Taba. It had not been a very satisfying visit, but from the Hobbs book I understood better why it had changed. It was useless to complain that our first trip to the monastery had been just after the return of the Sinai by the Israelis, when the roads were bad and the accommodations Spartan. Or, that there had been a time at the top of the mountain when I was the only one there. Someone could always top that, with a tale about the *really* old days when there were no paved roads or hotels at all, etc. etc. And not all that was new was bad. The drive to the coast had originally been on a dirt track. It was now paved and the spectacular sights—in places it looked like Wadi Rum in Jordan—could be comfortably seen, instead of the teeth-rattling, half-day journey it had once been.

The Helnan Hotel at Nuweiba' was the old Israeli-built facility refurbished. They had a room available. In the afternoon I lay on the beach. After the bitter cold of the previous two days the warmth seemed almost sinful. Dinner was a crowded buffet with a live band playing pieces like "Misty". It was the eve of the feast and the new crescent moon was briefly visible over the mountains to the west. I returned via the center of the peninsula, something we hadn't done before. The road went north for fifty miles from Nuweiba', before meeting the direct road from Elat to the tunnel at Suez. At first the drive, through the mountains in the southern part of the peninsula, was interesting. But the stage through el-Themad and Nakhl was dreary, enlivened only by the thought that it was the old pilgrim route. Nakhl meant "date palms" and it was a famous way-station. Twenty-five miles short of the tunnel was the Mitla Pass, famous in the wars between Egypt and Israel. There were still remnants of Israeli earthworks making their serpentine way over the hills. It wasn't as storied or as scenic as the Khyber or Malakand passes in the Northwest Frontier Province in Pakistan. But it was a relief after the endless sand with only an occasional view of the highlands of Tih away to the south. On the other side of the pass the scenery was actually pretty, with pink dunes a little like the Nefud, before the level of the canal and the tunnel.

After the tunnel it was a straight shot to Cairo. There were a few drops of rain along the way but not enough to clean the car. I was a just under six hours, door-to-door from the hotel at Nuweiba' to the apartment in Dokki. All things considered, the trip had been a success. I had finally found Serabit. And, for all of the negatives, and in spite of our worst efforts, we really couldn't spoil Sinai. It was still one of the most spectacular places on the planet.

7

Wadi Natroun

I picked up Maurice on Ramses street early on a Friday morning. He was an old friend from the 1980s, although with Egyptians friendship could sometimes be inconvenient as I would discover on this trip. We had often discussed a visit to the monasteries in Wadi Natroun and this would finally be an opportunity to see them with expert guidance. From Cairo the sixty miles to the turnoff at the rest house on the Alexandria Road was broken only by a stop to buy the day's newspapers—*Al-Ahram, Al-Akhbar* and *Al-Wafd*—for the monks. Maurice called them "munuks," with that inability of some speakers of Egyptian Arabic to pronounce, un-voweled, two consonants in succession.

The next fifteen miles was featureless desert with a few villages before we reached a fork in the road where a sign announced the monastery of St. Bishoy to the left and El-Sourian to the right. Maurice wanted to visit St. Bishoy first and confessed that he "loved" the place. Like many speakers of Arabic he often confused the English words "love" and "like," but I think that in this case he meant it. His wife had died several years before and he now felt that his life was empty. His work had given him an ulcer and I think the desert and the monastic life represented a kind of refuge. So I began the visit with a great deal of sympathy for him. But by the end of the day the sympathy had largely evaporated. Like most Egyptians Maurice was voluble and opinionated and I eventually grew tired of his constant hectoring.

As we approached, the complex of St. Bishoy was all masonry domes and simple plaster walls. The glare from the whitewash was overwhelming and when I later came out of the church it would be several minutes before my eyes adjusted to the light. Maurice had friends among the monks and we were able to park on the monastery grounds: "Park over there," he directed, "in the shade." The first order of business was prayer, and we walked through passages that looked like they belonged on the set of *Star Wars* or *Dune*, then several low, five-foot doors to the main church. The Friday service had already begun. The interior of the church was the usual Coptic warren of chapels decorated with icons, paintings, and tapestries displaying scenes from the lives of the saints. Maurice pushed his way to the front of the congregation and prostrated himself like a Moslem before a tapestry of St. Bishoy. Then he moved to a little shrine, touched a cylindrical casket covered in red velvet that was said to contain the uncorrupted body of the saint, and pressed his fingers to his lips.

Like most Egyptians, Maurice was very tactile and there was a great deal of touching and kissing in his religion. By the end of the day I was tired of being prodded and poked, told to do this or that, and led around by the hand, if not by the nose. But, at least during the service I was left alone. Maurice monopolized a place at a lectern next to the priest and held his head in his hands with obvious emotion. There were three lecterns side by side on the main altar, beneath panels of icons, fourteen icons on a side. In the center was a curtained door leading into a kind of recess through which the officiating priests periodically came and went. For the next two hours Maurice remained near the lectern and I occasionally caught a glimpse of the back of his bald head when eddies in the congregation—people were constantly coming and going—revealed the scene at the altar.

It was easy to see why he was developing an ulcer. In the management culture of ARENTO every decision rose to the top and he spent most of his days in the office trying to talk on three telephones at once, while simultaneously conducting a conversation with the latest of many claimants who had just thrust a paper requiring an instant decision on his desk, and bellowing at Salem, his little hunchback teaboy. He never spoke, but bellowed. He was very Egyptian in that regard—Muslim and Christian alike—and the sound of the unamplified Muslim call to prayer was astonishing in the halls of the Ramses building. Like many Copts, Maurice came equipped with two thick pair of glasses, one pair for reading and one for distance.

Meanwhile, the officiating priest was groaning in an odd, singsong kind of chant and the congregation occasionally broke in with what sounded like the Kyrie Eleison. Then he passed the microphone to another priest who broke into song, accompanying himself with the rattle of little brass plates like a *karkaday* vendor on Muski Street. This kind of thing went on alternately, first one priest and then the other, until I grew tired and retreated into the middle part of the church where straw mats were spread on the floor. There were several men in the area where I sat down, most of them asleep. They lay flat on their backs, their bellies rising and falling as they breathed. There was nothing remotely familiar about the service, except that it was all very Egyptian. Children played between the feet of their elders, people arrived late and left early, women sat on the floor, and men slept. In the vestibule where, like the Moslems in their mosques, we had removed our shoes, families ate picnic lunches. I had hardly seen a fat man in West Africa but fat men, and women, were the rule here.

We had arrived at about nine fifteen and it wasn't until nearly noon before the service was over and Maurice emerged from the church. I had left an hour earlier to look around the grounds. But now Maurice wanted to show me the interior of the church again. He took me by the hand and led me back into the several little chapels, detailing the history of each. In the baptistry he told me that three angels had appeared during the christening of his youngest son, eighteen years before, and that it had caused a stir among the "munuks." The monks, incidentally, struck me as anything but paragons of "love, joy, peace, goodness, patience, kindness and gentleness," the monastic ideal. When it came time to clear a part of the church during the service, they did so with considerable brusqueness and efficiency. With their unkempt beards and black bonnets—each bonnet with twelve crosses on the sides for the twelve apostles and one in back (for Christ?)—they looked like Sunni zealots.

We completed our tour of the inside of the church and then inspected the fifth-century keep with the drawbridge the monks raised when there were Berbers in the area. The first depredations against the monasteries had been from the Berbers and the west, long before the coming of Islam. Then we wandered or rather, drove, around the grounds. The monastery was self-sufficient and contributions from the faithful had paid for land reclamation and a considerable increase in the cultivated area. I could see a modern center-pivot irrigation system operating in a field half-a-mile away. Actually Natroun did not seem particularly green or lush. But there was clearly fossil water in the area and it probably had been settled for millennia. The monasteries dated from the fourth century.

We then visited the dispensary where Maurice had a friend, a monk who had been a doctor before entering the religious life. The dispensary was well staffed since there were many former doctors among the monks. They came from Cairo and Alexandria and contributed their time on a regular schedule—some on the first Friday of the month, others on the second Wednesday, and so on. There was an internal medicine clinic and Maurice visited it whenever he came because of his ulcer. His friend had miraculous curative powers and Maurice asked him to pray for his health. He also gave me a special blessing, a set of little cards daubed with the Holy Chrism, "a mixture of oils, fragrances, herbs and spices, which was placed on the body of our Lord Jesus Christ in the Tomb." A batch was periodically prepared in the monastery under the supervision of the Pope, who made his official residence in the complex. The incumbent was Shenoudah III who was kept here under house arrest during the Sadat years.

Attached to the dispensary was a kitchen and Maurice ushered me in for lunch. It was a "help yourself" arrangement, he explained, with pots of *fool medammes* and condiments on a central table, along with mounds of the monastery's excellent whole-wheat bread. Maurice washed two plates, ladled them full of beans, and cut limes for each of us, before directing me to sit and eat. We flavored the *fool* with oil, cumin, salt, pepper, and the limes and set to work as only Egyptians can, eating not so much for pleasure as for business, stoking our furnaces. Everything on the table was offered and then offered again: *fool*, more *fool*, jam, limes, oil, bread, more bread, more *fool*. Then Maurice made tea. After finishing the tea we moved outside to make space for other visitors.

For Maurice this visit was obviously more than a religious experience. It was also a social occasion. He simply wanted to *be* here. We sat for several minutes in the little courtyard between the dispensary and the kitchen, letting the *fool* settle. Then he abruptly asked me if I was happy. He clearly was. It was now about noon and he said that he saw no reason why we should go anywhere before, perhaps, seven o'clock that evening. This was not what I had in mind, and over the next several hours I often had to remind him of our original program to see the four monasteries in the cruciform plan. But he always seemed to have forgotten something that took us back to that peaceful scene at St. Bishoy: he hadn't given a newspaper to Father *Fulaan*, he hadn't made a donation in the church, Father *Mishaarif Min* had letters to be posted.

Finally he agreed to leave, provided we first paid a visit to a sick monk he knew. The monk was at the monastery farm, and we drove the several hundred yards from the church complex: "Slow down," Maurice instructed, then "turn left" and finally "stop!" There, a kind of dormitory overlooked a large open corral surrounded by stables. There were donkeys, dairy cattle, buffalo, sheep, and goats in the stables and the odor of large ruminants dominated the living area. At first, the monk didn't answer but Maurice persisted, eventually entering and finding him in his bed. The little apartment was full of bric-a-brac, pictures of saints on the walls, plastic flowers, and stacks of cages with parakeets all singing in unison. We had, of course, forgotten the newspaper and Maurice sent me back to fetch one from the car: "*Al-Akbar*," he directed. By the time I returned a family had arrived and the children were eating popsicles amid the parakeet droppings. The family mercifully cut our visit short. Finally, after one last stop at the main entrance—Maurice had forgotten to make a donation—we left St. Bishoy.

The monasteries of El-Sourian and St. Baramous now followed in rapid succession. In both places, without Maurice's personal interest, the visits were more businesslike. El-Sourian, or "the Syrian," was close to St. Bishoy but St. Baramous was about five miles distant over a dirt road. On the drive Maurice was still in full form: "slow down," he would say, or "watch out for the hole," and then "turn left." But when we arrived he permitted me to look around unchaperoned. The director of the monastery gave me, two Belgians, and two Germans a tour. His English was excellent—although when he searched for a word he almost always found a German one—and we learned some interesting details. St. Moses the Black had been a Nubian bandit prior to converting to Christianity, and his cylindrical, felt-covered coffin was the object of pious visitation in the little church of St. Baramous. At one time, his uncorrupted hand could be seen extending from the coffin. But it caused such a rush of penitents that it had stopped.

The interior of the domed church was separated into the three sanctuaries characteristic of the day, one each for believers, penitents, and sinners. It was a reminder of the Franciscan missions in California, with the same crude paintings and religious impedimenta. There were several layers of frescos, preserved in places and looking like they belonged in Central Asia. Outside were several olive trees, under one of which I found Maurice waiting patiently for me, sitting in an old stuffed chair and sipping tea. Maurice wanted to return to St. Bishoy, but it was getting late and I wanted to be back on the road. The fourth monastery, St. Macarius, lay at some distance from the other three, would have to wait for another time.

On the way to the main highway we were flagged down by a frantic-looking boy with an overnight bag. I couldn't understand much of his Arabic—his accent was unfamiliar and he used the soft "g"—but it seemed he was a Christian from el-Minya and was about eighteen years old. Maurice asked him what his problem was and this loosened a torrent of miserable complaints: he had come looking for work at one of the monasteries but, without a letter of introduction, he had found nothing. No one seemed to care. There was no one to help him. He was in the back seat of the car, but leaning forward so that he had positioned himself between Maurice and me. The discussion between the two of them went on for about fifteen minutes. Periodically Maurice would bellow at him "*Inta aiz aye?*"—"What do you want?"—and the same pitiable tale would pour out again.

By the time we reached the Alexandria road they had narrowed his choices to two: he could go with Maurice to his home in Shubra, where he might find work at one of the churches in the city, or take the train back to el-Minya where he would get the necessary letter. He decided he would return to el-Minya, except that he didn't have any money. So Maurice gave him ten pounds and that seemed to settle his mind, because he broke into a long chant like one we heard in the church that morning. After a while, I began to count and it lasted for over twenty minutes. He was still leaning forward, and so was chanting into my right ear. Maurice later told me that he was a good Christian boy and that life was particularly difficult for Christians in Upper Egypt. Eventually his song ended and we left him at the station in Giza, where he would catch a train home. His gratitude was palpable and he stood waving to us until we were almost out of sight.

I dropped Maurice where I had found him that morning, on Ramses street: "Slow down," he said. "don't turn there!," and finally "stop!" As he left we agreed that the visit had been a great success. But I was glad I hadn't taken him up on the offer of a visit to his villa on the north coast.

Maybe next time.

8

Cairo on Foot

The Cemeteries

It was called *al-Qarafa*, according to Hans Wehr "specifically, the graveyard below the Mokattam Hills near Cairo." Among the several meanings of the Arabic root word was either "to peel, pare, or derind" or "to feel disgust for, to be nauseated by." Either meaning could apply to a necropolis, although today's Egyptians, unlike their Pharaonic forbears, were not elaborately prepared for the afterlife. The body was washed and cotton wads inserted into the orifices, before it was wrapped in a shroud and buried, generally on the following day.

Egypt could almost be called a country of cemeteries. Much of the Pharaonic legacy consisted of elaborate monuments to the dead and the ancient Egyptians mummified not only human beings but also dogs and cats, crocodiles, and ibises. The pyramids are probably the largest memorials to the dead ever built. Later the Mamluks, who dominated the city for 600 years between the thirteenth and nineteenth centuries, would also build elaborate memorials to themselves. These were originally outside the walls of the city, in the desert and several miles from the inhabited area. But as the city spread—especially with the shortage of housing for the rural poor who were increasingly attracted to the metropolis—people moved into the environs of the tombs and eventually into the buildings themselves. By the middle of the eighteenth century the sprawling complex of Qaytbey's mausoleum had become a village. Later, the urban area spread to include the cemeteries and created the phenomenon of the "City of the Dead." But this particular city was very much alive, with grocers, butchers, bakers, and other purveyors of life's necessities. By the late twentieth century they had jury-rigged water systems, electricity grids, and telephone connections amid the monuments to the Mamluk tyrants.

There were two major Muslim cemeteries in Cairo, requiring use of the dual form in Arabic: they were the *Qarafatain*, both to the east of the Fatimid city and the Nile. The ancient Egyptians always buried their dead to the west of the river, in the direction of the setting sun. One of these later necropolises was to the north and the other to the south of the rough quadrangle of the Fatimid city, and so they were known as the Northern Cemetery and the Southern Cemetery. Together they constituted one of the more interesting walks in Cairo, a combination of spectacular but decaying Mamluk tombs and everyday Egyptian life that still existed in their midst. They were off the beaten path and outsiders, even those who ventured south as far as the Street of the Tentmakers, were rarely seen among them. But many of the jelly-mold or ribbed domes were still visible above the bridge that carried *Shari' Salah Salem* over the remains of Salah ed-Din's wall and on to Heliopolis and the airport.

But it wasn't only the Mamluks who built memorials to themselves and average Egyptians had for centuries segregated their dead in a way that was increasingly difficult in life. It was as if the old Ottoman confessional, or *millet,* system were still in place. Muslims, Christians, and Jews no longer lived in segregated areas of the city, but they continued to bury their dead in their own cemeteries. They were not only Christian, but Orthodox, Catholic, and Protestant; and not only Orthodox, but Coptic, Greek, and Armenian Orthodox. Sometimes the segregation was by nationality, but that broke down because there were separate cemeteries for Greek Orthodox and Greek Catholics, Armenian Orthodox and Armenian Catholics. There was a German cemetery, an American cemetery, and a cemetery for the British war dead. It was like the area around el-Alamain. There, everyone visited the British cemetery, but there were even more spectacular sights in the nearby German and Italian ossuaries. Even Greece had erected a classic little building bearing the names of the several hundred Greeks who fell in the battle. These were truly cities of the dead.

Cemeteries were interesting because they were a window into the life of the city. I started with the Southern Cemetery. It was easy to find a parking place near the mosque of Nur ad-Din, under the overpass and near the Sultaniya, one of the best preserved of the mid-fourteenth-century structures. It had been recently restored. An advantage of restoration in Cairo was that the effects of dust, air pollution, and neglect soon returned even a restored building to something like its previous state, so it blended easily back into the surroundings. Here, the freestanding minaret—with just a hint of the original pink in the zigzag pattern of the base—had not been restored and was much the worse for its 600 years of wear. Children played among the tombstones and were not so used to strangers that they still asked for pens or *bakshish*. Most tombstones looked old but I saw one dated January 27, 1996. *Al-Qarafa* was a working cemetery, just as it was a living community, and Muslims were still interred in its dusty environs. The Christian and Jewish cemeteries lay farther to the south.

People were generally friendly and, on a Ramadan morning, greetings were returned with evident feeling. South of the Sultaniya was a dirt road that ran in a straight line for nearly a kilometer to the southeast, flanked by houses and an occasional tomb, first that of Sudun (1504), then al-Sawabi (1285), and then Tankizbugha (1350). Trash was everywhere. Niebuhr says that in 1762 the rubbish was carried outside the city walls and piled in mounds that grew to huge proportions. The garbage collectors today, among the most wretched of Cairo's poor, still struggled with rubbish. But even with the Toyota trucks that had largely replaced donkey carts they were not up to the task. In 1762 there was no plastic and little paper refuse. But the bones, feathers, and chicken entrails, offal, peelings, parings, and rinds must have been the same. Scrawny dogs and cats picked through the piles of organic waste, alive with flies.

Tankizbugha with its spiked collar looked like something in a magazine catering to sadomasochists. Afterwards there was little to see before the jog to the west and another six hundred yards, before a turn south on *Shari' Imam el-Shafei* towards the mausoleum of the same name. Shafei was the founder of one of the four orthodox schools of Sunni Islam. His mausoleum was the largest in Egypt and a place of pious visitation by Muslims the world over. It was originally built in 1211 by Salah ed-Din's nephew, al-Kamil, and restored several times during the intervening centuries, notably by Qaytbey in the fifteenth century and Abdel Rahman Katkhuda in the eighteenth. I wandered through the mosque and then into the mausoleum. The interior of the dome, two wooden shells with a lead covering, was decorated geometrically like the Taj Mahal, after whose pattern fine carpets were now made. Marble panels lined the walls and bands of calligraphy and stalactite squinches were all brightly colored.

The tomb was especially popular with women, and on this day many were pressing their hands against the sandalwood latticework that enclosed the catafalque. Several even prostrated themselves in prayer. It was an unfamiliar sight, as women generally prayed in private. But no one objected to the presence of a foreigner and I sat on the carpet by the west wall and read the piece on the mausoleum in the *Islamic Monuments in Cairo*. It was what a mosque or mausoleum should be, a place of reflection or contemplation. Outside in the *suq* were of sellers of oranges, tangerines, bananas, sticky mounds of dates, pottery-ware, and cheap fabrics. The little road continued south, but it narrowed and soon filled with animals: fat-tailed sheep, lambs, goats, kids, and cardboard boxes of fuzzy ducklings. There were also geese, goslings, chickens, chicks, turkeys, rabbits, cattle, and young buffaloes with their pink-gray hides and soft, almost silken hair. Teenaged girls methodically slit the throats of chickens and tossed them in pots of boiling water. Hobbled sheep ate *birseem,* men bellowed, donkeys brayed, and businesslike butchers in bloody smocks went about their stern tasks.

It had rained heavily the day before and the street soon became a quagmire of straw, mud, blood, and manure. I walked on in what I thought was the direction of the Hosh el-Basha, or the tomb complex of Mohammed Ali and his family. But it was in the other direction, behind el-Shafei, and the Cairenes, ever helpful, sent me back to the west. The Hosh el-Basha was an odd grouping of nineteenth-century domes that housed the tombs. Inside, there were monuments in the Turkish style, raised masonry boxes surmounted by turbans, although they lacked the clean lines of the Turkish originals. Even so, it was spotless and spare, empty on this particular day. The lavish decoration seemed out of place in this remote corner of the cemetery. The tombs of Abdel-Rahman Katkhuda and Ali Bey el-Kebir, both powerful in Niebuhr's day, were just around the corner. But the owner of the house in whose courtyard they were now located was not in, and I didn't see them.

I walked back to Salah Salem past piles of refuse, occasional ruined mosques or Mamluk facades, and scruffy little shops. I bought some excellent *'aish baladi,* the loaves a foot in diameter, and three kilos of oranges under the bridge. I was home in time for lunch.

Today I looked for Niebuhr's *Turbet el-Yahud,* or the "tomb of the Jews." One of his companions, the Swedish botanist Peter Forsskal, had been told by the Egyptians in "Kaidbey" that there were several places near Cairo where Jews had once lived. So I went to Qaytbey, the sprawling mausoleum complex in the City of the Dead, captured by David Roberts as the "Tombs of the Caliphs" and appearing on the Egyptian one-pound note. There, the keeper of the mausoleum recognized the name as *Turab el-Yahud,* or the plural "tombs of the Jews." It was in *Bassatin* he said. Bassatin meant "gardens" and I would soon discover how far from a garden the area now was.

I had earlier looked for the Jewish cemetery in the vicinity of Fostat. I walked through the underground passageway to the Ben Ezra synagogue, the best-known Jewish monument in Cairo, where a man told me that the tombs were south on the autostrade just before the Ma'adi exit. He seemed to know what he was talking about, and sold me a couple of booklets on the synagogues of Cairo, one in English and one in Arabic. But he had a prominent *zebiba*—a "raisin," or prayer mark—in the middle of his forehead, and so was obviously a Muslim. On the way out of the synagogue a policeman told me that there were no tombs of the Jews nearby, but only in Bassatin. There was that name again, and I probably should have followed the earlier lead.

So I drove to the autostrade and turned south past where, the day before, I had seen the mosque of Agha Shaheen, an extraordinary structure built into the western face of the Mukattam. It was inaccessible except with a series of long ladders. The minaret was unlike anything like the traditional configuration, polygonal in the first two courses, with fluting that looked almost Pharaonic, like a lotus. The last course was round before becoming conical. It apparently dated from the Fatimid era.

Further south, near Ma'adi, I turned off just before the bus station at Bassatin. A man selling bread and he said yes, this was the area of *Turab el-Yahud,* but that it was a name only and there were no tombs, of Jews or anyone else. But I persisted, leaving the main road and driving into a poor neighborhood where I asked a group of men smoking *shishas* if they knew about the tombs of the Jews. A general discussion ensued, before we all agreed that I was looking for the Jewish cemetery. They said it lay under the highway bridge.

One man in the group, Yahya, said he would show me the way. So we drove through the little village, on potholed roads full of children, chickens, cats, dogs, goats, and sheep. Yayha did what I would have done under the circumstances, and asked questions every hundred yards or so. The answers were unfailingly polite and helpful. Finally, we exited near a highway overpass under construction, parked, and walked under the I-beams for fifty yards to a spot overlooking the *turab.*

It was an extraordinary sight. The cemetery was maybe three hundred yards on a side—or nearly twenty acres—and covered with low-lying masonry tombs, the occasional monument rising very prominently out of the flat. It was impossible to see much from this vantage point, so we walked toward what looked like the entry gate. The gate was made of wrought-iron, with a Star of David in the upper half. But it was locked. A little boy said that if we wanted to go in he knew where there was a key. So he climbed the gate, slithered over the pointed spikes at the top, and dropped to the ground. After a few minutes he came back on our side and said that there was another gate, a hundred yards away and that a woman would let us in.

Inside, most of the flat gravestones were old and badly weathered. Most had Hebrew inscriptions, also badly weathered on top. But some were some relatively new—I saw one dated 1950—black granite with scrolls on the side, with names like Cohen and Katz. The oldest date I saw was 1870. But most had to be much older than that. I wandered amid fallen-down columns and one standing obelisk about eight feet high with an inscription in Hebrew. On the way back to the entrance we were met by the woman who had let us in, now frantic with worry since Yahya had told her he was with the highway department and that clearly was not the case. The man in charge of the cemetery was *barra*, or outside the country, but still she insisted there could be a problem. Yahya told her not to worry and we left her, clearly still distraught He had been muttering pious ejaculations throughout the visit, about how I had been sent by God because he had a nephew who needed medicine that would cost ten pounds. I gave him twenty.

As I drove away I could see that the highway bridge—a part of the autostrade coming from the west—intersected the cemetery. There were several freestanding tombs on the other side of the bridge, boarded up like the tombs in the *qarafatain* or Muslim cemeteries to the north. People were still living among them. I measured the distance from the cemetery to the citadel on the odometer and it was just under three miles. It was here that the Jews in the *Haret al-Yahud*, the Jewish quarter another half-mile to the north, carried their dead. In times of popular unrest they could not pass through the *Qarafatain* but were forced to go west to the river before turning south. It looked like the cemetery had been neglected for years. But soon every motorist on the autostrade would be able to survey its dusty environs.

Today I was no the trail of three churches Niebuhr showed in his map of the city. Instead, I found another collection of cemeteries. Just short of the Rhoda subway station the east side of the street was lined with cemeteries, including the American cemetery and the German cemetery, all enclosed by high walls. In the latter I found the grave of Theodor Bilharz, the Hungarian who discovered the parasite that caused schistosomiasis, or Bilharzia, once the scourge of Egypt. There was also an English cemetery, at the end of which lay an unfamiliar sight in the urban sprawl of Cairo, the "BRITISH PROTESTANT BURIAL GROUND." On the gatepost a sign read:

>"1914-1918
>CAIRO MEMORIAL
>WAR CEMETERY
>1939–1945."

Inside the locked gate lay immaculate grounds with beautifully tended lawns, memorials, and row after tidy row of headstones. Flowers were placed on many of the graves. None of the headstones was fallen down, and none of the thousands of graves was fallen in. It was amazing, all the more so for being utterly unexpected. It was like the cemetery at El-Alamain, except that there it was in the desert with no lawns. This was on the fringes of Old Cairo.

It was what the Gezira Club or the Ezbekiyya Gardens, signature features of European Cairo, must once have looked like.

The Churches

Today I looked for the Patriarchal Church of the Copts in the precincts of the old Fatimid city. So I walked south to Muski Street and then east to the Khan el-Khalili. I crossed over the pedestrian bridge to *Shari' Muez li Din Illah* and walked east to the Bab Zuweila, then north to the vicinity of the mosque of Qajmas al-Ishaqi, a beautiful little *Burgi* Mamluk structure. There was a vaulted passageway and the road underneath was just high enough to admit vehicular traffic. Past the vault I began to refine my search and asked a man outside a barbershop if the Coptic Patriarchate was in the neighborhood. He called another shopkeeper and together they confirmed that it was still there. The first man would show me where it was. This was helpful as in many of the neighborhoods in Cairo there was only one way in or out. It was the case here, and on my unescorted way out I came to several dead ends. The names posted on the walls were interesting, including *Haret er-Rum*, *Rum* here referring to the Romaeans or Byzantine Greeks. We walked past a high wall behind which an interesting European-looking facade appeared, before reaching the Patriarchate.

A sign in English on the compound wall announced it to be the "COPTIC ORTHODOX BATRIARCHAT, Church of St. Vergin the Relief." Inside, two men were helpful but their knowledge was limited. Yes, the church was old, having been established in the 6th century AD. It had been restored, however, and the interior of the structure was modern. A plaque outside the entrance stated that the restoration had taken place between 1978 and 1995, "in the reign of His Holiness Shenouda the Third, the 117th in the line of the Popes of Alexandria". Nothing inside was of particular interest.

On the way back I stopped at the building I had seen earlier. Inside the gate was a kind of courtyard where several shacks of cardboard and wood had been built against the wall. The mystery building sat beyond the courtyard. The facade was striking, unlike anything I had seen before in Cairo. It looked like one of the California missions, with four pilasters separating it into three bays. In each bay was an arched opening on the ground floor and an arched window on the second story. The two outside pilasters extended above the surface of the facade and became capitols. The two central pilasters came together in a little arched structure with two and then one opening. The openings looked like they might once have contained bells, although bells would have been forbidden in Cairo. The structure was about forty feet high. It looked to be Spanish or Italian Baroque.

The tenants, a couple of men and a woman, were friendly and let me look around, so I sat and made a sketch of the facade. Then a man came to the door of one of the shacks and motioned me inside. He was sick or crippled, because when I entered he had returned to his bed. A Cairo soap opera was showing on a color television set. After I declined a cigarette, the man gave me a brief history of the place. It had been *tekiyya arwaam*, or hospice of the Romaeans, again meaning the Greeks or Byzantines. The *ghalban,* or poor, came here for food, clothing and a place to sleep. Then the story became complicated: someone by the name of Khaled now owned the property and was looking to sell it. They were living there with his permission.

I asked if I could look inside and they said yes. The woman went to another shack for the key and we all entered the building. In a city where every square foot of living space was precious, this place was empty. It was about a hundred feet long by forty wide. An elevated pulpit sat half way along one wall. The walls had little bays and arches at the top, and in the ceiling there were paintings, faint but still recognizable: an obvious Christ in the center and four saints, probably the four Evangelists, on the sides. We all agreed that the figure in the center was *Sa'idna Eissa*, and when I suggested that the others were probably *Matta, Morcos, Luq,* and *Hanna*—Matthew, Mark, Luke, and John—they allowed as how this might be so. But they were Muslims and really wouldn't know. The paintings were not icons and so not Greek, and were not recognizably Coptic. They looked European.

So what was this thing? It looked like it had been built as a European church in, maybe, the seventeenth century. It later became an almshouse, under whose aegis I didn't know. Why was it now deserted and who was this Khaled who apparently owned it? The three tenants accepted ten pounds gratefully for their information.

Niebuhr's "Residence and Church of the Greek Bishop of Mount Sinai" was shown in his map just inside the Bab en-Nasr. So I entered the old city through the gate and walked east for maybe a hundred yards before a little alleyway led to the left. A sign on the wall in Arabic said it was *Haret 'Atoufa,* or "the quarter of His Grace." This looked promising and I asked a man at a dry-goods store if there was a Greek Orthodox church in the vicinity. He said no, but there *had* been one that was now a ruin. He said that just ahead was the *Shari' al-Gawaniya*, where the church once stood.

Sure enough, after another fifty yards, lay the ruin. There was nothing left but the shell, walls about five feet high. Everything else was gone and the site was now a rubbish heap. An old man in a shop nearby said that there had been a church there but it was gone *min zaman*, a long time ago, before his lifetime. Boys were playing football in the unpaved street and a vegetable seller with Giza plates was trying to maneuver his Toyota past the ruin. But there was a car parked in his way, and he eventually gave up and stayed where he was, hawking his beans, cucumbers, eggplants, onions, tomatoes, tomatoes, cabbages, and cauliflower. Another twenty-five paces further on the street turned right, past what looked like an outbuilding. Inside a ruined door a wary teen-aged girl was cooking over an open fire, and she said that the building had once been a villa. So I had probably found the residence of the Bishop.

On the way back to the Bab Nasr I stopped to see the inside of the old Fatimid walls. Portions were being restored, and that required excavation since the base of the walls was probably several meters below the surface of the city today. A woman let me through her little clapboard shack and then the corrugated tin wall they had put up to separate the construction site from the neighborhood. In the little nearby machine shops boys in filthy clothes were operating presses, stamping machines, and lathes. I didn't ask them if they were connected to the Internet yet.

The Mosque

Today I went looking for the Mosque of "Abu Fakir" who, Niebuhr says, built the aqueduct. In his map it lies about six hundred paces to the southeast of the *fum al-khalig*, or the place where the canal exited from the Nile. I took the metro to the Al-Malek es-Saleh station and emerged south of the Rhoda overpass and north of the cemeteries where I had been the week before. I wasn't sure that I would find a mosque of that name. Walking east over the Salah Salem underpass, I stopped and asked a group of men smoking *shishas* in a tea-shop about the mosques in the area. The little bubbles stopped long enough for them to wrinkle their noses. After we had established the name I was looking for—it was "Abu Saki" or maybe "Abu Zaki" but surely not "Abu Fakir"—they all said they hadn't heard of it. There was the Amru mosque to the south but I said that wasn't it, and showed them the map where the mosque was supposed to be. They all agreed that it must be there since, as one man told me, from the beginning of Islam in Egypt there had never been a mosque that, once established, had subsequently disappeared.

There was also the mosque of Hassan el-Anwar to the north, and to the east there was Abu Sa'ud, but other than that they couldn't help me. Finally, one man said to walk in the direction of Amru and I would find it. So I walked to the south, past the extensive Maronite cemetery where they were holding a funeral, to the Catholic cemetery where I had a brief look. It was a repeat of the Greek Orthodox cemetery, except that the inscriptions were in French and Arabic. In the distance lay the Amru mosque, but this was clearly not what I wanted. Niebuhr showed the Abu Saki mosque five hundred paces to the north, by slightly east from Amru. So I walked a block east into a wretched little neighborhood and then turned north again. The street was six inches deep in gray water and children were hopping between little islands in the middle. Vegetable and fruit stands lined the street. Pomegranates, or *romaan,* had just come into season. I crossed Salah Salem and continued north for another five hundred yards, asking directions several times along the way, until I came to the mosque of Hassan el-Anwar, lying under the aqueduct. The call to prayer had just begun and the amplified sound was deafening. Of all the discomforts that Cairenes endured—noise, air pollution, traffic and dust—noise always seemed to me the most difficult.

I asked a man sitting outside about "Abu Saki" and he wrinkled his nose like the others. But he was interested in the question and I sat on the stoop next to him and showed him Niebuhr's map, hoping that might help. But like most Egyptians he had trouble orienting himself and didn't seem to understand a map. The characteristic response was to send me to one of the best-known mosques in the area, or to the citadel. It was always the first, and easiest, answer. Hassan el-Anwar, in spite of its antiquity, was not what I was looking for. It was close to the river, literally under the aqueduct, not the several hundred yards to the east where Niebuhr had shown it.

So I walked east, parallel to the aqueduct towards a little square minaret. It seemed to be a light manufacturing area, because there was fluffy, brightly-colored industrial waste of some kind piled to the left of the dirt path, in which children were playing. Everywhere, there were scraps of what looked like styrofoam, maybe the remnants after the soles of shower thongs had been cut. After two hundred yards or so I turned south again. I asked two boys where the mosque of Abu Sa'ud was and they said *dogri,* or straight ahead. To the right and left were what looked like discarded hides, mounted on wooden frames. Then I realized that they were not discarded at all but were curing, because now there were hundreds of them, stacked on both sides of the dirt path. They were stretched taut, nailed to the wooden frames, and the holes showed that the frames had been used over and over again. The path wound through piles of refuse and little streams of odd-colored effluents. Around the large factory-like structure to the right, everything was black. The scene was Stygian and covered what appeared to be several acres.

The piles of garbage were now ten feet high, and included dirt, organic waste, plastic, paper, and chicken feathers. After a couple of hundred yards, I asked a man straightening nails in a little shop about the mosque and he pointed straight ahead. And then I recognized where I was. I had moved south again towards Salah Salem, but was now considerably east of where I had started. After another two hundred yards the mosque appeared up the hill to my left, just where Niebuhr showed it on his map. I crossed the dual carriageway and approached a modern-looking structure without identifying marks. The *khatib* was in the middle of the sermon and it was impossible to ask questions over the din. So I went down the hill to a little park where I sat on a bench and waited for the service to end.

The mosque was an architectural hodgepodge. The minaret was a combination of a classic Mamluk base—octagonal with stalactites—and simple modern upper sections. Above the stalactites was a plain gallery, then a round section made of plain stone, topped by a final little structure that gave it the look of a lighthouse. The rhythmic admonitons of the sermon continued, broken now by prostrations. They were close to the end of the service. An old man came up the hill and shuffled across the little park. He was a human wreck, his clothes filthy, the pants wrinkled and several sizes too big, gathered at the waist by a belt, shoes with no socks, and a torn shirt. He was carrying a sack of cheap *baladi* bread, not the big, puffy loaves for sale near the Citadel, but the flat things that seemed to lose their shape and taste as soon as they came out of the oven.

He was maybe sixty and had several days' growth of white stubble on his cheeks. His steps were labored, and as he made his way up the hill it looked like he had a problem with one of his legs. Or maybe it was his prostate, because he walked with his legs apart, as if he were bowlegged. When he died, his pitiful body would be washed, before they placed cotton in his nose and ears and tied his mouth shut. Then, they would wrap the corpse and place it in a cheap wooden coffin like I had seen earlier that morning near the Maronite cemetery, and lay him in the ground.

A pair of little girls came up and sat next to me on the bench and welcomed me to Egypt in English. But that was the extent of the language because they dissolved in giggles when I asked them where they learned it. Then they asked me if I had eaten: "*fatirt?*" They were beautiful, doe-eyed little creatures and one followed me up the hill asking for *monaye*. The sermon was now over and the congregation—all seemed to be overweight men—was emptying. So I sat on a little stone bench near the entrance and an older man asked me what I was looking for. I told him and he said that this mosque had been built in 933 of the *Higra*, or 1527 AD, and that the full name was Abu Sa'ud el-Garhi. He had been a descendant of the Prophet, "peace be upon him". He knew nothing about Abu Fakir or Abu Saki or Abu Zaki. He suggested I ask at the *Azhar*. But the information turned out to be a gold mine. Because it suddenly dawned on me that the name el-Garhi was very close to el-Guri, the el-Ashraf Qansuh el-Guri who *had* built the aqueduct. Niebuhr had simply confused the names. The mystery was solved.

Matariya

Today I looked for the obelisk of Senwosret and Mary's tree in Matariya. They were close to one another according to the guidebook. None of the maps of the city showed Matariya and the guidebook did not list the obelisk as an historic site. But the entry in the *Atlas of Ancient Egypt* under "Heliopolis" listed *Iunu* as the capital of the 13th Lower Egyptian nome around "Tell Hisn, northwest of the modern el-Matariya" where "the temples of the sun god Re' . . . were among the most important and influential religious institutions in the land . . ." It want on to add that despite the site's importance not much of it remained today.

I had never been to the area but it looked like it was northeast of Abbassiya. So I left the flyover where the new extension continued toward the airport and turned north just past the new Coptic Cathedral, "Al Botrossia." It became increasingly *shaabi*, or folk, as I moved deeper into the warren, frequently asking directions and often being sent in opposite directions. After much back and forth I eventually reached a large empty field at the head of which the obelisk stood in a small enclosure. The entry in the *Atlas* stated the area was 1,100 by 475 meters, making it nearly 120 acres in extent. It was barren, *'ard faadiy*, with the exception of large mounds of trash. A bucket-loader was loading the trash into trucks.

The hieroglyphs on the obelisk were worn or defaced in the lower third but sharp towards the top. It was one of a pair placed near a new temple of the sun god by Senwosret I of the 12th dynasty, in 1942 BC. The temple was long gone and only this obelisk remained, the second having fallen in the middle of the eighteenth century and apparently having been carried away in pieces. Both were of Aswan red granite. This one was over sixty feet high and weighed 120 tons. In 1950 it had been raised by two meters to protect it from the rising water table. Flinders Petrie had done a little excavation in the field in 1912 and recovered a few fragments.

An office of the Ministry of Antiquities was nearby, staffed by the usual fat kerchiefed ladies, just now finishing their *iftar*. A few bored-looking soldiers were posted around the perimeter of the enclosure, presumably a precaution after Luxor. I was the only one there. A sign pointed to a small open-air museum, located about six feet below the surface on which the obelisk now stood, and so probably at the original elevation. It was full of green water, in which a few plastic cups floated. There were broken fragments of basalt and granite lying around the periphery although none of the ladies knew anything about them.

But one, Saraya, flirted a bit and asked for a photo. Afterwards she offered to take me to *shaggarit Miriam*, Mary's tree, that she said was within walking distance. Along the way she told me that she had five children, the oldest a girl of fifteen years and the youngest a boy of six. We walked for a quarter of a-mile, through streets full of schoolchildren, piles of garbage, minibuses, and stands offering unappetizing-looking produce and little fish, alive with flies. We passed what I later found to be a small Catholic Church before turning left down a side street to the tree itself. It was a sycamore, now dead and gnarled and spread to a height of about ten feet. During the Christian period in Egypt pilgrims had carved their names in the trunk. A new sycamore—*hadith*, or new, said Iman who gave the lecture—towered above it. The Holy Family was said to have taken refuge under the original. The well from which the Holy Family supposedly drank was located fifty yards to the west. The water looked about as potable as that in the little museum.

Entrance to the trees cost six pounds. After the lecture Iman refused a tip. It was her job, she said. On the way back the caretaker let me into the mystery church and I found the walls covered with murals showing scenes of the Holy Family during their sojourn in Egypt. The Church was not Coptic, but thoroughly Roman and decorated to Western taste. It was an oddity in this neighborhood. I gave Saraya twenty pounds for the children.

The Sarcophagus

Today I visited the Egyptian Museum, on the trail of a black granite sarcophagus Niebuhr had seen in the city in 1762. I didn't find the sarcophagus I was looking for, but several others similar to it. On one with the same inlaid decorative motifs but slightly different hieroglyphs, there was an Arabic catalogue number. So, I asked a girl in the office on the first floor what the number meant. She led me into the bowels of the museum where a young man named Adil told me that the number I had seen was not the one I wanted. But if we went back and looked together we might find it. Sure enough, a small number in English, in red—No. 29302—was on the top of the sarcophagus and that was the key. So we returned and entered an office where eight overweight women sat, eating pastries.

With ill grace one of the women brushed aside the crumbs and allowed Adil to open her desk where he found a long ledger, looking like the accounting books in ARENTO. In the ledger was a listing of the numbers and we scanned them until we found No. 29302. Next to it was a picture that identified it as late Persian or Ptolemaic. However, that was only step one. We would have to wait for Mustafa who had the key to the bookshelf we needed to continue the process. He would be there in five minutes, said Adil, who then disappeared. Now, in Egypt "five minutes" really meant nothing except that Mustafa wasn't there and probably wouldn't come that day. Sure enough, Mustafa didn't come and Adil never returned. But much longer than five minutes later someone else did. We found No. 29302 in a chart on the wall that identified it as having been catalogued by Maspero in 1914 and we would find it in catalogue forty-eight. And there it was, in volume forty-eight of the *Catalogue General des Antiquities Egyptiennes*, fully described in French with a translation of the hieroglyphs.

I didn't see Niebuhr's sarcophagus that day and, in fact, I later found it in the British Museum. But I did learn enough to know where it had come from—certainly Saqqara—and what it might have represented. I also found one stele from Sinai. But the visit was interesting for another reason: they were beginning to build a computer database in the museum. A couple of girls sat in the room where I was reading and they correlated the hieroglyphs with codes from a handbook—a separate number for an arm, two arms, leg, trunk, torso, etc.—before laconically entering them in the database. The general complaint about the Egyptian Museum was that the exhibits were not properly displayed and catalogued. But it looked like all the information was there. It was just a matter of making it available to the public. Someone suggested that it was purposely withheld to give scope to the rogues who lead tour groups through the museum. But I resisted the impulse to be righteous since I had seen Martha that morning as I wandered among the catafalques, escorting a group of American ladies through the exhibits on the first floor. We passed like ships in the night.

9

David Roberts

We were all familiar with the story of unrecognized artistic talent, of artists living in garrets, laboring in obscurity, unappreciated until after their death. It seemed to be part of the artistic experience, at least in the West. However, we were less used to the reverse, of successful practitioners who were also unappreciated for the quality of their work, but primarily *because* of their success. David Roberts seemed to be an example of the latter. What was it about Roberts that made us so indifferent to his work, so willing to dismiss him as a glib purveyor of unreality? A look at the portraits of Roberts that have come down to us may explain part of the reason: the calm, almost bland look with which he regards us seems to speak volumes about the man.

The portrait by R.S. Lauder that hangs in Scottish National Portrait Gallery shows him "masquerading" in his Turkish dress. But we see no Byron here, no hint of towering rages, of uncommon passion or unusual inventiveness, the commonplaces of the nineteenth-century romantic personality. Instead we see what appears to be an uncomplicated, workmanlike man who probably spent most of his time quietly plying his trade. That was another part of the problem with Roberts. However skillful he may have been, he was a practitioner of one of the lesser arts, that of illustration. It was a fine art, admittedly, but almost a trade, and had never been considered *real* art by some. His early training was as a theater scene-painter, and the need to produce results regularly and on schedule may have leant a discipline and rapid technical facility to his work. And he was very good at what he did. He seems almost to have been *too* good, too fluid, too facile, and therefore somehow undeserving of the attention paid to him during his lifetime.

It must have been a combination of these perceptions that led to his remarkably patronizing obituary in *The Times*. There, Roberts was characterized as "a kindly, canny Scot . . . liked by all who knew him . . . He gave a grand broad effect, a truthful general result, and did not much trouble himself with the minuteness of workmanship." Now, Roberts was certainly a Scot and he may have been kindly, but the rest of the characterization is about as wrong as it could be. As we will see below, the general result was often *not* truthful, but his skill in capturing the minuteness of the workmanship was nearly photographic.

There may also be something a little provincial about our appreciation of Roberts. There is hardly a visitor today to *Egypt, Syria, and the Holy Land*—to give them the titles of the volumes published over the years 1842-49—who hasn't seen or doesn't own a reproduction of a Roberts. For years the big hotels in Cairo have sold inexpensive copies of his Egyptian series and there is even a series of full-sized reproductions that sometimes appear in offices or apartments furnished for expatriates. The real thing, lithographs from the 16" x 27" edition of 1842, are expensive in Cairo at 6,000 pounds, or about $1,600 a copy. Individually, they are about the same price in London, although many of those are from the subscribers' edition identified by its finer paper and the absence of titles on the pages. A full-sized original from his lesser-known 1837 Spanish series, *Picturesque Sketches of Spain*, costs 40,000 pesetas, or about $330, in Madrid. The complete set of six volumes that make up *Egypt, Syria and the Holy Land* would command a figure today in the neighborhood of 100,000 sterling pounds. But, whatever the price, it is almost as if Roberts is ours, and we resent any disparaging of him. By "ours" I mean, in general, expatriates. In spite of the fact that he could almost be called the national artist of Egypt, Egyptians are not particularly interested in this "Orientalist" phenomenon.

When Roberts made his tour of Egypt and Palestine in the winter of 1838–39 he had already done tours of France, Belgium, Holland, Germany, and Spain. He was, among other things, an architectural draughtsman and legatee of a European tradition that probably reached its height in Giovanni Battista Piranesi (1720–78), the son of a stonemason. There were many parallels in the careers of Piranesi and Roberts, including early training in a craft that, in Piranesi's case, reflected the practical cast of mind and artisanal background from which he came.

The principles of scientific perspective had been developed in the fifteenth century and they were used to render, as through the eye of a camera, the architectural detail of classical ruins. Piranesi's pictures of ancient Roman buildings had enormous influence not only on contemporary architecture and the applied arts, but also on the work of foreign architects. The *Vedute di Roma*, published in 133 plates in 1743, delineated classical structures with unprecedented accuracy. They were a precursor to photography.

And if photographs sometimes lied, even more scope for exaggeration was given to the practitioners of this tradition.

They made ample use of that scope to glorify the classical remains they saw. Words like "monumental," "elevated," and "heroic" captured their reaction to the "overwhelming experience of the antique." What made Egypt different was that to the elevated or heroic was added a hint of the exotic, so that the scenes, both Pharaonic and Islamic, became "monumental" and "Oriental" at the same time. But even with this emphasis on architectural accuracy, earlier European portrayals of the Orient had always suffered from a lack of immediacy. In a painting like Claude's *Seaport with the Embarkation of the Queen of Sheba*, dating from 1648, we see a seventeenth-century galleon awaiting this very European-looking monarch as she debouches onto a Venice-like quay for her trip to Jerusalem—the painting purporting to depict the voyage of a south Arabian woman a thousand years before the birth of Christ. Claude had probably never seen the Yemen or Jerusalem of his imaginings.

Roberts, however, saw at first hand the sights he depicted. He has been criticized, with some justice, for the "heroic" nature of many of his lithographs of Egypt and the Holy Land. There is no question that he was enthusiastic about what he saw in the East and that this enthusiasm sometimes led him to exaggerate the color and particularly the scale of the sights he recorded. But Egypt *was* exotic, and that is what fired Roberts's imagination. We have since become apologetic about the western fascination with things "Oriental," as if it served only to further European colonial schemes. But we forget that initial European contacts with the Orient took place at a time when European superiority was anything but assured. Early visitors to cities like Delhi and Samarkand were astounded at what they saw. And if later colonials like Clive were unashamedly exploitative, at least they made up in directness and vigor for the suffocating superiority of the Victorians. Roberts was a Victorian, albeit an early one, but he was enthusiastic about the visual richness of Egypt. If he was swept away by the grand vistas, and didn't scruple to make them grander still, at the same time he was a draftsman of the first water and that is what set him apart from others working in the same genre.

Because it is the architectural accuracy of Roberts that stands out in the plates. Take, for example, the lithograph entitled *Tombs of the Khalifs, Cairo*. It is, in fact, the mausoleum of Qaytbay in the northern cemetery and the fidelity of the representation is astonishing. The edifice is slightly changed today from what Roberts saw in 1838, with the entrance stairs no longer walled-in and only a fragment remaining of the high wall that intersected the facade next to the entrance. But, with a few predictable exceptions, the architectural accuracy of the portrayal is remarkable. A photograph taken today and blown up to the size of the lithograph provides a ready reference. For example, the error in the height of the arch over the entrance—from the underside of the horseshoe to the landing—as compared with a standard selected arbitrarily as the height of the double lintel to the left of the entrance, is less than one percent of the height as it appears today. The overall height of the facade in the Roberts print is in the same range, and the variation in its width is less than 4 percent, compared with the same standard. The height of the minaret is only 2 percent less than it should be.

Arithmetic comparisons between the lithograph and the photograph could be continued indefinitely, with an examination of windows, doors, minaret sections, etc. The result would be largely the same. There are a few minor errors. The rows of *ablaq* courses of masonry lining the entrance portal are fourteen in the Roberts print, but fifteen in the flesh. The crests over the entrance facade were fewer in 1838 than they are today, but this is surely a case of their having been replaced. The details of the horseshoe arches and the *mashrabiya* in the upper window are very accurate, although there has been ample scope for the wood of the latter to have deteriorated over the intervening years.

The minaret is late Burgi-Mamluk, and a variant on the classical square, octagonal, followed by circular sections. There are slight inaccuracies: the square section supporting the base is about 25 percent too wide. This is surely a result of Roberts' seeing two walls as one and missing the fact that the full width as shown in the print is a combination of the base itself and another wall slightly recessed from it. The spaces between the eight columns in the pavilion at the top, below the pear-shaped finial, are filled in with *ablaq* masonry rather than open as they appear today. But the proportions in the print are faithful to the original, with the exception that the first circular section—or the third overall—is too long in about the same proportion as the forth is too short. But, again, it is not only the arithmetic that is impressive. The detail—from the slightly different stalactite patterns supporting each circular section, to the final section with its eight columns—is carefully recorded, with the exception noted above.

Given the care with which Roberts recorded these details, we might expect that the departures from accuracy are *not* accidental. This is where he seems to have run afoul of critics. The most frequent device used by illustrators to emphasize the monumental nature of structures—and one practiced by Roberts—was to reduce the size of the human figures who, more than anything, established the scale of the buildings. So, in the *Tombs of the Khalifs* the figures in the foreground are about one-third smaller than they would be in real life. It is as if the square in front of the mausoleum were peopled by adult figures, none of them over four feet tall. The effect is to increase the apparent size of the building by a third in comparison with this most common of scales.

A second departure from literal accuracy is related to the first and together, they combine to increase the size of the vista in the plate. The dome has been moved forward, towards the plane of the facade, the effect of increasing its size by just over 17 percent in comparison with the same standard we used above. At the same time, the wall that serves as one of the supports of the dome has been pushed back by the same 17 percent as measured by the size of the two windows that appear vertically, one over the other, in the same wall. That is, the left supporting wall of the dome is now farther away than it should be and becomes a part of the grand panorama that Roberts has sweeping away for hundreds of feet into the distance. The actual dimensions of the building measure in the scores, not hundreds, of feet. At the same time, the size of the dome has been increased, in effect, by being moved forward. We suspect this was done so that Roberts could carefully detail its carved star pattern and floral arabesques. They are drawn very carefully and it is difficult to detect a difference in the detail from the photograph taken today.

There is a slight problem with the perspective. If the horizontals on the now-absent wall are projected, the vanishing point constitutes a cluster of points just above the two sitting figures in the foreground. This does not agree with the lines of several of the lower courses that show the horizon to be slightly above this cluster. But, again, these are minor defects in an otherwise faithful reproduction of the building. The fidelity is all the more remarkable when we realize that Roberts spent just one day— October 5, 1838—visiting the "tombs of the Khaliphs," calling them "little better than ruins and inhabited by the poorest wretches . . ." The alleged state of disrepair and the wretchedness of the inhabitants are difficult to detect in the print of the Qaytbay mausoleum.

It was this facility of seeing detail at a glance and reproducing it faithfully at a distance that sets Roberts apart from other illustrators. In his pharaonic prints the hieroglyphs—arguably the most beautiful system of writing ever devised—are rendered with the sureness and facility of the originals. And we should remember that the original sketches for the scores of prints made by Roberts on Egyptian subjects were all done in less than four months—from September, 1838 to January, 1839—with often less than a full day at each of the sites. They may have been worked up later in the studio, but his ability to record the mass of architectural and decorative detail in such a short period of time is remarkable.

Roberts was, of course, fortunate in his lithographer, Louis Haghe. There is some question about the level of detail in the original Roberts sketches, from which he and Haghe produced the finished plates in what must have been a very close collaborative effort. If they were sketchy, he must have stored an immense fund of standard decorative detail from which he could draw in the production of the finished lithograph. But, as we saw with the minaret of Qaytbay, these were not stock motifs drawn from a standard repertoire. Instead, the slight differences in the stalactite patterns were faithfully rendered. The same is true of the hieroglyphs in his Pharaonic prints.

Roberts was also fortunate in his medium. In the early nineteenth century lithography was a recent development, having been invented by a German, Aloys Senefelder, in 1796. The first lithographs appeared in Britain only in 1807. Where earlier work had been by means of etching, the greater spontaneity afforded by the new medium was soon exploited by artists. Whether the medium was largely responsible for the quality of the Roberts prints is questionable. What is undeniable is that where earlier etchings— even those of Piranesi—were dense and sometimes ponderous, the Roberts lithographs are light and airy, which lends them their particular charm. It was an ideal medium in which to capture the celebrated light of Egypt.

So, yes, Roberts sometimes took liberties with dimensions and often reduced the human scale in his prints to make the buildings appear more monumental. But his skill as an architectural draughtsman made them faithful reproductions that, in some cases, remain as the only records of structures that have not survived, such as the minaret of Sheikh Mohammed al-Ghamri in Cairo. But lest we be tempted to see him as only an "Orientalist" phenomenon, his pieces showing Romanesque, Gothic, Moorish, and *Mudejar* architecture in Spain are of a piece with his Egyptian series. The *vaqueros* lounging in the foreground of his *Correo de los Morros* in Granada are vintage Roberts, their serapes a bit too flowing and the brims of their sombreros a bit too wide. Perhaps he should be accused of a latent Occidentalism. But in the print there is no trifling with the architectural detail.

The "art" Roberts practiced was considered a lesser one, and his facility is discounted in the same way that first-rate talents working as illustrators have always been discounted: they are not practitioners of "high" art. But the liberties Roberts took make the prints something more than mere architectural renderings, and raise them to a higher level. I have a nice photo of the Qaytbay mausoleum and keep it in an album. But I am going to keep my *Tombs of the Khaliphs* on the wall.

10

Malaysia

When a cellular telephone conference was announced in Malaysia we thought it would be an excellent venue for representatives of ARENTO and the Ministry of Transport and Communications. Unlike a similar conference to be held about the same time in Cannes, it would take place in the developing world. The new chairman of ARENTO was the former Egyptian cultural attaché in Paris, parachuted in to break the back of the old guard who came from within the ranks of the company. Like most Egyptians he bridled at the suggestion that there was anything undeveloped about the country and he naturally would have preferred the conference in France. But for a couple of reasons we thought the Malaysian conference would be more relevant to Egypt.

In the first place Malaysia was a predominantly Muslim country and we felt that a "Islamic model"—if there was such a thing—might appeal to the Egyptians. There were sensitivities even in the relatively straightforward world of telecommunications, and issues of sovereignty, security, and content had already raised their troublesome heads in Egypt. They were all important, but content was particularly controversial, given the images available on the web. In addition Malaysia had recently liberalized the telecommunications market and opened the cellular sector to competition. In that respect it was *ahead* of France and most European countries and we saw it as a potential case study in what the Egyptians wanted to accomplish.

So we won their grudging consent and made the necessary arrangements for the trip. We would fund the conference fees and living expenses and ARENTO would pay for the air tickets. We wrote letters to two organizations in Malaysia—Jabatan Telekom Malaysia, JTM or the regulator, and Syarikat Telekom Malaysia, STM or the fixed-line operating company—saying that we would like to visit them while we were in Kuala Lumpur. We tried to express our interest in terms that were not patronizing to either country. But no one seemed too concerned with the wording, the Malaysians probably because they had better things to do. If the minister himself were to attend, it would require an official invitation from the Malaysian Minister of Telecommunications. But he did not, being unwell. And, anyway, he was probably more interested in his metro project. The chairman of ARENTO was also busy, attempting to establish his authority over the increasingly refractory company, and he begged off.

So the Egyptian delegation consisted of two senior employees of the ministry, two central department chiefs, or CDC's, from ARENTO, and one consultant. As it turned out it was pitched at the right level, ministers or chairmen not being used to sitting for days at a time listening to presentations on such topics as "Carrier Network Service Performance Systems" or "Advances in Mobile Satellite Applications throughout Asia." But we were still an official delegation and, as we would learn in Singapore, matters of protocol were important.

We flew Singapore Airlines via Dubai and Singapore to Kuala Lumpur. I had last been in Singapore in 1988, after stopping over briefly in Kuala Lumpur, and had visited the office of the consulting firm I then worked for. They said that doing business in Singapore was like doing business in Europe, but that the Malays were a little too laid-back for the American taste. The implication was that Malaysia would never quite equal Singapore. It may have been true, but Singapore was a one-of-a-kind phenomenon, more a Chinese city-state than a country. And the change in Malaysia over the eight years was remarkable.

Kuala Lumpur was now a beehive of activity, with new high-rises going up everywhere. There seemed to be energy in the air and the sense of it was palpable. The driver of the cab from the airport was a Malay who said that the population of the country was roughly 50 percent Malay, 35 percent Chinese, and 15 percent Indian. I later learned that the Indians were mostly Tamils who had been brought in as rubber tappers before the Second World War. It wasn't clear how much the new developments involved the different ethnic groups but a paternalistic government apparently made sure that everyone got a piece of the action. There was an official policy of indiginization, a carry-over of the anti-Chinese feeling from the "troubles" of the 1960's. But beneath the official line, there were probably still the old clichés, of industrious Chinese, devious Indians, and lazy Malays. The classic book on the area, *The Malay Archipelago* by Alfred Russel Wallace, spoke of the mix of the Malays, Chinese, English, Portuguese, Indians, Arabs, Bengalis, Parsees, and Javanese in the middle of the nineteenth century. It was the Chinese who made the greatest impression:

By far the most conspicuous of the various kinds of people . . . and those which most attract the visitor's attention, are the Chinese, whose numbers and incessant activity give the place very much the appearance of a town in China.

More recently, the Americans had used the British experience in Malaya as a model for our counterinsurgency efforts in Vietnam. The "Malayan emergency"—it was never called a war since insurance for the rubber and tin interests didn't cover acts of war, but did cover terrorism—lasted from 1948 to 1960. It was, we thought, the classical example of how to deal with a communist revolution in Asia. In retrospect it was easy to see how important Malaya would have seemed at the time, and how the lessons learned there would become important later on. The emergency spanned the triumph of the communists in China, the outbreak of the Korean war, the ejection of the French from Indochina, and the initial American involvement in Vietnam They all seemed to be related, and some alleged they were part of a sinister communist plot.

The British battle for "the hearts and minds" of the people in Malaya (although the quote was from John Adams) became the pattern for the Americans in Vietnam. The jungle refuges for the rebels, resettlement of large segments of the population in compounds, the declaration of safe areas, and the political nature of the war, all seemed a prelude to Vietnam. But in reality the differences between Malaya and Vietnam were far greater than the similarities. At any one time the Malayan insurgency never involved more than five to six thousand "CT's", or communist terrorists. And although they sometimes found a refuge across the border in Thailand, there were no safe havens in surrounding countries.

There had been no prelude to the war like the exodus of the hundreds of thousands of Vietnamese from the north to the south, no regular army involvement like that of the North Vietnamese, no major supply effort by the Soviets and the Chinese, and no naval and air operations on the scale of the American effort in Vietnam. The CT's were homegrown and dedicated communists—how anachronistic the term sounded today—largely confined to the jungle. They finally gave up because they grew tired of the harassment, the privation, and ultimately their lack of success. Now, Malaysia was a byword for progress of the capitalist sort and it was hard to understand how some Malayans could have been so single-minded. But most of the CT's had probably been Chinese.

The drive from the airport took about forty minutes, through an area of thick jungle and periodic rubber plantations before we reached the outskirts of the city. There were scars in the red-brown earth, denuded by what looked like torrential rains. There wasn't really a rainy season, we were told, only more rain at some times of the year than others. Then a river appeared, meandering behind a line of bamboo shanties with corrugated tin roofs. Kuala Lumpur meant "muddy confluence" and there was another river that joined this one further on. Both were the color of tea with milk and, for some reason, this gave the water a clean, almost appetizing look.

In the distance high-rises announced the center of the city. As we neared the commercial district it became obvious that many of the buildings were unfinished. The driver told us that they were working on the venues for the Commonwealth Games in 1998. And they were building what would be the two tallest towers in the world when they were completed in time for the games. The city seemed to be in a state of feverish activity.

Our hotel, the Istana or "palace" in Malay, was also where the conference would be held. It was also a reminder that Asians were still the best hoteliers in the world. The Istana was like Singapore Airlines, with an endless supply of courteous staff, ever ready with the guest's name and a polite inquiry as to what they couldn't do next. The rooms were large and comfortable, although it was surprising that in a country with seven mobile telephones licensees and everyone plugged into one electronic device or another, there was no remote for the television.

The conference would start the day after our arrival, so we had a little time to acclimatize ourselves beforehand. It was still humid in the early evening when I took a turn around the center of the city. There was that first breath of night air in an Asian city, the mingled odors of exhaust and sewage, the exudations of millions of people, and of something ineffable that faintly suggested wickedness and excitement. But this was not Kaosiung or Bangkok and I was approached by only one prostitute in several days in the city. The main order of business seemed to be business and people were shopping with a single-mindedness that was astonishing.

The opening session took place the next morning. The conference lasted only two days, but packed into that short period were sessions covering most aspects of deploying cellular networks in a developing country. Some of the material was highly technical. But the Egyptians found the Malaysian model, with its seven licensees, unsettling. In their opinion, Malaysia had moved too far, too fast in its liberalization. Surprisingly, Singapore—pristine, efficient, organized Singapore—was the model they found more attractive. That was probably because Singapore Telecom had moved more slowly and there were only two cellular licensees.

English was the *lingua franca* of the conference and it was not difficult to see why. The attendees—Americans, Egyptians, Malaysians, Singapore

Chinese, and Australians—were all from former British colonies or dependencies. But the English used by each was slightly different. The Malaysians had their own interesting lilt, characteristic of the archipelago. The keynote speaker, a Malay, was dynamic and warmed gradually to his subject, "Establishing the Potential of Mobile Communications Applications and the Framework for Effective and Rapid Deployment of Mobile Services in Malaysia."

Even with such a dry topic he carried the audience along with him. When told by the moderator that his time was up, he dismissed him with a wave of his hand: "don't interfere . . . I got my own style." And he did. But he was also typical of Malaysian speakers of English. The most common problem seemed to be with plurals. There were "potentials for growth" and "rooms for improvement" on "the roads" to development. How often during the conference would we hear about "an interim measures" or "in conclusions."

Malay had once been written in the Arabic script and Arabized newspapers were still available on the street. But it was now Latinized phonetically, which produced some oddities: "teksi" for "taxi," "sen" for "cent," and "kalej" for "college." It was strange to see a shingle advertising "fisioterapy." In some cases they had Latinized the Arabic as well and we saw signs left over from the feast, wishing us well on the "aidilfitri." Several of the Malaysians opened their presentations with the full-blown "*Salaam aleikum wa rahmat Ullahi wa baraktu,*" and littered their speech with "*insha'ullahs.*"

The Australians had the flat accent that was their national signature and they were straightforward in an almost apologetic way. It was as if they acknowledged that the rough edges in their character had still not entirely worn off. It was very refreshing. They said all the right things, alluding to the absence of a body of jurisprudence in Asia to deal with disputes, and to inadequate guidance to operators, notwithstanding government-mandated terms in the tenders. One of their advantages over the Malaysians is that they were expressing complex thoughts in their first language and did not have to struggle with translation. The earnestness of the Australians made them particularly believable.

The single American speaker, a former senior executive of one of the Bell operating companies, was almost a caricature of the type, down to his impeccable grooming and lapel pin. His presentation was the best organized and the best delivered of the conference. It was characterized by good enunciation, pauses at the right places, and clear emphases. It was also full of management speak—allusions to "the funding community," to "success enablers," to "downstream opportunities for optimal integration." He used the word "impacted" as a verb instead of an adjective describing wisdom teeth. It was all very logical. First there was market research—"where it all begins"—then planning, planning, and more planning, then funding, then launch and, finally, rollout. It was unlike our experience in Egypt, where the sequence seemed to be decide, implement, *then* plan. But it all seemed a little too pat, as if he had been wound-up. If interrupted, he would have to be rewound and started over again.

The British came in two types. The first was a retired Royal Navy communications expert. Given his accent—"mixin'" instead of "mixing," and "readin' from the same hymn sheet"—he had probably been a senior enlisted man or maybe a warrant officer. He clearly knew his subject—fraud in cellular networks—but his delivery seemed oddly dated, almost Victorian. There were "fraudsters" intent on perpetrating subscription fraud, or roaming fraud, or conference-call fraud. Then, there were those who were guilty of aiding and abetting the fraudsters, and they also needed to be apprehended. It was as if we were listening to some latter-day Holmes or Watson. At the end of the day, he was a simple policeman. But he also had a matter-of-fact community-of-interest with the Australians and the Americans and a modern approach to the problem. Fraud was like substance abuse: the necessary first step was to recognize that there *was* a problem.

The second British type was the bane of people of color the world over. It was not the topic, which had to do with the demand for cellular services in Malaysia, or what he said, which was unexceptional enough. It was *how* he said it that grated. His manner of calm, understated assurance was as much a learned behavior as the American's studied forthrightness. But where the American spoke directly he drawled, where the American paused he mumbled, where the American emphasized he continued as if emphases should be self-evident. He went on and on and I found myself struggling to hear him, particularly the asides which were uttered smilingly under his breath, as if he were indulging a private joke to which the rest of us weren't privy. The performance was aggravating to the former colonials in the room and the reason why the most abiding legacy of the British in their former colonies was a profound inferiority complex.

After the conference we had a day's stopover in Singapore, where we had arranged to see both the operator and regulator. Not surprisingly, Singapore was the more formal of the two places. At the ministry there was a ritual welcoming ceremony for the official delegation from Egypt. We were led by the First Undersecretary of State for Communications in the Ministry of Transport and Telecommunications and he replied on our behalf with appropriate expressions of gratitude and interest. Name- plates for each of us were arranged around a conference table that might have come from a

James Bond movie. We exchanged business cards, but not in the American way, handing them out like candies.

Instead, each was offered and accepted with both hands, carefully read, and a short comment was considered appropriate for each name or title. Mr. Khan, we learned, was simply the Anglicization of a Chinese name, and was not "a prince, nobleman, Lord; a Persian satrap . . ." This was followed by video presentations that were slick and professional. Later, we met the regulator, the Telecommunications Authority of Singapore (TAS) and if it was less high-tech, at least they offered to train Egyptian regulators in the disciplines they were developing. After the formal meetings there was time to look around the city.

Singapore was also changing, feverishly building the new and razing its old Chinatown, and there were only a few areas recognizable from eight years before. But it was still possible to find a little outdoor Chinese restaurant with pork and rice for breakfast. The best hotel in town was still Raffles, but it had been restored and the arcade was now full of couturier outlets, Armani, Vuitton, and Gucci. A wide range of touristy stuff was available in the hotel gift shop, and the playing cards were just as flimsy but much more expensive than they had been in 1988. The price of the rooms was now astronomical and old-timers lamented the passing of the place they had once known and cherished. St. Andrew's, the Anglican Cathedral in the center of the city, was still there and was also being renovated. It occupied an entire city block, most of it open lawns and gardens. With the price of real estate in Singapore the grounds must have been worth hundreds of millions. The cricket pitch across from the government buildings was alive with activity, the men in loose white sweaters and an odd assortment of hats, going through their leisurely paces. But part of the field was occupied by Chinese girls in spandex uniforms playing softball. The metallic "thunk" of aluminum bat on ball was undoubtedly the sound of the future.

If the shopping in Kuala Lumpur had been purposeful it was even more so in Singapore. There were many bookstores and I bought books on the Malayan emergency and *The Pregnable Fortress* by Peter Elphick, the story of the fall of Singapore to the Japanese. A cruise to the southern islands provided context: a good view of the jade-colored sea, white sand, and coconut palms that, along with the heat and humidity, were probably unchanged from 1942. I tried to visualize the scene of the Japanese arrival, of the cruel, arrogant little men as they swarmed across the straits. The fall of Singapore was the greatest military disaster in British imperial history, but the only thing remarkable about it was that it had been so inevitable.

According to Elphick the "fortress" had been deficient in almost every military necessity. The aircraft were obsolete, there were no tanks, and ammunition was severely rationed. The troops were mostly new levies, the sweepings of Sidney and Melbourne, and seventeen-year-old Punjabis, some of whom had never fired a rifle. The Japanese didn't penetrate the dense Malayan jungle, but drove down the western side of the peninsula on the best road in Southeast Asia. Many came on bicycles and the tires burst in the heat. The sound of thousands of metal rims on the pavement was so alarming that the Indian troops broke and ran.

From the British side, infighting was rife: between the civilian and military authorities, between the services, between the Indian and regular armies, and between the Australians and everyone else. They were no match for the Japanese who had a singleness of purpose and a fervor that seemed to make them invincible. Some suggested that Churchill, with his hands full in North Africa, simply wrote off the Pacific, knowing that when the Americans came in they would put it right. Even so, the loss of the *Prince of Wales* and *Repulse* came as a shock. Singapore was doomed and maybe everyone knew it from the start. The Indians were receptive to the propaganda of the Indian National Army, whose representatives were attached to Japanese units, and there were cases of large-scale desertion.

But it was nothing like that of the Australians who simply walked away one night, leaving the Japanese to land on the island unopposed. It was a scandal, next to that of the Russians in 1917, perhaps the greatest example of desertion by a regular army in military history. It was hushed up at the time, and there was never an official inquiry into the fall of Singapore. But there were the inevitable questions about the Australian character, about their individuality and lack of discipline. It seemed to be true. The Australians knew they were doomed, without armor and air cover, and if the English and the Indians would put up with these conditions, *they* would not. But it was more than simply walking away. There were many cases of looting stores of alcohol, drunken binges, rapes, and the forcing of civilians—European women and children—at gunpoint off evacuation ships. It was an ugly episode and to this day remains suppressed by both governments.

At the airport on the return trip one of the Egyptians tried to change his reservation to attend another conference in Bangalore. We spoke first with Singapore Airlines that had a flight to Madras. But they would have to refer to the ticketing office in Cairo. Then we looked into domestic flights in India and we raced through the airport looking for the office of Air India. For once, Singapore let us down and it took several abortive turns before we reached an unmarked office in a back corridor. There we spoke with a Sikh, a sour man who was clearly not interested in helping. He worked for Air India and the domestic carrier was Indian Air, or maybe it was the other way around. In the end, Cairo wouldn't let Singapore Airlines change the ticket anyway, but the behavior of the Sikh put Air India, or was it Indian Air, on our personal blacklist.

On the short stopover in Dubai we were welcomed back to the Arab world by Emirati security staff. Like Saudi airport employees they were thoroughly unpleasant. They especially liked to taunt the Indians, Pakistanis, and Sri Lankans. One lectured me about my boarding pass and transit card. He eventually threw them back at me with a leer. Cairo airport was a breeze by comparison and I was back in the apartment forty-five minutes from the time the wheels touched down.

The conference was actually very useful and for several years afterwards the Egyptians referred to the trip as a kind of benchmark in the liberalization process. It was supposedly Hosni Mubarak's own trip to Malaysia the following year that finally broke loose the logjam in mobile deployment in Egypt. Prior to that there had been too many concerns about security and—more importantly—too many sons involved. So maybe the choice of Malaysia had been right after all. Incidentally, the new chairman of ARENTO didn't survive to see it happen. The old guard rose up and threw him out. Better yet, they simply hunkered down and outlasted him. In the end Egyptians always did things their own way.

11

The Meeting

The eighty-twenty rule applied in spades in ARENTO. At a senior level maybe it was even ninety-ten. That is, 90 percent of the work of the company was done by 10 percent of the employees. Authority was not delegated and senior managers were overwhelmed with claims on their time. This day was no exception and I was ushered into the vice-chairman's office along with another delegation from Booz-Allen, two expats and an Egyptian. There were already visitors sitting in the armchairs in front of his desk, a tall Brit and an attractive Egyptian woman. She was probably his translator and factotum. I sat in an armchair by the wall and the other newcomers arranged themselves around the conference table.

We were obviously interrupting something, but that was the norm in ARENTO. There was a foot-high stack of papers on the vice-chairman's desk—some of them important—and the phone rang continually throughout the next hour and a-half. Promotions to general manager had just been announced by the minister and the hubbub filled the halls of the Ramses building. Women ululated and men slapped each other on the back and exchanged kisses. The two secretaries, Ahmed and Tareq, couldn't screen out the callers since most of them had to do with the promotions. The vice-chairman took them all:

> *Aiwa, ya Bash Mohandis, alf alf mabrouk . . . ya'ani da'iman kidda tamam ya seedi . . . Ullah ya khaleek . . . salaama ya seedi, alf alf mabrouk . . . salaama ya seedi. . . Ullah ya khaleek . . . alf alf mabrouk . . . salaama salaama . . . kidda tamam . . . maa salaama . . .*

or

> Yes, oh exalted engineer, a thousand congratulations . . . that is, may everything always be well . . . God keep you . . . goodbye

oh my good friend, a thousand congratulations . . . goodbye oh
my good friend . . . God keep you . . . a thousand congratulations, goodbye, goodbye . . . may everything always be well . . .
goodbye. . .

They were formalities but they were anything but perfunctory. Promotions were important in the lives of these underpaid civil servants. One of the new general managers made about as much as we paid our drivers. So the congratulations were heartfelt.

But the vice-chairman gave them his own spin. He was a talker and not a listener. He had the habit of repeating back to you what you had just told him, and then asking— very helpfully—if you understood what he was saying. In a meeting with him two weeks before, we made a little progress before he suddenly veered off into uncharted waters. The words were familiar but none of it made any sense. I knew him from our trip to Malaysia and Singapore when the other ARENTO people just tuned him out when he began one of his dissertations.

The phone rang again:

Aiwa, ya seedi, alf alf mabrouk . . . ya'ani da'iman kidda tamam ya seedi . . . Ullah ya khaleek . . . salaama ya seedi . . . alf alf mabrouk, salaama ya seedi . . . Ullah ya khaleek . . .alf alf mabrouk . . . salaama salaama . . . .kidda tamam salaama . . . maa salaama

But he was good-natured and his light-blue eyes danced around the room behind a kind of mischievous grin, sharing with everyone the absurdity of his situation. The job really was impossible. There simply weren't enough hours in the day to do all the things he had to do. We all understood how hopeless it was: meeting with us, answering the telephone, dealing with the pile of papers on his desk, along with countless other demands on his time. His front teeth were white and regular but most of his molars were gone. Occasionally he would break into a raucous laugh and throw back his head. That's when you noticed the missing molars. The phone rang again:

Aiwa, ya Bash Mohandis, alf alf mabrouk . . . Ullah ya khaleek . . . salaama ya seedi . . . alf alf mabrouk. . . salaama ya Bash Mohandis . . Ullah ya khaleek . . . alf alf mabrouk . . . salaama salaama . . . kidda tamam . . . ma'a salaama . . .

As if the six of us weren't enough, a secretary now introduced two new visitors, a man and an older woman. They found seats near the conference table. Then, the Alcatel agent arrived. We were now fifteen minutes into the meeting and no business had been conducted by any of us. The Brit was looking increasingly petulant and aggrieved: after all, he had been here first.

The final straw was when two new general managers swept in with their ululating retinue. We all stood and congratulated them. The vice-chairman was already standing—he had not had a chance to sit down since we arrived. Out came a special box of chocolates, and they were passed around. This led to a discussion of Egyptian chocolates and the vice-chairman swore they were the best in the world. Then the phone rang again:

> *Aiwa, ya Josef, alf alf mabrouk . . . Ullah ya khaleek . . . salaama ya seedi . . . alf alf mabrouk. . . salaama ya seedi . . . Ullah ya khaleek . . . alf alf mabrouk . . . salaama salaama . . . kidda tamam . . . ma'a salaama . . .*

When he hung up his eyes danced around the room again, as if to say to all of us "you see what I have to put up with?" The Brit had finally had enough. He drew himself up to his full height and announced:

> Mr. vice-chairman, my bank is interested in serious business with ARENTO, which you have *not* given me the opportunity to discuss with you. Now, we can help with financing and we have GSM expertise. When you are ready to give me your full attention . . .

The phone interrupted him:

> *Aiwa, ya Bash Mohandis, alf alf mabrouk . . . Ullah ya khaleek . . . salaama ya seedi . . . alf alf mabrouk . . . salaama ya seedi . . . Ullah ya khaleek . . alf alf mabrouk. . .salaama . . . salaama . . . kidda tamam salaama . . . alf salaama . . . salaama . . . ma'a salaama"*

This time the vice-chairman threw back his head and laughed that infectious laugh as he hung up. He hadn't even heard the banker. Of course, it was nice meeting him. The Brit exited the room feeling much better, I'm sure, for having registered his displeasure. But he might as well have saved his breath. He had made no impact whatsoever. It was as if he didn't exist.

The departure of the banker and his translator made room and I took a place near one of the armchairs. I didn't sit. For the next hour the vice-chairman and I stood and talked across his desk when he wasn't answering the telephone. We had been working on ARENTO's financial plan and I began to explain to him what we were doing. They wanted to build a million lines per year—that would cost about a billion US dollars—and could self-finance only about a third of it. But no one had given much thought to where the rest of the money would come from. We wanted to give them an idea of the gross magnitudes, having factored in the timing of the revenue streams from the old and the new lines. Then, there was the matter of the back taxes that ARENTO owed the government. The vice-chairman listened and then repeated back to me a little of what I had outlined. And, by the way, did I understand what he was saying? The phone rang again:

> *Aiwa, ya seedi, alf alf mabrouk . . . Ullah ya khaleek . . . salaama ya seedi, alf alf mabrouk . . . salaama ya seedi . . . Ullah ya khaleek . . .alf alf mabrouk . . .salaama salaama . . . kidda tamam salaama . . . alf salaama ya seedi . . .*

Then the chairman's secretary arrived with the minutes from the weekly meeting with the minister. For the next twenty minutes the vice-chairman reviewed the minutes against the copious notes in his datebook. He showed me the notes:

> I was trying to write in a kind of shorthand because—do you understand me?—our Mr. Minister talks very quickly and I had to take it all down.

He used the colloquial Egyptian word for "quickly," before explaining its etymology. Then he threw back his head and cackled at the absurdity of trying to take notes while this man—"our Mr. Minister"—went on at a furious pace. The phone rang again:

> *Aiwa, ya Bash Mohandis, alf alf mabrouk . . . salaama ya seedi . . . Ullah ya khaleek . . . alf alf mabrouk . . . salaama . . . salaama . . . kidda tamam . . . salaama . . . alf salaama ya seedi . . .*

I left after an hour and a half. I had the vice-chairman's attention for a total of about five minutes during that time. But I had introduced one of the topics I wanted to discuss with him and he had parroted a little of it back to me. That was progress. All in all, it had been a very good meeting.

12

The Movies

In nearly six years in Egypt I had never been to the movies. I had seen an occasional western film at a special showing in one of the big hotels. But I had never been to an Egyptian movie theater. That was a little odd since, measured by the number of films made on a yearly basis, the movie industry in Egypt was second in the world only to India's. It was the primary source of movies and soap operas throughout the Arab world, and in 1995 the local film industry was celebrating its one-hundredth anniversary. An Egyptian friend from Alexandria—where everything, of course, was smarter—said that it had been a regular ritual to go the movies when he was growing up. It was also the fashion to wear shoes that made your feet look smaller and he always took off his shoes after he was seated. He spoke of the agony of trying to fit into the shoes after his feet had swelled during a double feature.

Movie stars had always been household names in Egypt: Abdel-Halim Hafez, Laila Murad, Shadia, Michel Shalhoub—otherwise known as Omar Sharif—and his former wife Faten Hammama, the most famous actress of her day. I had actually seen Omar Sharif, minus his mustache, in an old black-and-white film on television earlier in the year. They dated from a more innocent age, and now there was a new generation of actors and actresses like Adel Imam and Zeinat Sidky. To judge by the billboards in the streets in Cairo, the movies were different too, with more mayhem and a surprising amount of flesh displayed. Even the latest American pot-boilers eventually found their way to Cairo.

There had been several recent features on Egyptian movies in local magazines and newspapers. One article spoke about the different kinds of theaters in Cairo and the difference in the behavior of the audience. In the poorer districts there was a constant stream of talking, shouting, laughing, and even throwing of food. In the nicer places—and they had recently built or renovated several movie palaces in the downtown part of the city—they were more restrained. Another article dealt with censorship. It stated that "sex is definitely the censor's' current preoccupation." Scenes with women in bathing suits were sometimes permitted "assuming the camera angle is appropriate." This had not always been the case and, in the more socially relaxed but politically zealous Nasser years, the preoccupation was political. Nasser himself may have been a bit of a prude and he had been scandalized by Sukarno's philandering in the old days of the Bandung Five. But the generally leftist and secularist tone of the revolutionary period probably permitted a certain amount of sexual explicitness on the grounds that it was "modern" or "artistic" or "European." Now, the pendulum had swung back the other way and the censors were intent on protecting Egypt—and Isalm—from the corrupting influences of the West. And the sexual assault today was very different from the naive, almost innocent, sophistication of the 1960s and seventies.

To someone who knew only the Egypt of the last decade of the twentieth century, it was difficult to imagine how wild and licentious a place it had once been. Flaubert was in some respects a typical nineteenth-century visitor, and he reveled in the sexual freedom of Egypt. He minutely reported everything he saw, from the coupling of a man with a monkey in Shubra, women masturbating mad *marabouts* in the streets of Cairo, to the grotesque symptoms of Mamluks suffering from unnaturally-acquired syphilis in Qasr el-'Aini hospital. For Flaubert, Egypt was all bardashes, prostitutes, and public indecency. He slept his way to Luxor and back and never became used to the Egyptian woman's habit of depilation. It was the kind of thing that Westerners in the late twentieth century found in Tiajuana or Olongapo City or Bangkok.

But even in this century, during the wars and occupation, Cairo had been full of prostitutes. Naguib Mahfouz captured the atmosphere in some of his early novels. It was difficult to imagine an Egyptian prostitute today, just as it was hard to imagine a mob burning down most of European Cairo in 1952. They seemed like such nice, slightly prudish people. But if Europeans once came to Egypt to escape the pruderies of their own societies, it was the opposite today. Now, Europe and America represented freedom and not just freedom of ideas. There was a whole world of explicit sexuality out there. Not surprisingly Egyptians seemed to believe that Europeans and Americans actually behaved the way they were portrayed in movies. We often talked about the man reported breaking into a European woman's bedroom in Alexandria. He was surprised when she objected. It didn't seem to be that way in the movies.

At a dinner party an Egyptian friend mentioned the Cairo Film Festival, beginning that week, and it planted the seed. He said the advantage of the festival was that the censor wouldn't dare touch works of art from the rest of the world. The *Al-Ahram Weekly* ran a feature on the festival—Sarah Miles would be there in person at the opening—and the list of participating countries read like a mini United Nations. There would be entries from Poland, Austria, Italy, Brazil, India, Canada, Estonia, Japan, the UK, Australia, Croatia, Tunisia, the Czech Republic, Sweden, Belgium, the United States, France, Hungary, Russia, Sri Lanka, the Netherlands, China, Spain, Germany, Switzerland, South Korea, Greece, Slovenia, Lebanon, Turkey, and Armenia. The paper carried a complete listing of the venues, times, and features. There was a note that "past experience suggests that changes in the programme are likely to occur. It is therefore advisable to check with the venues first."

There were participating theaters in Ma'adi, Heliopolis, Nasr City, and Giza. But most were downtown and within ten minutes of Dokki by cab. On the night I decided to go, the nearby Tahrir was showing an Italian film called *Jonathan of the Bears*, something that didn't sound very interesting. So I decided to try the Radio theater on Tal'aat Harb. It was scheduled to show the French film *La Vengeance d'une Blonde*. Parking would be impossible so I took a cab and it deposited me at six twenty outside the theater, with the feature scheduled for six thirty.

There was a large crowd already waiting outside and a long line to the booth where a single attendant sold tickets. The ticket line didn't move for ten minutes, before gradually inching forward. The discipline was not bad for Egypt and no one seemed concerned about the time. As long as the mass of people at the entrance didn't move, there was nothing to worry about. When I reached the booth I paid fifteen pounds (or about $4.50) for a ticket. The attendant wrote the number of the assigned seat—I11—on the back of the ticket after consulting a large plan of the theater.

The crowd at the door had grown by the time the previous showing began to empty, and it must have eventually numbered in the hundreds. After a few minutes the mass surged forward and we began to move up the stairs. I remembered a similar experience in Jidda at a performance of the Harlem Globetrotters. It turned out they weren't the real Globetrotters at all, but the crowds had been so heavy in halls leading into the arena—and the Saudis locked all the doors behind us—that if there had been panic hundreds would have been trampled. Here, at the top of the stairs—maybe a hundred feet away—was the source of the problem: the crowd, four or so abreast, was reduced to a single line and everyone was frisked twice, first by hand and then with a metal detector, before being allowed to pass. Finally, the press eased and the theater opened up to the left and right. Although it was still lighted, nicely dressed ushers with flashlights showed us to our assigned seats.

The theater was large, very modern and clean, and graduated like a chemistry lecture hall. It seated about 500 and was quickly filling. The audience was almost all male and young, most of the men looking to be under forty and middle-class. There were no *gallabiyas*. Everyone was in good spirits but not boisterous. At about seven fifteen the lights dimmed and went out as previews were shown. One was a Hollywood B-flick about teenagers in a haunted castle, and the second was an Egyptian film about a man whose family washed cars in Cairo. It was called *The Garage*. Then the lights came on again and we waited for another five minutes for the beginning of the main feature.

As the lights dimmed it immediately became obvious that it was not going to be the French film. The credits began before the curtains were fully parted but it took scarcely that long for the audience to react. The English text on the screen said something about Europeans moving to the Americas and old sepia stills of immigrant scenes provided the backdrop for the names of the cast, producer, director, etc. But the crowd was having none of it. First there were individual shouts, then more shouts and then rhythmic chants and, before long, half the theater was on its feet. By the time the sepia had turned to color and an old priest had remarked in Portuguese—with English subtitles—how soon the sparkle faded from newlyweds' eyes, there was general pandemonium. No one could see or hear anything on the screen. Then the lights came back on.

This was not what everyone had come to see and the management had gotten the message. A couple of ushers and then the theater manager made their way to the back rows where most of the noise came from and tried to appease the ringleaders. A kind of negotiation took place and the manager finally held out his hands to the audience in a good-natured kind of way as if to say: "OK, you win." Wild cheers broke out, subsiding into a kind of expectant buzz as everyone congratulated everyone else on the victory. For a few minutes it was quiet. But then there were cheers again as the lights dimmed and the introduction began to Yannis Typaldos's *Terra Incognita*, the competition entry from Greece. The crowd settled into a kind of hungry silence. It didn't take long to see why.

The credits seemed to be Greek but the dialogue was in English. It was not dubbed. In a crowd of this size there could have only been a few whose English was good enough to understand what was being said. But no one had come for the dialogue. The film opened as a writer with a five-o'clock shadow sat and pecked away at a manual typewriter. A cigarette dangled from his lips and he looked a little like Albert Camus. Then the camera cut away to a bed where a naked girl lay and it played slowly over her breasts.

Back to the writer tapping away and then the girl walked past him, her naked buttocks disappearing into the bathroom, followed by the sound of a shower. By the time the credits were finished she had come back and stood provocatively next to him, in full frontal nudity. Without looking up from the typewriter the man told her to dress and leave. There wasn't a sound to be heard in the theater.

That was just the introduction but it set the tone for the next two hours. The plot had something to do with a toxic spill, official efforts to cover it up, and the murder of another writer who knew the truth. There were flashbacks to crowds of refugees leaving what looked like the scene of a battle—donkey carts and small children and old people on foot—looking like something by Fellini. There were half-naked people running through the streets of a city that looked like it had been bombed, with prostitutes on every street corner. The plot was predictable, with official villains, the writer as hero, a female photo-journalist as a kind of Robin to his Batman. He, of course, drank heavily and she, of course, loved him. The federal police were after him, or after the manuscript of his murdered friend, or after *something*.

The dialogue was wooden, littered with little bits of half-baked philosophy in the French fashion. There were villainous heavies and romantic dinners by candlelight and more flashbacks and beatings by official thugs. There was even a visit to an ailing father that appeared to be lifted out of *Five Easy Pieces*. It was sometimes hard to follow because much of it seemed to have been cut out by the censor. But, even so, there was enough soft-core pornography to keep this audience on the edge of their seats. It was the West in all its tawdriness, but with an odd sense of deja vu: sexploitation, the bodies firm in the nineties style, but in a sixties setting. It was all cheap thrills and morality on the cheap. But that didn't matter to the audience.

Oddly, the names of the actors and actresses all seemed to be Russian and the hero had been tossed from a Russian limousine when the feds were through with him. So where did this thing come from: a Greek movie, filmed in English somewhere in the Caucasus with a Russian cast? Maybe it represented not the West but the new Russia in all of its tawdriness. When it was over we all filed out, dispersing individually into the heavy night air in this sexually repressed society. There was another expectant crowd of young males surging up the stairs as we left.

If it was the official Greek entry in the festival I doubted that the jury would be very impressed. But a later review in the *Al-Ahram Weekly* spoke of the "important and controversial" films that Cairo audiences would not have seen without the benefit of the film festival. Among those listed was *Terra Incognita*. It was probably considered to be "modern" or "artistic" or "European."

Some things never changed.

13

Al-Andalus

In spite of nearly twenty years in the Muslim world I knew very little about Islamic Spain. The story of the Omayyad remnant that had established the empire and the broad outlines of the *Reconquista* were familiar enough. But for the most part the history of the country was a blank page. So when I had a couple of weeks of unused vacation time Spain was an obvious destination, with Portugal tossed in as an extra-added attraction. A first question was whether Americans needed visas. You couldn't always be sure, and we had once spent a frantic weekend in Singapore getting visas for, of all places, Australia. There had been a recent article in the *International Herald Tribune* entitled "In Border-Free Europe, A Weekend in Limbo," where the writer had tried to enter Spain without a visa. He had been stopped at the airport in Madrid and sent back to Geneva where the flight originated. But it seems that he was Australian and Australia required visas from the citizens of every country except New Zealand. The European Community had simply reciprocated.

So I traveled visa-less through Spain, then Portugal, and back to Spain with hardly a glance at my passport. I was stamped in and out in Madrid but crossed the Portuguese border on a bus somewhere between Huelva and Faro, identified only by a row of exchange kiosks. The bus didn't even stop. It was a very European experience. Even in early September, after most of Europe had returned to work, there seemed to be an army of backpackers, bicyclists, and campers on the move. I took every form of public transportation, from streetcars to high-speed trains, and they were clean and efficient. To an out sider it was amazing: no matter where or at what time you wanted to go, there always seemed to be a train waiting to take you there.

There was probably a phenomenon called "Eurotourism" and the Dutch girl in Sagres who worked for an American dating service in Amsterdam seemed to be the epitome. She was about thirty, bleached blond and tough looking, and seemed to have been everywhere: Bangkok was dirty, Jakarta was interesting, Los Angeles was big, and Mexico City was huge. She felt freest in Brazil but Peru had been the most interesting from a cultural point of view. Her boyfriend, part Indonesian and a bartender, had just finished his higher studies in management, the new European buzzword. Both complained about the superficiality of visitors to Amsterdam. Everyone saw only the drugs and prostitutes and forgot about the museums. Actually, they were not typical in that they both had jobs. Everyone—especially the Dutch—also complained about the number of young people without jobs, who probably would never have jobs, but were still traveling around Spain on the public dole.

Germans were everywhere. Charter airlines brought planeloads to the Algarve, and still they came even after several highly-publicized accidents. There would later be the burned-out hulk of a German charter to Portugal, lying next to the runway in Faro. The German girl in Sagres was probably *not* typical. She had a good job in the laboratory of a pharmaceutical firm and wanted to move into research. She had the kind of skin that seems to turn to gold on first exposure to the sun and that, combined with her delicate features and rich brown hair, should have made her very pretty. But she looked perpetually preoccupied and the occasional smile only made her look sad and vulnerable. The story was a little confusing, but it seems that her boyfriend had been a heroin addict and they had given him methadone. He later committed suicide. One of the last pictures she had of him was on Cape St. Vincent and she had come to the Algarve on a kind of pilgrimage. It *was* sad.

In another sense, the trip was anything but European. Madrid was in the north but I spent most of my time in the south, in the old province of *al-Andalus* in Arabic, or Andalucia in Spanish. In Jidda we had lived in *Ronda* in the Arabian Homes compound and the ambiance—from the white stucco villas with red tile roofs to the grounds heavy with citrus trees, bougainvillea, and frangipani—had been determinedly Andalucian. The stucco was actually not out of place in Jidda, although the old part of the city had been coral block underneath. And a major artery in the city had been *al-Qurtuba*, or Cordoba, Street. The Saudis were supposed to be everywhere in Spain, especially in the *Costa del Sol*, but I saw little evidence of them away from Marbella and other watering holes. I did see an Arab family in Cordoba with the women smugly veiled in the Egyptian fashion. After days of displays of feminine beauty they looked out of place. Instead of being religiously correct the veil seemed a kind of *sin* against nature and I had to check an impulse to become righteous on the subject.

In Spain the Muslims had been the authors of much that was delicate and beautiful, by comparison with which the monuments of the *reconquista* would seem only powerful and crudely assertive. But today they seemed to have forgotten what made Islamic Spain beautiful and it was a sad commentary that the best-preserved Islamic monuments were in places like Samarkand or Granada or Cordoba, which were either secularized or in the hands of non-believers. Islamic Cairo was deteriorating faster than Polish or German—or occasionally Egyptian—efforts to preserve it, although Cairo may have been a special case. There, the Fatimid city was still a city, not a museum, and serious restoration would displace thousands of people who lived and worked among the monuments. But even allowing for a place like Cairo, too often it was outsiders who were preserving the finest remnants of Islamic civilization.

To Madrid

I had no set schedule, beyond a general plan to see Granada, Cordoba, the coast, the Algarve, Lisbon, and maybe Porto. But I had booked a hotel in Madrid for the first night to be sure I had a place to stay. The travel agent had provided a listing of three- and four-star hotels in the other cities. They were all in the eighty to a hundred-dollar range, but I had not made any bookings and was glad I didn't. Spain was full of small, very clean hotels for much less, and in September there was always space available. The room at the Plaza in Madrid was just as small but much more expensive. I paced it off—if that was the term— and it was all of eleven by seventeen feet. Into that tiny space they had managed to fit a double bed, two end tables, a desk, a luggage stand, a bathroom with tub, a shower, and a washbasin. The television was suspended from the ceiling. There was just enough room to maneuver between the furniture.

For transportation my first thought in Cairo had been a rail pass. A first-class pass cost just over $300 and it would eliminate any worries about ticketing, backtracking, or missed connections. But the travel agent called later to say that Portugal didn't subscribe to the convention. There was another pass for $500 that covered both countries. He had no idea how much individual fares were but suggested that I buy them on the spot. It was good advice and I traveled very comfortably, first class when available, for two weeks for under $200.

In Madrid the first order of business was a train to Granada. That meant the Atocha station, about ten minutes away from the hotel by taxi. The schedule listed daily departures, leaving in the morning and arriving in Granada in the afternoon. So I had the rest of the day in Madrid. The hotel was within walking distance of the Prado and the Plaza Major, and I was able to see them both. It was an interesting neighborhood with several small restaurants and a nice little hotel. I made a note of it for my return. Lunch was at the counter of the *Museo de Jamon*, a sandwich of a hard roll like San Francisco sourdough with *Serrano* ham, and a beer. The ceiling of the restaurant was hung with whole hams and I stopped counting at 300.

In the evening, I walked the broad *Paseo de Recoletos* before dinner. The stores were full and the merchandise, particularly the clothes, was surprisingly inexpensive. Dinner was a tossed green salad, roast suckling lamb, and braised green peppers. The house red was good and the bread was hard and crusty. It became softer farther south. Surprisingly, food was *not* inexpensive and I reverted to my practice in Paris several years before: almost nothing for breakfast, avoiding hotel buffets which served mostly carbohydrates; a sandwich and a beer on the street for lunch, and a good dinner with wine. But this was not Paris and the food was surprisingly pricey. It was difficult to find a main course anywhere in the next two weeks for less than fifteen dollars and, with wine and a starter, it rarely came to less than thirty.

To Grenada

I was at Atocha at nine o'clock the next morning for the nine forty-five train to Grenada. About fifteen minutes before departure the computerized status board showed the platform and I found my coach and reserved seat in a non-smoking car. The price for a first-class seat was 3,500 pesetas (about twenty-nine dollars) and it was like flying first-class. The seats were wide with plenty of leg-room. A steward appeared with headsets for the movie that showed on the overhead monitor. There was an inflight magazine, which I kept since it showed the rail system throughout the peninsula. Incidentally, I spoke no Spanish and no one in Spain spoke much English so it was a dumb-show for most of the week. Portugal was different as English was widely spoken. The Portuguese attributed this to the arrogance of the Spaniards, but it probably had to do more with the armies of English who traditionally descended on Portugal for their holidays. And there had always been that special connection anyway, the English viewing the Portuguese as the enemy of their enemy, and vice-versa. The connection led to a dangerous dependency and an Englishman, William Beresford, had been the virtual ruler of Portugal during the Peninsular War in the early nineteenth century.

This was not the high-speed train and the trip would take just over six hours. But it was restful and these interludes became increasingly welcome over the next two weeks. Outside of Madrid the landscape had the barren look of parts of California, maybe east Contra Costa or Alameda counties. There were even windmills, but not the high-tech devices that mounted the Altamont. They looked like something out of *Don Quixote* and, up closer, the scene really didn't resemble California at all. There were flocks of sheep grazing among tumble-down houses and the shepherds, with their felt caps and staffs, looked like peasants. Dogs kept the sheep away from the tracks. But then the scenery changed and California returned again: the same golden fields and rolling hills covered with pine and scrub oak. There were cottonwoods and eucalyptus near the streams that came down from the mountains. The soil was first white and calcareous but then it turned brown or red-brown and it was carefully turned over in many areas. Wild artichokes appeared to complement the pines and oaks.

After about four hours we began to climb through the *Sierra Morena* and it became very rugged, like the area around the Pinnacles near Soledad. An hour from Granada rows of olive trees appeared and they marched in formation over the hills as far as the eye could see. There must have been thousands of square miles of olives. They were followed by fields of sunflowers, their millions of individual heads all demurely turned down, away from the direct rays of the sun.

Granada

We pulled into Granada at 3:49, two minutes late. I found a small hotel near the center of the city and by five o'clock was settled enough to have a brief look around before a serious excursion the next morning. The Alhambra sat on a hill overlooking the city. At first, I went up the hill but too far west before a couple of Americans put me right. On a wall near a large horseshoe arch there was a crude drawing of a door labeled "Ceuta" and graffiti inviting the North Africans, the architectural authors of this little jewel, to go back where they came from. They were shown as black rats carrying suitcases.

Back in the town someone said that a regular bus went to the top of the hill and I located the stop for the next day. Dinner was a mixed salad and the Granada specialty, *jamon con habas,* or ham with broad beans. The whole ham was sitting upright on a table in the center of the room and the waiters snacked on slices as they made their way back and forth from the kitchen. Raw, it was dense and salty, like Egyptian *basterma,* but cooked with the beans it was soft and moist and the meal was filling. The house wine was very good although the bread was not as crusty as it had been in Madrid.

Granada had been the last Muslim holdout on the peninsula, the kingdom falling to Ferdinand and Isabella in early 1492. Before that, Spain had been Arab and Muslim for over 700 years, longer than it has since been Christian and European. But the *reconquista* was actually a long drawn-out process and some would say it began as early as 722 when the Christians stopped the Arabs at Cavadonga. From that date the pressure was inexorably southward and, beginning with the enclave of Asturias—nearly as small in extent as Muslim Granada in the fifteenth century—Christian rule was gradually restored in the peninsula. The map in the Michelin guide-book showed advancing, east-west lines of Christian dominance in 850, 1040, 1150, and 1270. By the time Granada fell Muslim rule had been reduced to about 5 percent of Spain.

But it was still interesting to compare the history here with that of the other contested peninsula at the opposite end of the Mediterranean, Anatolia. Each was finally conquered in the fifteenth century, the last Christian enclave of Constantinople falling to the Turks in 1453. It had been even smaller than Grenada. Each had experienced large population movements—ethnic cleansing in twentieth-century terms—before settling into its present composition. The Byzantines made population resettlement an official policy, and had moved large numbers of Slavs into the peninsula over the thousand years of their rule. Anatolia had been overwhelmingly Greek and Slav—and Christian—before Turkic peoples began to displace them in the twelfth century. But parts of the peninsula remained Greek into the twentieth century, and Smyrna was a Greek city before war, massacre, and large-scale population transfers changed it into Turkish Izmir. As recently as 1923 Greek and Italian armies had bloodily reasserted their right to parts of Anatolia before Ataturk threw them out.

In the sixteenth century the giants of the two peninsulas—the Spain of Philip II and the Ottomans under Suleiman the Magnificent—faced off before the next century witnessed their exhaustion and the beginning of a long process of decline. Philip, the Most Catholic King, simultaneously built an overseas empire in Asia and the Americas, absorbed Portugal, and waged war against the Protestants in France and the Low Countries. At sea he fought the English with his grand armada in the Atlantic and the Turks in the Eastern Mediterranean. It was a magnificent effort but even the infusion of American silver couldn't save him. Overextended and bankrupt, Spain fell back in defeat to become what it is today, the poorest country in western Europe.

Suleiman mounted thirteen major campaigns, ten in Europe and three in Asia, and presided over an enormous expansion of empire. The Turks were at the gates of Vienna in 1529, controlled the Balkans and much else in Europe, sent naval expeditions against the Christians in both the

Mediterranean and the Indian Ocean, and simultaneously fought the Safavids in Persia. The Ottomans lasted longer, largely because of *realpolitik*: the end of the empire would have ramifications for the European balance of power and they were permitted to linger into the twentieth century. But it was a long, slow agony of decline before the sick man of Europe finally succumbed to his infirmities in 1919.

Comparisons like this could be carried too far. But in an atmosphere where Muslims today talk of their lost patrimony in Spain, I wondered whether they would consider a trade of Andalucia for Anatolia. What was once the greatest church in Christendom—Aya Sofia in Istanbul—became a mosque and then a museum. I was reminded of Aya Sofia in the Great Mosque at Cordoba. There was now a cathedral in the center of the building, although the Emperor Charles V told his architects that they had destroyed something unique to build something commonplace. In fact, it took three turns around the expanse of 800 double-horseshoe arches before I found it. But, of that, more below.

I awoke at about five AM to the sound of thunder and then a light fall of rain. The weather report on television showed the system. They did it the American way with a meteorologist who looked professorial, and the peninsula was covered with little yellow suns, in places partially covered by clouds. Most of the southwest was cloudy and I decided to watch the movement of the system and plan my movements accordingly. The bus to the Alhambra arrived on schedule and it was a ten-minute climb to the top of the hill. Outside the city it soon became very green, with oaks, cypress, and ground cover, ivy and ferns. After one abortive attempt I found the *Puerta de la Justicia* that served as the entrance to the complex.

The *Alcazaba* on the left was the original building, dating from the ninth century although it had been considerably enlarged in the early thirteenth. Massive and stone, it was nearly deserted. From the battlements there was a good view of the city below, including the oddly-shaped Cathedral. But if the Alcazaba was deserted, the *Nasrid* palace was not, nor was it massive and stone. Instead, it was light and delicate stucco-work with hardly a surface not covered by stalactites, filigree, or the odd Andalucian calligraphy—neither Maghrabi nor resembling anything to the east. Lines of tourists snaked through the beautiful little galleries and halls, with hardly room to stand back and take in their full effect.

This was the real center of the complex. In its final form, it dated only from the late fifteenth-century, after the fall of Cordoba. There was something transitory and almost deferential about this little jewel, as if it represented the last breath of an exhausted civilization, crowded now into its final refuge in the peninsula. It was probably no accident that the founder of the dynasty had been a vassal of Ferdinand III of Castile. To their credit, the Alhambra survived intact because of the insistence of Ferdinand and Isabella that it "be well repaired and maintained, in order that it stand forever as a perpetual memorial . . . and that such an excellent memorial and sumptuous edifice as this not fall into disrepair and be lost." Later monarchs followed suit and it was declared a national monument in 1870. Emperor Charles V's palace next door may have been, according to the guidebook, one of the most successful Renaissance buildings in Spain. But it suffered by proximity and seemed crude next to the *Nasrid* palace. The impression was reinforced at the cathedral in the city below. These Spanish cathedrals were not garish or rococo. They were massive and surprisingly spare, powerful statements by the victor in this long war of religions.

It was still overcast but that made wandering through the extensive gardens restful. There were other buildings in the grounds, including the *Parador de San Francisco*, but so integrated into the gardens, terraces, and pools that they seemed a natural part of the scene. As a backdrop there was the *Sierra Nevada* and the *Pico de Veleta*. At 11,148 feet it would be covered with snow in the winter. It was hard to imagine a more picturesque setting. Back in the city I had lunch in a little cafe on the *Plaza del Campillo*, tormented by a plague of shoeshine boys. They were persistent, refusing to take no for an answer. Dinner was *bacalao viscaieno*, salted codfish soaked and then cooked in a tomato sauce, with a carafe of the house wine. Everything on the menu seemed to be served with chips. There were eggs with chips, sausage with chips, eggs and sausage with chips, steaks with chips, fish with chips, hardly anything *without* chips. It was probably a product of the English contagion.

To Cordoba

On television the next morning the little suns were partly obscured in Almeria but clear in the vicinity of Malaga. The system seemed to be moving eastward and so I decided to go south and west. I arrived at the station at 7:49 and found the 7:50 connecting to Malaga waiting on the platform. There wasn't time to buy a ticket in the station, but just enough to race through the tunnel to the other side and board the train. Across the aisle sat an American couple I had seen two days before on the train from Madrid. He looked to be about forty with a ponytail and goatee, rimless glasses, and an earring in one ear. She looked about the same age, wore no jewelry or make-up and was dressed seventies-style in a shapeless smock that looked like it might have been made out of last year's drapes bought at Cost Plus.

It turned out that they were from Santa Cruz, California where he was a computer consultant with his own business. She was a systems analyst in Silicon Valley but had quit her job to make the trip. They were a common-law couple, had been together for six years, and had last been in the Balkans and Greece. We chatted about the University of California at Santa Cruz, where she had done graduate work. The school was violently Marxist and feminist and she said that without previous exposure at Illinois and then Texas at Austin, she might have been seriously infected. She seemed the more reasonable of the two, lamenting the lack of communication in the typical Silicon Valley office. People sat in cubicles across from one another but sent emails instead of just talking.

He was less flexible and made several remarks that betrayed a hard ideological edge. They read only the *Daily Worker* and had been amused at my absorption in the *International Herald Tribune* two days before. Yes, the intervention in Greece in 1947 had probably saved that country from the likes of a Ceaucescu, but it had seriously disrupted the political system in the country. Their friends in Greece were scornful of the American health-care system, and much else besides. On more general subjects he counseled me to be wary of Windows 95, at least as a main application interface. They were a California phenomenon, a cutting-edge anachronism, a cross between *Easy Rider* and *2001, A Space Odyssey*. The conversation ended abruptly when I had to change trains in Lineares-Baeza.

The wait for a connecting train was half-an-hour, unusual in this very efficient system. Soon, we began the climb through rugged mountains that looked like they might have been a spur of the Sierra Nevada. We passed through many tunnels. The houses were yellow stone with red tile roofs. On the other side of the mountains the soil looked poor but everywhere there were century plants, vineyards, cactus with the fist-sized fruit just ripening, pomegranates, oranges, avocados, and cotton. A crude concrete irrigation channel ran alongside the tracks, identical to ones I had seen in Uzbekistan several years before. The outskirts of Malaga announced themselves by drab apartment blocks that looked like they belonged in Cairo. We arrived in the city just after noon and when I asked for a "beer" in the little cafe outside the station the waiter was uncomprehending. So I added *cervesa* to my short list of Spanish words. After checking in at the Hotel Malaga Palacio I had a look around the city.

The *Alcazaba* was closed for restoration but there was a path to the top of the hill on which the fort sat. Below, the sixteenth-century Cathedral was another testament to the power of the triumphant creed, with clusters of columns twenty feet in diameter. Inside, there was chapel after chapel in the cavernous space and a massive eighteenth-century organ. Afterwards, I walked down to the beach and suddenly realized that I was on the *Costa del Sol*. The Mediterranean lapped at the brown beach and it was peaceful this particular September. But it could be treacherous in the winter and the naval campaigning season for the Turks and Venetians had always been limited to the spring and summer. I remembered the navy and out of Gibraltar a storm that was the heaviest weather we had encountered, the South China Sea not excepted.

There were a few sunbathers, but not the wall-to-wall worshippers of the tourist brochures. The port was interesting and a Cunard Line cruise ship was tied up alongside the dock. In the terminal the schedule was posted for the ferry to Melilla, a Spanish dependency in Morocco. I was tempted but only briefly, if I was to see more of Spain and Portugal. Picasso was born in Malaga in 1881 and there was a little museum with a few prints in an unmarked, second-floor walkup. After the shops opened in the afternoon I bought a bottle of Malaga sweet wine as an aperitif. Dinner was a whole avocado in a salad and *merlu Visca* or hake, Basque-style, with white asparagus, shrimps, and clams. As usual, the house wine was good and the bread, although it now came in little sticks about an inch long, was plentiful.

The next morning I was at the station in time for the 7:45 train to Cordoba. The brochure said that it was the *Garcia Lorca*, offered only second-class service but had a dining car, and was scheduled to arrive in Cordoba at 10:02. The ticket cost 1,900 pesetas, or about sixteen dollars. In the dining car a couple of stiff Spanish coffees in tiny cups, about the size of a Turkish coffee in Egypt, was sufficient preparation for the day. The direction was nearly due north, back towards Madrid, but we seemed to be west of the Sierra Nevada and the terrain was not particularly mountainous. The fields were carefully turned over and, as we approached Cordoba, the city seemed to lie at the base of a tall range of hills looking like those behind Addis Ababa. At the station the man at the Avis desk said there was no need to rent a car to see the city. Even the ruins of *Medina Azahara*, a nearby royal city sacked by the Berbers in 1013 and the old part of Cordoba, were only a few hundred pesetas away by taxi. So they were, and the taxi dropped me at the Hotel Conquistador on the east side of the great mosque.

Cordoba

There were several lodging options: the Hotel Maimonides, after the twelfth-century Jewish physician and philosopher; the Hotel Averroes, after the Arab sage of the same period and the same catholicity of interests; and the Hotel de los Omayas, after the dynasty that spawned Spanish Islam. The names had gone through interesting metamorphoses as they passed from one language to another. Maimonides came from the Arabic *Ibn Maimun*, in Hebrew *ben Maimon*, and it was odd that he was not today something like "Avimon," *Ibn Sina* having become Avicennes. Averroes had originally been *Ibn Rushd*, and it would be interesting to know how the harsh sounds had been dropped, although I didn't know enough about Spanish to speculate. The word "Cordoba" emerged relatively unchanged from *al-Qurtuba*, the Arabic consonants betraying its Mediterranean origin, along with *Saqaliyya* or Sicily, *Qubrus* or Cyprus, *Malta,* and *Balqan*. Andalucia was originally *al-Andalus*, although the accent in the Arabic was on the second syllable. Then, there was the Guadalquivir, the great river that lay a few hundred yards across the boulevard from the mosque. It was certainly *al-wadi al-kabir,* or "the great (river) valley", the "v" and "b" still interchangeable today to Spanish and Arabic speakers. Oddly, they appeared next to one another on a standard keyboard. In Cairo *Al-Ahram* reported the news from Israel under the dateline "Tel Abib."

I settled on the Conquistador whose entrance was opposite a magnificent horseshoe arch on the west side of the mosque. The room was small but nice and overlooked a garden done in the Moorish style. The entrance to the mosque was on the north side, through the Orange Tree Court. Inside, several passes were required to do it justice. The first circuit through the maze of 800, softly-lighted, *ablaq* or "piebald" double-horseshoe arches, was to accustom myself to the light and form a general impression. A second pass was needed to gauge its size. It looked like the equivalent of about three football fields. The recesses around the periphery had been walled in and filled with chapels dedicated to saints, familiar names like San Marcos, Santa Ana, and San Juan Bautista. On the third pass I consulted the guidebook and traced the successive additions in the building program. It was begun in 785 AD, but the original structure was only a fifth of the final size. Additions in 848, 961 and 987 contributed the remaining four-fifths. But it was only after an hour into the visit that I noticed that there was something in the center of the massive space: people were clustered together, illuminated by clerestory lighting, and they all seemed to be looking upward.

It was the cathedral, built over a period of seventy-seven years from 1523 to 1600. There were undoubtedly details to be appreciated, from its Gothic beginnings through Renaissance additions to the final Italianate vaulting and dome. The cherubs were admittedly skillfully executed, the baroque choir-stalls were finely done, and the marble, jasper, and mahogany pulpits were beautiful. But this was a little like the difference between the eastern and western arms in the museum in the Tower of London. There, the south-German crossbows with their compound systems of pulleys were technologically beautiful, but they didn't match the color and variety of the oriental weapons.

However, here it was the East that was simple and spare and the West that was more ornate, and the cherubs, choir-stalls, and pulpits were no match for the arches. Surprisingly, even though the steeple dominated the building from the outside, the cathedral was unobtrusive within. That was probably because it occupied only about 5 percent of the surface area of the mosque. The steeple was closed for restoration. It had originally been a minaret, later topped by a sixteenth-century bell tower. The addition was a testament not to understanding but to triumphalism in this clash of civilizations, the bell being not only unfamiliar but abhorrent to Muslims. In Islam bells were used for animals, not human beings. Among the conditions of the Caliph Omar the ringing of bells had been forbidden to Christians in Egypt to announce the beginning of their services.

In fact, if size were the measure, the mosque remained the dominant party in this architectural fusion of Christianity and Islam. I later saw the little fourteenth-century synagogue in the *Juderia* and, although there were some interesting decorative details, it represented even less in the equation. It was tiny, a cubicle only about twenty feet on a side, and so less than one percent of the size of the mosque. We still remembered wistfully those infrequent times when the Muslims, Christians and Jews—the three "People of the Book"—lived together in harmony and tolerance, drawing on the strengths of each community. Andalucia in the fourteenth century had represented one of these ages, as did twelfth-century Norman Sicily.

But both were brief and transitory and the arithmetic showed how disproportionate the relationship had been. Jews may have been accepted in fourteenth-century Cordoba but, crowded into their tiny synagogue, they must have felt little sense of permanence. The pressure to convert had been unremitting, although they shared that with the Muslims. The following century would witness the coming of the Inquisition to Spain, although the Inquisition tried Catholics, not Muslims or Jews. The main concern of the Church was with the *conversos*—*maranos* and *moriscos*—"new Christians" originally Jewish and Muslim. They were suspected of secretly practicing their old rites, and the presence of large numbers of unconverted Jews and Muslims was thought to encourage backsliding. After an unsuccessful attempt at isolation they were all expelled from *Sepharad* in 1492. It was a memorable year.

There were other sights to be seen and I wandered down past the Roman gate—Cordoba had been the capital of the Roman province of

Baetica—to the Guadalquivir, halfway along its sluggish course to the Atlantic. It was dun colored, like tea with milk. The bridge was just under 300 paces wide and there was something about the river's volume and quiet flow that made it a worthy complement to the mosque. The rest of the old city was quaint and, at first glance, touristy. There were souvenir shops everywhere selling ceramics, leather goods, T-shirts, and postcards. But away from the vicinity of the mosque people actually occupied these little places. At the entranceway to one, through the wrought-iron gate, appeared horseshoe arches, yellow columns, ceramic tiles, a marble fountain, bougainvillea and ferns in earthenware pots.

But they had not been assembled just for my edification, and the scene was repeated all over the town. The interiors may have been small and poorly insulated, food was probably expensive in the little shops, and you could hardly get your car down one of these streets. But as a picture of quiet serenity the area was unmatched. The Alcazar—in Arabic, *al-Qasr*, or the fortress—was originally Omayyad but had been extensively rebuilt by Alfonso XI in the fourteenth century. The most interesting part was the gardens. For dinner there was paella as a starter, then fried fish and a salad. The bread continued its metamorphosis as I moved south, coming here in small individually-wrapped packets advertised as "*Palillos Santa Elvira*" by Rafael Rodriguez, complete with address and telephone number.

Away from the mosque Cordoba was just another big city with people going about their everyday chores. The map in the guidebook showed remnants of the old city walls and I traced them before returning to the vicinity of the mosque. In the distance, just to the north of the *Avenida de las Ollerias*, there was a tall, circular brick tower that looked like it belonged one of the old slave khanates of Central Asia. But, up close it dated from the late nineteenth century and was probably just the smokestack from a defunct factory. Near the *Plaza del Porto* was a posada described by Cervantes and several museums displaying work by local artists.

Dinner was in a restaurant in the old city. The ground floor was packed and we made our way up three floors to the roof, which was not. There was a good view of the city from the level of the bell tower in the Cathedral, fifty yards away. It tolled the hour and half-hour, which I noticed since the service was slow. But the pork steak was good, with braised red pepper, scalloped potatoes, and a bottle of rosé. A group of academics sat at the next table, all specialists in insect microbiology and representing a little bit of America set down in this corner of Spain. One taught at the University of Arkansas, although he was not from the state, and he said that in some of the rural areas where he did his research it was impossible to understand the speech of the locals. He wore his ball cap throughout the meal. Another in the group was a Sikh studying aphids at the University of California at Davis. After sunset the wind picked up and it became cold. But the lighted bell tower and minaret against the black sky made for a rare picture.

The next morning I had a half-day in Cordoba before the train to Huelva. I had decided against Seville and would press on to Portugal. After breakfast I walked down to the river again and across to the *Torre de la Calahorra* on the other side. Ducks were afloat in the pools among the rushes. Back at the mosque there was evidence of the same deterioration that appeared everywhere in Cairo: the soft sandstone or limestone was being eaten away, probably the result of air pollution. A blue carpenter's chalk line at a height of about three feet ran along the length of the east wall. It looked like restoration was in the offing.

To Portugal

There has been recent revisionist history about the Portuguese of the fifteenth century and their role in opening the way to the East. Yes, they had been intrepid explorers but it was not as if they decided one day to sail to India. There had been over a hundred years of "coasting" before they ventured into the open sea. Prince Henry "the Navigator" was not a navigator at all, having left Portugal only once, for the siege of Ceuta in 1415. He really didn't plan the conquest and mapping of the world, and when he died in 1460 the Portuguese had only passed Cape Palmas and entered the Gulf of Guinea. It would be another forty years and 3,000 miles before they rounded the Cape of Good Hope and opened the way to India. The enterprise had always been commercial and exploitative and Henry was its main beneficiary, claiming title to the gold, slaves, and other commodities they found along the way. And who could be sympathetic to the Portuguese after the mess they left behind in places like Angola and Mozambique?

These things may have been true, but somehow they didn't detract from the Portuguese accomplishment. In years of cautious probing to the south they were dealing with deep-seated fears of the unknown and uncertainty about the prevailing winds. There was no guarantee that if they passed Cape Bojador they could find their way back to Lisbon. The ships used by these mariners in the early part of the century were little more than fishing boats with lateen sails and they were increasingly out of the sight of land. Models of these ships were shown in the Maritime Museum in Lisbon and they were tiny. In fact, the Portuguese were the first true ocean sailors and they began the age of sail. Two hundred years later the Genoese and the

Turks, with their more parochial outlook, would still be using oared galleys in naval engagements in the Mediterranean.

The Prince Henry "myth" may be part fiction, but he was the epitome of what motivated the Portuguese. The easy pickings of the *reconquista* were a thing of the past, the Algarve having fallen to the Christians in the thirteenth century. Henry was not a first-born and would never be king. Like other lesser nobles he sought an outlet for his abundance of restless energy and the ventures he sponsored, first into Morocco and later down the west coast of Africa, harnessed that energy. The Portuguese had missed the Crusades and by the time they became fired with religious zeal crusades had passed out of fashion. But they pursued the Muslims with a crusading spirit anyway. By the beginning of the age of exploration they had been fighting the Moors for hundreds of years and, even in a cruel age, they added their own refinements to the conflict. They expected no quarter and gave none. Accounts of some of their early actions in India are bloodcurdling.

Their efforts had been commercial ventures with the prospect of great gain or great loss. But the wonder is that anyone should have expected anything else. Prince Henry set in motion the series of steps that carried the Portuguese ever farther south before rounding the Cape: there were the Madeiras in 1419–20, then Cape Verde in 1444, followed by Fernando Po in the Bight of Benin in 1472, the mouth of the Congo in 1482–83, and finally the Cape of Good Hope in 1488. After that, the east coast of Africa and then India followed with a rush. The Moluccas, China, and Japan came soon afterwards. The Portuguese were tough, fearless, and cruel, but there was no denying the scale of their achievement. They were in the open ocean for as many as ninety days at a time, out of the sight of land. Columbus's men nearly mutinied after only thirty days on the first voyage to America, while sailors in the Mediterranean were still clinging to their familiar shores.

Exploitation, not rule, was the Portuguese aim and the schemes for milking their conquests were not enlightened. But they had little of the racial feeling of the northern Europeans and miscegenation might almost have been described as a national policy. They bankrupted themselves in the East in a hundred years and by the time English formed the new East India Company in 1600, the handwriting was on the wall. Domination of the Indies would pass to the more progressive Dutch and English. After 1595 Portuguese trade with Asia declined by two-thirds. Hormuz fell in 1622, Mombasa and much of Ceylon in 1630, then Malacca in 1641, the rest of Ceylon in 1644, Muscat and the Persian Gulf in 1650, and Negapatam in India in 1660. Independent again from Spain in 1640, the Portuguese spent the next thirty years, at tremendous cost, in an effort to preserve their independence. The reinstated crown realized that they would probably have to give up the East in order to save Brazil, whose exports of sugar and Brazilwood made up for the loss of the India trade. Somehow their insolvency seemed to make them, finally, only more human.

The train left for Huelva, the end of the line, in the early afternoon. The schedule showed that the same train also went to Cadiz in the south and I wondered which of us would have to change. We hurtled off in what I thought was a westerly direction before pulling onto a siding and then, inexplicably, hurtling back in the same direction we had come. But at two thirty-five we pulled in to Huelva and I'm still not sure how we got there. And here, at last, the train system in Spain broke down. There was nothing beyond Huelva except a bus to Faro in Portugal. The bus station was a fifteen-minute walk through the gritty little city. The next bus left at six PM so there were several hours to wait. I read a pair of *Herald Tribunes* from cover to cover, wondering if there wasn't another pair of Communists watching me.

When the bus came it was air-conditioned but there was almost no legroom. It was like flying economy again and I had become used to first-class. In the dying light the area still looked like parts of California, maybe the East Bay. There were vineyards, sunflowers, olives, dates, figs, oranges, almonds, and peaches. It was probably no accident that so many of the little San Francisco delta towns had been settled by Portuguese.

At the border the bus hardly slowed and there was no document check. This was the seamless European Community in action. We arrived in Faro at eight-thirty but there was a time change so it was really only seven-thirty. It was a short walk to the train station where we waited for the eight-ten to Lagos. I was hungry and bought a large roll at the counter in the station. It was dense and contained bits of something unidentifiable in the center. The Dutch girl I had first seen in the bus station in Huelva also bought one. When she got to the middle she blanched, if the Dutch can be said to blanch, and stopped. I was hungry and ate the rest of mine.

The station was a contrast with the Spanish stations. There, everything had been modern and efficient. Here, our train was sitting on the siding and the engineer, dressed in a pair of Levi's and checkered shirt, sat in the cafeteria and chatted with his cronies. About ten minutes before the scheduled departure he climbed into the locomotive and fired it up. I was sleepy and the trip was a little surreal. Just before we arrived in Lagos a woman approached and offered a place to stay in her house for 3,500 escudos, or about twenty-three dollars, a night. The guidebook—I had been unable to find anything on Portugal in either Egypt or Spain—later said this was common practice in the Algarve. It was late enough and I was tired enough that

I decided to have a look and was glad I did. She had a car and we drove the mile to her very clean apartment. I was given a key to the main entrance, to the apartment, and to my own room. The double bed was spotless and the private bath was furnished with everything except shampoo.

The morning came early with the garbage men and a cacophony of barking dogs. The bedroom was on the sixth floor and, as the sun came up, Lagos revealed itself below. It was very pretty, with whitewashed houses and tile roofs, narrow streets, and the port away in the distance. The oldest slave market in Europe had been somewhere near the port, but I didn't see it. I had decided to go to Sagres and Cape St. Vincent that day and Maria told me where to find the bus stop. It was a five-minute walk from the apartment and the posted schedule said that trip would take an hour. For some reason it took half that time, maybe because it was a special bus, articulated in the middle and twice the normal length. It probably couldn't squeeze into the little towns along the way.

In Sagres Henry's castle looked monolithic and, in fact, dated from a much later restoration. Cape St. Vincent was about five miles away. I decided to walk and by the time I reached it I had developed serious blisters. This view at the southwestern-most corner of Europe was very rugged. But it was clear and sunny and the water was calm. Back in Sagres I decided to change money as I was nearly out of escudos, the bank would not accept a new hundred-dollar bill. I asked that if a bank wouldn't accept a hundred dollars who would? He didn't know and it wasn't his problem. But across the street a little kiosk selling, nick-nacks, post cards etc. did, and the rate was good.

Afterwards I lay on the beach until the early evening, before taking the last bus back to Lagos. The beach was a soft golden color and the water was calm. This was, after all, the Atlantic and we had left the rocky little Mediterranean beaches behind us. Back in Lagos Maria was preparing *bacalhau*. She gave me directions to the center of town and I set off, very gingerly, before stopping at a little restaurant along the way. It was a good decision. The waiter was the husband and the cook seemed to be his wife. Everything in Portugal appeared to be family-run, and they were friendly and almost embarrassingly deferential. The swordfish steak fried in garlic was huge, after starters of green olives, bread with anchovy paste and a large green salad. The man asked apologetically if the house wine would be good enough. It was.

In the city center lay the Lagos of the tourist brochures. It was alive with people and at ten o'clock that night all the shops were open. Sidewalk stalls hawked portraits, watercolors, T-shirts, and postcards. There had been a piece in the *Herald Tribune* in August saying that tourism in the Algarve had declined sharply compared with the year before, but you would never know it by the scene that night. Back at the apartment Maria and Johnny, her husband, were still up and Johnny was leaving early the next morning for work. If six-fifteen wasn't too early he could give me a ride to the train. That was perfect because the train for Lisbon left just after seven. These Portuguese were getting better and better.

I was at the station in plenty of time. It was a repeat of the night in Faro, the engineer hobnobbing with the passengers before climbing to his place in the locomotive. The ticket to Lisbon cost 2,010 escudos or just over thirteen dollars. It was actually two tickets stapled together, the second for the ferry that would take us to the *Estacio Fluvial* on the other side of the *Tejo*. Outside Lagos there were rolling hills covered with oaks, many of them with a raw, orange look as if their skin had been stripped away. In fact, they were cork oaks and we later saw yards with stacks of the bark waiting processing into those little adjuncts to the wine industry. The train arrived at the *Barreiro* station in Lisbon at eleven o'clock and the ferry was waiting at the dock. A thirty-minute ride took us to the other side of the estuary where I set out to find a hotel.

Lisbon

We landed near the *Praca do Comercio*, the heart of old Lisbon. The earthquake of 1755 had destroyed most of the twenty thousand houses in the city and this area, the *Baixa*—about seven oblong blocks wide by eight long—had been rebuilt under the severe strictures of the Marques de Pombal: all buildings would be no more or less than five stories high and landowners who couldn't afford to rebuild within five years would be subject to expropriation. This gave the Baixa a geometric and uniform look. I walked three blocks north until I saw ensigns flying from a building down a side street. Sure enough, it was a hotel, the *Residencial Duas Nacoes,* and it would do, if only for its location.

The price was 6,000 escudos, or about forty dollars, for a very clean room with a private bath. Over the next few days I dealt with several desk clerks, all Portuguese, but all having been born somewhere else. Their English was that of their countries of origin. The Canadian who sometimes spelled the South African, was a typical North American: he wore wire-rimmed, purple-tinted sunglasses, day and night, and when I said that I wanted to stay an extra night he shrugged and said "that's cool." The Mozambican who sometimes filled in for the other two had a typical South-Asian anxiousness to please. He was Indian, his parents from somewhere on the west coast, but he wasn't sure where. When I said that I had grown up with many second-generation Portuguese and wondered why their parents had left, they all narrowed their eyes and said that things were better now but had not been so good under the dictatorship.

I spent the next three days in Lisbon and saw much of the city. I was still on the trail of the Portuguese of the fifteenth century and that meant books and a visit to the maritime museum at Belem. The bookstores were in *Chiado* and *Bairro Alto* to the west of *Baixa* and it took several trips before I found them, all near Garrett Street. I was looking for a history of Portugal in English and maybe even Richard Burton's translation of *Os Luciadas* of Luis de Camoes, the national poet and chronicler of the age of discovery. I was interested in Camoes largely because of the Burton connection, and had seen his memorial several years before in Macau. There was even a Camoes bookstore but inside my inquiries brought only mute shrugs. Finally, I was directed to a little place where I was admitted only after ringing a buzzer. The pretty woman inside spoke excellent English and she helped me to look up the various versions of the Luciads. We found that *Os Luciadas* had been "Englished by Richard Francis Burton: (edited by His Wife, Isabel Burton)" in 1881. The last bit was unfortunate, but they didn't have a copy anyway. There were a few books in English and I bought a little Everyman edition of Henry Fielding's *The Voyage to Lisbon*. I later found a good general history of the country through the age of empire by a Portuguese professor at Columbia University.

Belem was a ten-minute trolley ride to the west. I had never understood the attraction of the cable cars in San Francisco, why people came thousands of miles and stood in long lines to ride them. Some of these bright yellow trolleys looked like the cable cars, although less open to the elements. But there was something bracing about the fresh air and even the jolting as the little car made its way up the hill. The *Museo de Marinha* was in a complex dominated by the sixteenth-century Hieronymous Monastery, built by Manuel I with proceeds from the India trade. It took sixty years to complete and was massive, of gray limestone. It had survived the earthquake and the fretted and carved facade, full of gargoyles and saints, had survived later air pollution.

Inside, the first exhibits were of the early discoveries before moving into the seventeenth century and the Napoleonic Wars, the age of sail, then steam and, finally, twentieth-century ships including American destroyers of the Adams class. The early stuff was fascinating: models of the tiny ships that had first taken the Portuguese down the west coast of Africa and then to the Madeiras, the Canaries, and the Azores. They were at first little more than fishing boats, followed by *naus,* adaptations of the European round ship designed to withstand the pounding of the Atlantic. Only later came the galleys and galleons. The ships were well suited to the task, and so were the men. The Portuguese were fearless to the point of recklessness and contemptuous of death. That's what made them so formidable, even in the face of overwhelming numbers of the enemy.

Shipbuilding had been only one of the reasons for the Portuguese success. Another had to do with navigation. The development of the magnetic compass meant that with a relatively accurate system of navigation they could now sail in the open ocean. The longitude problem would remain unsolved until the late eighteenth century and the development of the chronometer, but latitudes were relatively simple and had been known for hundreds of years. And the initial Portuguese forays were in a general north-south direction. Increasingly, tables correlating the season, latitude, and celestial phenomena would be made available. In the southern hemisphere the southern cross replaced the pole star. The combination of latitudes and the compass meant that simple dead-reckoning could be used and positions at sea known with increasing accuracy. The wind was still a problem, but the fact that they had to sail so far west to pick up the trade winds eventually meant the discovery of the Azores and then Brazil.

There had been a lull in activity after the death of Henry. They had just turned slightly east of south at the Bijagos Islands off the coast of what is today Guinea Bassau, but it would be another twelve years before they discovered that the trend to the southeast and then due east would not take them directly to India. Africa turned south again and there would be another 3,000 miles before they reached the opening to the Indian Ocean. It took sixteen years to cover the distance from Fernando Po to the Cape of Good Hope. The commodities they sought were slaves, gold, and spices, profitable in inverse order. Slaves had been the original attraction, along with the "fabulous" gold of Senegal. There were also spices in West Africa, largely red and black pepper. But the real profit came from the spices of the Indies. They were the big six—pepper, ginger, cinnamon, cloves, mace, and nutmeg—and they were found on the Malabar coast of India, in Ceylon, Sumatra, the Comoros Islands, and the Moluccas.

At first the Portuguese controlled access to all of them. In return, they provided manufactured goods, metals, specie—Fernand Braudel maintains that the Iberians simply recycled American silver to Asia—and textiles. Where the African trade had been farmed and the spur to much of the early activity had been the prospect of private gain, spices presented new opportunities. The terms of trade meant that there were fortunes to be made and the early voyagers to India came back to Europe loaded to the gunwales with spices. The average profit over many years was nearly 90 percent. So great was the attraction that early in the sixteenth century the Portuguese monarchy made spices a crown monopoly. Individuals—from captains to simple seamen—could still trade on their own account in India, but now the goods, transported at crown expense, had to be disposed of officially at fixed prices.

But among the reasons for the ephemeral Portuguese success in the East was that, unlike that of the English and the Dutch, it was not based on a strong, commercially-minded middle class, able to reinvest their profits in new ventures. Too many of the Portuguese middle class were New Christians and, as targets of the Inquisition, had been frozen out of the trade. Too much of the money made in India went into land, luxury goods, and royal excesses like the Hieronymous Monastery. As a great power the Portuguese spent themselves into eclipse. But they didn't leave without a trace. They stayed on in coastal enclaves like Goa, Diu, Timor, and Macau. In the seventeenth century Goa had a population equal to that of Lisbon and it only reverted to India in 1962. Macau went back to China in 1999. They left half-caste descendants with names like deFreitas and Fernandes and deSousa in India and Sri Lanka, and they were often members of government or world-class cricketeers. Portuguese Jesuits opened Europe's eyes to the languages and civilizations of Asia, and Portuguese remained the *lingua franca* of commerce in the East well into the nineteenth century.

Lisbon was a pretty city, looking very much like San Francisco. The estuary of the *Tejo* was broad and the April 25 Bridge could have been the Golden Gate. From the *Castello de Sao Jorge* on a hill to the west the city spread out below, all white and pastel with orange tile roofs. There were undoubtedly drab sections as well, and I rode the No. 15 trolley to the end of the line to see what it looked like from ground level. It went through a working-class district full of pimply teenagers, toothless gossiping housewives, and old men in felt caps rushing to catch the train. It looked picturesque enough from above but living in Lisbon probably wasn't easy for the working poor. The food was good. For breakfast I generally had a couple of tiny espressos and a little custard in a pastry cup. The coffees cost the equivalent of about seventy-five cents. There were many outdoor restaurants in the Baixa and lunch was generally a beer and a sandwich of ham and cheese, or pork. For dinner, I continued my practice from Spain: eat the local fare and avoid beef and chips.

Most restaurants served starters and they added a considerable amount to the bill. But they were worth it: plates of sautéed squid in oil, little sharp, round cheeses, anchovy pâté, fat green olives, and crusty sourdough bread. The house wine was always good enough. As a main course there was *bacalhau, or* salted codfish, the Portuguese national dish that came from the waters off Newfoundland. On the second night it came *assada,* or broiled, a fat piece from the midsection, moist and tender like a swordfish steak. It had to be soaked for days, beforehand to return some of the moisture and reduce the salt. Later there was salmon and then swordfish. The prices were about the same as in Spain: around twenty-five dollars for the starter, a main course, and a bottle of wine.

There were surely many things I missed in three days in Lisbon: the sardines, for one, and the fish market for another. The South African at the hotel given me instructions to the market but it was the vegetable market that I found. I didn't see many parts of the city, or Sintra and the royal palace to the west. I did buy the *History of Portugal, Vol. I: From Lusitania to the Empire,* by A. H. de Oliveira Marques, as well as a kilo of dried bacalhau. The latter came in a packet about six inches by nine inches by four inches thick, and was hard like kindling. Triple-wrapped in plastic it gave off no odor and fit nicely into the bottom of the duffel bag.

My last day in Lisbon was spent wandering the streets and riding the subway, which was was well laid out and efficient. In the morning I walked to the train station and bought a ticket to Madrid, the South African suggesting that it would be a good idea to be there early. It cost the equivalent of about seventy-five dollars. I also got a cash advance—in dollars—at the *Banco Portugues do Atlantico* and by the time they had sold me escudos at an inflated rate, then bought them back in exchange for deflated dollars, I was poorer by many of the latter. I missed Egypt where the difference between buy and sell was only a few piasters. The common European currency was supposed to end gouging by banks but it would be interesting to see if they abandoned their predatory practices. Dinner was at a working-class restaurant where they were watching a football match on a grainy, black-and-white television. After dinner I took a cab to the train station and, since I tossed my duffel in the trunk, there was a substantial baggage surcharge.

Madrid and Home

The train left at ten o'clock and I had a sleeper. There was an African in the top bunk across from me and beneath him a Portuguese man who put on his pajamas behind a little curtain before retiring. I lay down fully dressed and the next thing I remembered was being awakened by the porter at six thirty in the morning just outside Madrid. It was the soundest sleep I'd had in months.

I took the metro from the Chamartin station to Atocha and found the hotel from two weeks before. They had a room for 5,200 pesetas, or about forty-five dollars, a night. I had a day and a-half in Madrid before the flight to Cairo the next afternoon. So, I decided to see the Escorial, an hour away from Atocha by train. It was overcast and began to rain about halfway there. We climbed through rolling hills covered with oak trees and occasional deer sheltering under the oaks. A bus took us from the station to the monastery and I jogged through a downpour to the entrance.

The Escorial was a revelation. There was no blood, no weeping statuary, none of the reported excesses of Latin Catholicism. Instead, it was spare and severe, of gray granite and stupendous in conception and execution with nearly 1,200 doors and 2,600 windows distributed over the three acres of the building. Commissioned by Philip II to commemorate the victory over the French at St. Quentin in August 1557, it served as a royal palace, mausoleum, and monastery for the Hieronymites. The unaccompanied tour wound through the pantheons, chapter houses, church, and the Royal Library with its 40,000 volumes, all turned spine-backwards for preservation. But the real gem was the royal apartments. There we saw the apartment of Philip's daughter, the Infanta Clara Isabella Eugenia, in Fernand Braudel's touching phrase "his preferred companion in the last sad years of his life, his reader and secretary, confidant and private joy."

On the other side of the secretaries' rooms were Philip's own modest apartments. They overlooked gardens filled with citrus trees, and then the plains leading down to Madrid. In the distance lay Mount Abantos and the *Sierra de Guadarrama*. Inside was the bedroom, communicating directly with the church, and the bed where he died on September 13, 1598 of gangrene brought on by gout. And to the left of the bedroom was his study and the desk on which, in his small crabbed hand, he had written dispatches as he presided over an empire that included half of the known world. It was a stupendous but ultimately unsuccessful effort. After the study, the rest of the tour was an anticlimax.

For dinner it was back to the Plaza Major where I had seen many restaurants on the first stay. I was looking for something interesting and the fillet of kid sounded different, but it was dark and red and tasted like beef. At a nearby table an English couple were making their painstaking way through a paella. But at the table next to me were four Spanish who clearly knew what they were doing: the food came in relays, plate after plate of shrimps, calamari, ham, fried vegetables, and little sausages, all washed down with mugs of lager. After dinner I bought a bottle of dry sherry and a little packet of fat green olives as a memento of Spain.

The next morning brought another pleasant surprise. Among the shops near the Plaza Major I came across a window full of familiar-looking prints. They were by David Roberts, originals of his Spanish tour,

Picturesque Sketches of Spain, published in 1837. At nine forty-five the shop wasn't open and when I returned at ten fifteen it was still closed. I had the sinking feeling that I was going to miss the Roberts. But five minutes later the proprietor arrived and showed me several large folders that included the familiar-looking prints. They had come in both large and small editions, and the lithographs of Gothic, Romanesque, Morro, and *mudejar* scenes ranged from little pages six by nine inches to the full-sized sixteen by twenty-one.

I bought a very nice, full-sized *Correro de los Morros,* done in Granada. It was vintage Roberts with the horseshoe arches and architectural details very carefully rendered. The owner provided a certificate of authenticity. At 40,000 pesetas, or about $325, the print was a quarter of what I had paid in Cairo for a full-sized original from the Egyptian series. He took a credit card and I was struck, again, at how easy it had become to spend money in a foreign country: no more worries about exchange rates, rationing cash supplies or unfamiliar currency. Along with telecommunications and television it was another sign of a shrinking world.

At the *Museo de Jamon* I bought a kilo of Serrano ham to add to the bacalhau in my duffel. In the early afternoon I walked the mile to the Plaza Colon to catch the bus to the airport. The flight stopped in Barcelona for an hour. Afterwards I slept most of the way, having an exit seat with extra legroom. It took an hour to clear customs in Cairo since a *Saudia* jumbo arrived at about the same time. But the streets were nearly deserted and I was in my own bed by two AM.

The next day was a Friday, the shopping day in the city. I was looking for something to complement the Spanish ham. There is always an adjustment after travel outside Egypt and after two weeks of cleanliness, efficiency, and unveiled women I thought Cairo would come as a shock. But as I wandered through the crowds, mounds of rubbish, and derelict cars in the Dokki *suq*, I felt at home again. There were the *zaballeen* collecting the night's trash and the occasional man wandering the street in his pajamas, skinny *saiys* hustling through the crowds with trays of steaming tea, bearded men in skullcaps, and fat *fellahas* selling greens.

All around me there was that Cairo chaff, the verbal give-and-take that Cairenes love:

> *Sabah el kheir* " (Good morning)
>
> *Sabah el ishta' wa yasmine*" (The morning of sweet cream and jasmine)
>
> *Aiz kilo sukar* " (Give me a kilo of sugar)
>
> *Inta as-sukar* " (*You* are the sugar)

Mashi ya Basha? " (Is it all right, oh Pasha?)

Mashi wa la bi yadi" (It's all right, but not because of anything I've done.)

It was what made the days pass in their difficult lives, this apparently limitless fund of patience and good humor.

I bought a kilo of *fool* at the dry-goods seller and the sight of a *khawaga* buying beans brought the usual interrogation:

Min ain inta?" (Where are you from?)

Anna min Amrika" (I'm from America)

Bi gad? " (Really?)

Wallahi, bi gad" (By God, I am)

It would have been impossible to explain to him why I wanted the *fool,* how, if I was going to make Serrano ham with broad beans, I needed the beans. At the fruit-sellers I bought a kilo of bananas and the exchange was repeated, with a slight variation:

Inta min ain? " (Where are you from?)

Ana min Amrika" (I'm from America)

Ahsan naas" (They're the best people)

This, of course, was just Cairo chaff too. But I think he may have meant it because he gave me the bananas for five pounds and the posted price was six.

14

Democracy in Egypt

The president of the chamber barked out the aspirated "Hs" in his introduction: "AH-mad Fat-HI Serour." On this day His Excellency, Dr. Ahmad Fathi Serour, the speaker of the Peoples' Assembly, was the guest speaker at the monthly luncheon of the American Chamber of Commerce in Egypt. The chamber regularly sponsored addresses by prominent figures, both American and Egyptian, and over the last year we had also seen George McGovern, Stuart Eizenstadt, and a regular succession of Egyptian ministers and American cabinet members.

Serour was a cherubic little man with a faint mustache and a wave of sandy hair that was swept in a comb-over from one side of his head to the other. It appeared to be lacquered or plastered. He was introduced as having a masters degree in law from Cairo University, a PhD from somewhere in the United States, and was the head of several legal organizations, most of them Arab or Francophone. But it was clear that French must have been his second language because his English was painful to hear. The topic was "The Political Role of the Peoples' Assembly" and he started with a little lecture on the differences between parliamentary and presidential systems. He told us that the Egyptian system was a blend of the two, like the French system:

> We are not a PARliamentary system or a PRESidential system, but a combination of a PARliamentary system and a PRESidential system.

He sounded almost Japanese, the odd inflections coming from somewhere in the region of his solar plexus. He went on for about twenty minutes in heavily-accented English, barely tall enough to reach the microphone. From the sound system boomed the most unexpected modulations. At the end of the lecture we weren't much more enlightened about democracy in Egypt than when he began.

He then agreed to take questions and, with a grin, said that he wanted hard ones, "the harder the better." In the managed democracy of Egypt, before a notoriously hardheaded audience, the questions were predictable. Why did the constitution require that 50 percent of the representatives in the Peoples' Assembly be workers and farmers? What about businessmen? Why wasn't the constitution changed? What about the judiciary overturning election results without reason? Who did the Peoples' Assembly report to, the people or the president? Wasn't the government's overwhelming majority evidence of vote-rigging? Was it more or less difficult being speaker with a majority?

The answers were predictable. Farmers and workers needed protection, unlike businessmen who were well-connected and had considerable influence of their own. The constitution wouldn't be changed just because one or another group wanted it changed. The parliament represented the people, just as the constitution stated. Everything that had been done by the judiciary was perfectly legal. The majority in parliament of the National Democratic Party—Mubarak's party—was because that's what the people wanted. But none of his answers betrayed much evidence of a theoretical point of view. Things were the way they were because that's the way they were. Beneath that slightly ridiculous hairdo there didn't seem to lurk a rational thought process. Nothing he said seemed to reflect a training in the law—in three languages, no less.

But he was right about one thing. The harder the question the better he liked it. He wore a perpetual grin and sparred with the audience in Arabic before delivering the answers in English. It was just that the answers weren't answers at all. The odd inflections became more pronounced as the difficulty of the question increased. But he outdid himself when the Clinton scandal with Monica Lewinsky was mentioned:

> NO, No, I do not AC-cept this. AmER-ica has disgraced itself. We respect AmER-ica for its civilization and its TECH-nology, but THIS could not happen here. AmER-ica is home of privacy but THIS has SHAMED AmER-ica. No. NO.

He grinned again at the audience. He was thoroughly enjoying himself. He wasn't answering the questions, but everyone knew that he wouldn't. The fact of the matter was, he couldn't.

The session highlighted the problem of democracy in Egypt. In the late twentieth century the country had been a beneficiary of American largesse for twenty years. Just as with Israel it was a reward for Camp David. It had raised the standard-of-living—albeit unevenly—and improved the business climate, the beneficiaries largely being the people in the room.

But democracy it was not. In the first place, with an Islamist threat that had been largely driven into Upper Egypt, thousands in jail on the mere suspicion of Islamist sympathy, and a still-strong Muslim Brotherhood, there was no prospect of concession to the popular will. That will would certainly be Islamic, if not Islamist. There were periodic parades through poor-neighborhoods in Cairo, the marchers chanting the refrain: *Islam hu al-hal, Islam hu al-hal*. Nothing else seemed to have worked and for the poor Islam *was* the answer. Constitutional change was not an option, if only because of the Islamic factor.

The constitution was a relic of the Nasser years and enshrined socialism as the economic system of Egypt. All the privatization activity that had haltingly taken place during the 1990s was theoretically unconstitutional. But no one wanted to amend the constitution for fear of pressures to make it Islamist instead of socialist. These pressures were not necessarily due to zealotry or an enthusiasm for cutting throats. Among the things that made the butchery in Luxor so horrific was that it was *not* the Egyptian way. But millions of people had not benefited from the reforms and there were pockets of poverty in Cairo that would rival slums anywhere in the world. The poverty was endured by the Egyptians with their customary good humor. But their patience was not limitless and to many there had to be a better answer than the market, the Internet, and the American way. Why not turn to Islam, the most vital force in the lives of 90 percent of the people?

The growth rate of the population had dropped, some said, to just over 2 from around 3 percent yearly. That meant that it would *not* continue to double every twenty years. But demographic pressures had long-since outstripped economic growth and there were already too few jobs for the *shebab,* or youth, hundreds of thousands of whom entered the labor market every year. The government was doing its best to meet the challenge with schemes to provide jobs and apartments. But they seemed misguided or ineffectual. The economy was sputtering, insulated from the Asian contagion until the price of Asian goods dropped so steeply that Egyptian importers began spending hard-earned, hard-currency reserves on cheap imports. Meanwhile, exports were under pressure. The largest export earner was oil and the bottom had fallen out of the crude-oil market.

The Egyptians seemed to practice the nothing-ventured nothing-lost theory of macro-economic policy. They did everything their way, and that was slowly. When pressured into attending the Doha conference in 1998, they had reluctantly gone but warned: "We will do nothing. We are very good at that." Egypt had never been an attractive place to invest and it was said that bureaucratic inefficiency, inertia, and the lack of an enforceable commercial code imposed a 25 percent premium on the cost of doing business in the country. Foreign direct investment, or FDI, in Egypt averaged something less than a billion dollars per year, a tiny number in comparison with figures for Asian countries like Singapore, Taiwan, and South Korea. With no large inflows of foreign capital, there had been no massive outflows like there had been in Asia. But they learned the wrong lesson from the Asian collapse and it only reinforced their insularity.

There was plenty of liquidity in the country. But it was spent on luxury goods and real estate, things with little multiplier effect. *Al-Ahram* on Friday was full of advertisements for automobiles and housing developments. But it was said that 40 percent of the apartments in Cairo were unoccupied while there was a shortage of housing for the young. That was because they were unfinished. Landlords or parents built flats and left them empty until their children grew up and could occupy them. Parts of Cairo looked like the aftermath of a war, forests of highrises, empty husks, except that they were brightly painted and some of the exteriors looked finished. Billions of pounds were tied up in these empty investments. Most were probably financed with cash, so at least there was little danger of a real-estate bubble like Japan's or Hong Kong's.

The press was relatively open, but the groveling of people like Samir Ragab was an indication how far from free it really was. To him President Mubarak was the fount of all freedoms and Egyptian journalists and intellectuals felt secure under his wise leadership. Ragab was chairman of the board of the English-language *Egyptian Gazette*. It was often the first thing a tourist or visiting businessman in Egypt saw, slipped in the morning under the door of his five-star hotel room. But it was an embarrassment for a country that aspired to regional leadership. The front page consisted mostly of dispatches from the wire services, and the back pages—the paper was only six pages long—occasionally had reprints of articles or reviews from the British or American press, pieces on the pervasiveness of the Mafias in Russia or a review of Harold Bloom's latest canon.

But the inside pages were where Ragab and the editor-in-chief, M. Ali Ibrahim, held forth. M. Ali Ibrahim had been the author of a recent—and scurrilous—attack on the United States, citing racism, the plight of the American Indians, the Vietnam war, capital punishment, the prison system, pornography, etc. etc. as reasons why America's day in the sun had passed. The policies of the United States in the Middle East were difficult enough to defend. You didn't need to cite the persistent alcoholism of the American Indians or the breakdown of the African-American family to find fault with us.

Editorially the paper was an embarrassment. But along with the bootlicking there were malapropisms that made reading it a constant adventure for a westerner. Some of the articles were obvious translations of Arabic articles, with the syntactical difficulties that translation often involved. Most of the reportage had to do with domestic violence and the stilted English masked real pain. There was also the ritual reporting of state functions that represented the standard fare in most Arab newspapers, as well as national holidays to recognize and congratulatory telegrams to be exchanged between heads of state. These were all solemnly reported.

Egypt had enough talent to produce a good English-language daily and it was a puzzle as to why it did not. There were several good English-language weeklies or bi-weeklies. The *Al-Ahram Weekly* was the best thing to happen to Egyptian journalism in years. The English was readable, the articles often mildly controversial, and the paper carried a wide range of political, economic, and cultural news. It featured regular contributions by the likes of James Zogby, Edward Said, and Naguib Mahfouz. The only problem was that it soon lost its novelty. When you read the *Al-Ahram Weekly* once, you soon discovered, you had read it for all time. Maybe that was because of the intractability of the problems in the Middle East. It was like *Al-Ahram* itself. There, the constant headline in the 1980s had been the call for the withdrawal of foreign forces from Lebanon. In the 1990s it was coverage of the latest developments in the Middle East peace process. But there *were* no latest developments. Netanyahu had seen to that.

The *Al-Ahram Weekly* was interesting for another reason: one of the correspondents was Gamal Nkrumah, the son of Kwame Nkrumah by an Egyptian wife. The father, the president of Ghana, had been a prominent member of the Nonaligned Movement and the name was a reminder of the palmy old days of the Bandung Conference, when there was something to be nonaligned about. Now, there was only the hyperpower and the market. But anti-Americanism remained a reflex, increasingly ill-tempered as the Soviet alternative disappeared. Gamal didn't like America or Britain, and regularly wrote scathing articles about British intervention in Sierra Leone or the persistence of racism in America.

Another newcomer was the *Cairo Times*, a glossy bi-weekly printed in Cyprus. The Publisher was an Egyptian but the editorial staff was heavily expatriate. It was the closest thing to a real newspaper in Egypt. It didn't pull any punches and it was remarkable that it survived at all. But editions had occasionally been pulled and other publishers of the expatriate press were concerned that its outspokenness would provoke restrictions on everyone. The *Cairo Times* covered real issues: female circumcision, pollution, the state of the health care system, the vexed Coptic problem. Everyone else responded to the allegations of a Coptic "problem" with paeans to the unity of Egypt. But there *was* a problem and the *Cairo Times* recognized it.

Today, Copts and Muslims will tell you that they are all Egyptians and that there is no difference between them. But there is a darker side, and a deep Muslim-Christian animus lies just below the surface. Copts need presidential approval to build new churches and there always seems to be mosque nearby. Needless to say, there are no licenses needed for mosques and little Muslim prayer halls called *zawiyas* are scattered through every neighborhood in the city. The Islamists, having been driven out of Cairo, now target Copts in Upper Egypt, and there have even been *fetwas* ruling that it is lawful to kill and plunder Copts since they are unbelievers.

Like the early Copts themselves the Islamists have increasingly decamped for Upper Egypt and taken refuge in the cane fields around el-Minia and Malawi. Assiut, again, is a cockpit of contention. In its crackdown on the Islamists, who attempted to assassinate Mubarak in Ethiopia in 1996, the regime has imprisoned tens of thousands of people on the mere suspicion of Islamist sympathy. Amnesty International has been critical of police methods in Egypt. The Egyptians fail to understand how the West can see the threat, and still give refuge to Islamist firebrands in London or Amsterdam. But as long as Mubarak and his managed democracy remain partners in the cold peace with Israel America winks at the violations of human rights.

However, hostility to the Islamists does not mean sympathy for the Copts. And the Coptic Church has become aggressive of late, the hierarchy now made up of ex-professionals—doctors, lawyers, and engineers. Pope Shenoudah III was kept under house arrest in the Sadat years, although there was nothing unusual about that since Sadat locked up everyone else as well. But because of the unspoken and subtle prejudice in Egypt, many Copts have left the country and there are large enclaves in Canada, the United States, and Australia. For that reason, the minister of Expatriate Affairs in the Egyptian government is generally a Copt. Some of those that left have come back to work in Egypt as American citizens and often bring back with them a carefully-concealed-dislike of their Muslim brethren. The dislike is reciprocated, often carefully concealed as well.

The persecution today is mild, nothing like the old laws that included the Caliph Omar's "conditions:" Christians could not ride horses and had to dismount from an ass in the presence of a Turk; they could not ring bells in their Churches or read their scriptures in a loud voice; they could not marry a Muslim woman; and they could not drink wine in pubic. Other conditions imposed on local Christians included the wearing of distinctive clothing, the keeping of their crosses and swine from the public view, building their houses no higher than those of the Muslims, and the burying of their dead in silence. Some conditions remain in effect today, including the ban on a Christian man marrying a Muslim woman. A Muslim man can, of course, marry a Christian woman. A Christian cannot buy alcohol during

Ramadan, although a Muslim clerk will slip a bottle under the table for a small fee. Pork, the cash crop of the Zabaleen, is sold openly, but only in Coptic butcher shops.

It was traditionally said that a Copt could not be an important minister: Foreign Affairs, the Economy, Defense, Interior. This dates to the Dinshawi incident in 1906 when the British hanged four Egyptian villagers after they had chased British officers hunting pigeons out of their village. One of the officers died of a heart attack and it was ruled a capital offense. The foreign minister at the time was a Ghali, and he was assassinated by a zealot because he was a Copt and thought to be in league with the British. He was the grandfather of Butros Butros Ghali, lately Secretary General of the United Nations, also effectively assassinated with considerable zeal by Madeleine Albright. The Ghalis are one of the great Coptic landowning and political families in Egypt. The political tradition was recently broken when Youssef Butros Ghali, Butros Butros Ghali's nephew, was named Minister of the Economy in the current government. He is an egghead and, they say, a great brain. He was previously Minister of State for Economic Affairs, not technically a ministerial position. But in uncertain economic times even his religion could not keep him out of the government.

But voice any criticism of Egypt and a foreigner will find a Copt just as defensive as a Muslim. The Copts may be outspoken in their own country, but they resist the interference of others in what they consider national affairs. The bill in the United States Congress that would impose sanctions on countries violating the religious rights of their citizens includes Egypt, largely because of the Coptic problem. Pope Shenoudah denounced the bill, and with good reason, the Copts believing it would only complicate their lives. And, for all of their difficulties, the Copts are Egyptians first and foremost. The suggestion that they are different from Egyptian Muslims is unwelcome, especially since some believed that the bill's sponsors included AIPAC and it was really only an attempt to embarrass the country. But the aggressive expatriate Coptic community in the United States may also have something to do with it.

The largest-circulation Arabic dailies, *Al-Ahram, Al-Akhbar* and *Al-Gumhouria*, are government papers. I read *Al-Ahram*, the flagship, on a daily basis, but not carefully enough to know how good it really was. There were complaints that editorially it still followed a Nasserist line and it was said that Naguib Mahfouz now read it only for the obituaries. There were two main opposition papers, *Al-Wafd* and *Ash-Sha'ab. Al-Wafd* represented the old party of privilege, now dressed up as the "New Wafd," and back in business after a period in the doghouse under Sadat. The name came from the delegation that Egypt attempted, unsuccessfully, to send to the Peace

Conference in 1919, and the party newspaper with its green header now competed with *Al-Ahram* and *Al-Akhbar* for urban readership.

But there was something elitist and maybe even a little too Coptic about the party and, after a brief resurgence, it had gradually lost its allure. *Ash-Sha'ab*, or "The People," was originally socialist. But in a metamorphosis common in Egypt, it had become Islamist. That suggested that contention, not ideology, was the guiding principle and that the dispirited opposition was using whatever vehicle was at hand. The Muslim Brotherhood—not necessarily Islamist—was still strong and the Brothers had captured leadership of most professional syndicates in Egypt. Most people believed that in truly free elections, constituencies represented by the readers of *Ash-Sha'ab* and *Al-Wafd* would capture most of the vote. The NDP, the party of Mubarak and of Ahmad Fathi Serour, would finish a poor third.

It was said that Egypt under Nasser wrote the book on driving away foreign investment. Now, the country was doing everything it could to bring it back. The success was mixed. The Nasserist bureaucracy was still there, for all of the attempts at improvement. At a recent conference in Cairo, "Growth beyond Stabilization," Jeffrey Sachs solemnly intoned that Egypt was very good at bureaucracy, having been at it for 7,000 years. Soon, everyone in the conference, including the Egyptians themselves, took up the theme. Actually, 7,000 years would have overstated the case by a few millennia. But the Egyptians had clearly been at it for a long time. The Nasser period had also been a time of the pervasive presence of the *mukhabarat*, or secret police. We heard stories from old-timers of children being interrogated by the police because they were suspected of wearing underwear from America. The police had been everywhere and some Egyptians, in their nostalgia for the pride and assertiveness of the Nasser years, seem to have forgotten the darker side.

All of this meant that there wasn't much democracy in Egypt. The country had been run by generals since Nasser's time and anyone but a military man as president was hard to imagine. But no one knew what to expect after Mubarak, although his son Gamal was supposedly being groomed as the successor. Many didn't feel that nepotism was an improvement over militarism. Egyptian writers and intellectuals chafed under the restrictions and what appeared to be slavish deference to the dictates of the United States. In addition to the aid we gave Mubarak very little to sell at home. Wye Plantation provoked only the usual yawn from the man in the street, too little, too late and Netanyahu had no intention of implementing it anyway. Why Wye? Now there seemed no alternative for Egypt but the market and the American way.

And Ahmed Fathi Serour was still up to his old tricks. In an address to a student group in Alexandria he was combative, claiming "tartly" that election irregularities were the work of "thugs and hardened criminals" and that it was the people themselves who were responsible for election rigging. He "ridiculed," "seriously warned," and generally hectored his audience. "We (in Egypt) have a consolidated democracy," he claimed "which is unprecedented in the country." The statement was incomprehensible. In the government's defense, some of the opposition represented the old socialists dressed up in Islamist clothes and it was hardly responsible. But the best way to make an opposition responsible was to offer it the prospect of exercising power. As it was, the Brothers gnashed their teeth on the sidelines, hopelessly irrelevant, their time taken up debating such critical issues as whether or not the Minister of Agriculture was, in fact, a Jew.

Israel was a democracy, at least if you were Jewish. It was truly an outpost of Western values in the area, although I don't know what else we would have expected from a European colony in the Sunni Arab world. Surrounded and encysted like a foreign body, it still had not been accepted as a legitimate part of the Middle East, for reasons that were as much its fault as that of the Arabs. The Western values included some that were not very attractive, including a willingness to bring the latest military technology to bear on developing-world enemies. A Jewish life was precious and the Israelis were willing to trade hundreds of Palestinians for the remains of one Ron Arad, a clear indication of their valuation of the other side.

But in terms of democracy in the region, the recent developments in Iran were the most promising in years. The fact that a moderate had been elected and allowed to take office, followed by an overwhelming victory by moderates in local elections, represented truly revolutionary events. That presaged perhaps a new axis: a moderate Israel and a moderate Iran together exercising some restraining influence on the thugs in the area. Saddam Hussein and Hafez al-Assad were dinosaurs and dinosaurs were going out of fashion these days.

Israel had changed too. The latest wave of immigrants from Russia was educated and cyber-iterate. Some of them were even Jewish. Maybe the future really was the market and the danger to a country like Egypt was not military but educational. The Egyptians had been congratulating themselves on their splendid human resources for years. Meanwhile, as the Egyptian educational system imploded, other people like the Indians and the Israelis were simply getting on with it. But Egyptians, used for centuries to life on the margins, were not a revolutionary people and it was hard to say what would shake them out of their torpor. Maybe some American muscle could help. But American leadership was a commodity in short supply in the 1990s.

Democracy in Egypt had a long way to go before it played a part in the life of the country.

15

Budapest

It was the *Eid al-Adha*, the Feast of the Sacrifice, from the tenth to the thirteenth of the pilgrimage month, and I wanted a respite from Cairo. The streets of the city were awash in blood and water, and men with knives and bloody smocks strolled through the crisp spring air with unaccustomed importance. Little children in new clothes tiptoed through the gore while their parents portioned out the offal. No one who ate meat could object to the slaughter, but the public and workmanlike manner of the butchers made it an affair of the entire community and said something about the coarseness of the common taste. We preferred the plastic-wrapped product from Safeway.

It was too early for Greece and I had already seen Sinai twice that year. I originally thought of Isfahan and Persepolis. But an Iranian visa would take a month and I hadn't started looking in time. I would have to save Iran for later. Then I thought of Budapest. The Turks had taken the city in the sixteenth century and kept it for 160 years, and there must be interesting things to see. The Hungarians had thrown themselves into the breach countless times as Europe's bulwark against first, the Mongols and then the Ottomans, and the flower of Hungarian chivalry had been decimated by Suleiman the Magnificent at Mohacs in 1526. Besides, the Hungarians originally came out of Central Asia and Central Asia was always interesting. Before their settlement in the Carpathian Basin and conversion to Christianity, the Hungarians themselves had struck fear into the heart of Europe. The churches of Christendom once sounded with the prayer "From the arrows of the Hungarians, spare us oh Lord." Along with the Finns they had preserved their Finno-Ugaric language, related to Turkish.

The ethnic mix in Central Asia was probably no more complex than the mix of tribes in Central Africa. But waves of these people had washed over Europe for millennia and the little *HUNGARY, A Brief History* I later bought in Budapest showed a bewildering catalogue of peoples in the area to the north of the Caspian and the Black seas. There were Scythians, Ugrians, Ananino, Kaliz, Pechenegs, Cumans, Iazyges, Kangars, Permians, Ogur, Khazars, Alans, Abkhaz, Magyars, Mordvinians, Muroma, Merya, Krivichi, Vyatichi, Radimichi, Severyanye, Kipchaks, Polyanye, Drevelyane, Dregovichi, Livonians, White Khorvat, Duleb, Vlachs, and Finns. And that was just in the west. The steppes stretched another three thousand miles eastward to Mongolia, the fount of migration of these restless people.

The Hungarians, or Magyars, considered themselves descendants of the Huns and they settled in their present location to the west of the Carpathians in the tenth century. Since the time of "the Settlement" they had preserved traces of their original incarnation as shepherds and mounted archers. The horse was first domesticated in Central Asia and the Hungarians had kept elements of their equine civilization in their saddles, wagons, means of riding and driving, and in their range and mobility. Children in the steppes literally learned to ride before they could walk. Unlike Europeans further west, late converts to the horse, everyone rode, not just the nobility. The Magyars had been the most westernized of the nomadic horsemen. The culture of Central Asian horse-breeding and much else—the equestrian civilization that stretched from the Great Wall of China to the River Leitha in eastern Austria—had reached Europe through the Magyars: "Everything we now revere as a triumph of the human spirit has been bought somewhere, at some time, not only with human blood and tears but also with the sweat of horses." Miklos Jankovich told the story in *They Rode into Europe,* a book I found in Islamabad years several before.

In the great expanse of the steppes, covering eight modern time zones, there were also Uryanchai, Voguls, Ostyaks, Samodeyes, Chukches, Koryaks, Yomuds, Tekkes, Kirghiz, Kalmucks, Huns, Patzinaks, Kumans, Tatars, Tungus, Yakuts, Ephthalites, Avars, Turks, Massagetes, Budini, Koban, Sarmatians, Alans, and Mongols. It was the mobility of the horse that allowed them to penetrate Europe, the evolution that, according to Jankovich, led "... from nomadic reindeer-breeding through horse-keeping to the riding of the horse ... the answer to why Mongolia over the centuries has been again and again the calm heart of the hurricane out of which the storms of horse archers have blown so devastatingly."

Their horses were light and agile. They never developed the massive *destriers,* the huge chargers of the west, the cold-blooded horses capable of carrying a fully-armored knight into battle. There was a reason for these massive animals. By the time the steel chamfron for the horse, the bridle, bit and headstall, the remainder of the horse's armor, the saddle, the man's complete plate armor, the spurs, sword, shield, lance, dagger, surcoat, housing over the horse-armor, and helmet were added to the weight of the man himself, the horse had to be able to carry 440 lb, or 224 kg. By contrast, the later Austro-Hungarian cavalry manual listed the standard "all-up" weight to be 121 kg, which was also about the standard English-packhorse weight. The knight was so ungainly on the destrier that he rode another mount, a palfrey, until just before he entered the lists. The palfrey was like the tank transporter, the modern battle tank being so mechanically delicate and fuel-inefficient that it is carried up to the drop-off point before entering battle. Hungarian horses were of the lighter, "hot-blooded" type, and Hungarian cavalry rode farther and faster than the western European arm. They were the origin of the Hussars, the light cavalry later adopted everywhere in the West.

After their conversion to Christianity, the Hungarians became Europe's first line of defense against their brethren to the east. But there was always something "eastern" about them and throughout the nineteenth century they remained on the other side of the imaginary line that separated Europe from Asia. Not least it was in their tactics, which were those of the Turks, feinting and attacking in several places, then wheeling and withdrawing, to regroup before returning to the attack again. The stirrup allowed them to shoot from the saddle at full gallop and they rained showers of arrows on their enemy, with devastating effect. They simply wore down opponents who were used to standing, even if it meant perishing where they stood. It was not helter-skelter, but required a very high degree of discipline and horsemanship to execute the evolutions as a body. It was the same discipline and organization, passed down from father to son, that allowed Babar and his Moghuls to decimate the more numerous but less agile Indians.

Central Asia remained a mystery. In spite of two careful readings of Grousset's classic *The Empire of the Steppes*. I still didn't really know what a Hun or a Mongol or a Turk, not to mention the rest of them, were. But they had appeared everywhere, from the Moghul Empire in Northern India, to the successive Turkic peoples who overran Anatolia and then spread into Central Europe. The successive waves were based on rapine, plunder, and domination of the settled peoples. They left no institutions in Europe, only smoldering ruins and pyramids of severed heads. They made a pastime of casual butchery and I often wondered at the sheer hard work involved in the killing of hundreds of thousands of people without stand-off weapons. It was what Brill's *First Encyclopedia of Islam* termed "the holocaust."

Some of the easterners stayed and adopted the institutions of the conquered people. For those who remained in Hungary the original system of clans broke down, replaced by ownership of estates with a landed aristocracy and serfs. The Carpathian basin was rich in minerals, water, and agricultural resources and a classic European feudal system developed, with monopolies on the production of salt, fish, precious metals, and horses. Precious metals remained an important export until discovery of the Americas flooded Europe with gold and silver and led to widespread inflation. The traditional Hungarian affair with the horse remained, however, in the new setting and some of the serfs raised horseflesh, not wheat. The Hungarian plains were ideal for the herds, and breeders often turned their mares loose to be covered by wild stallions. Maybe some of the old independence, based on the horse, remained too, because the history of the country was full of peasant revolts.

That was all in the past. But there was also the present, and it would be interesting to see how the Hungarians were faring in the post-Soviet economic order. Everywhere, the free market was the byword, but there was a social Darwinism about it and all but the fittest were having trouble surviving. Everyone seemed just as slavishly addicted to this as they had been to earlier panaceas. There were now kleptocracies everywhere in the old Second World, the same old few making fortunes out of privatization while the masses were reduced to bare subsistence. We had become used to seeing pictures of pensioners selling old clothes or anything else of value on the streets of Moscow. But this was Hungary, one of the brighter spots in an otherwise dismal picture and a candidate for early NATO membership. It would be an opportunity to see, at least superficially, how they were adjusting.

Egypt Air offered the best price for a four-day excursion. I was looking forward to spring in Budapest but, as the departure date approached, the weather reports were dismal: sub-zero temperatures and cloud cover over most of Central Europe from the Baltic to the Balkans. But the die was cast and I left on schedule, just after eleven on a Friday morning, The map in the in-flight magazine showed Cairo to Budapest connecting through Kiev, but this was a direct flight and it arrived on time just over three hours later. Americans didn't need visas, but the lines through passport control were long and the wait was considerable. They were the old Soviet-style booths, with an angled mirror to allow the uniformed officer a full view of the supplicant. Outside, a shuttle service provided transportation to the hotels at a fraction of the cost of a taxi.

We were called individually by destination. I had reservations at the Ramada Grand Hotel and after about fifteen minutes it was called. The trip into the city was on an odd motorway, four lanes sandwiched around two lanes in the center, fenced off, with one lane in either direction. The van was new and Japanese, and a two-way radio crackled throughout the half-hour trip. There was also a mobile phone in a holder on the dashboard and the driver spent most of his time talking on one or the other. No one in the van wore a seat belt. Most of the cars in the streets were Japanese or German, with a fair sprinkling of Mercedes and BMWs, but there were a few old East Germen Trabants as well. From the look of the advertisements, the market economy had taken off and European, Japanese, and American brands—Mercedes, Sony, Kentucky Fried Chicken—appeared to be everywhere.

We reached the city center and the penetration of America continued, with McDonalds, Pizza Hut, New York Bagels, and Burger King. The Ramada was the last stop on the itinerary, located on Margit Island in the middle of the Danube, two miles from the center of the city. I had seen a list of about thirty hotels and asked the travel agent to check on availability. The Ramada was the only one that responded and I decided to stay at least for a night. It was old-style European and when I looked at the list again, I realized that it was a "thermal" hotel. Patrons padded through the common rooms in white bathrobes, on their way to various cures. The therapy menu was there in the room along with the room-service menu: selective impulse, diadynamic, interference current, ultrasound, infra-red, solarium, microwave, decimeter-wave, short-wave, individual medical gymnastics, group medical gymnastics, tube baths, carbonic baths, galvanic baths, four-cell galvanic baths, massage, hydromassage, underwater jet massage, underwater traction, inhalation, mud-pack, galvanization, and ionthoporese.

There were a few hours of daylight left on the first day, just enough time for a look around the city. Margit Island was heavily wooded and, even with the cold and damp, many of the trees had come into leaf. The oaks sported tender new leaves although the massive plane trees were still bare. The fruit trees were blossoming, a mass of white flowers. The walk to the end of the island was about a mile along a path used by cyclists, joggers, and strollers. At the end, the Margit Bridge led to Buda on the right and Pest on the left. The Danube was gray-green under the overcast and seemed to be about 400 yards wide, about the same width as the Nile at Rhoda. I turned left towards Pest and walked half a mile down Istvan Street to the intersection with *Bajcsy Zsilinsky ut* and another mile south along that street. There were several bookstores along the way, but they were all closed. The signs indicated that they were open at ten in the morning although, I was to discover, that didn't include the weekends.

I walked back the way I had come and by the time I reached the Ramada night was falling. The reconnaissance done, I made a rough plan for the next four days: Pest on Saturday, Buda on Sunday, bookstores on Monday any loose ends on Tuesday before the flight back to Cairo that afternoon. The remote location meant dinner at the hotel but the menu looked interesting and it was not a bad place to be stranded. The roast leg of goose, potato pancakes, and braised red cabbage were delicious and, even with a bottle of Hungarian wine, the bill came to less than twenty dollars. There was also live music, a quartet in tuxedos, made up of a violinist, a cellist, a clarinetist, and a timpanist playing an odd keyboard instrument, striking it with muffled sticks. They looked like a throwback to the Austro-Hungarian Empire, short, in patent-leather shoes and immaculately coifed. The fat pink fingers of the violinist were brilliantly dexterous on his instrument. They played mostly Mozart and Haydn.

The next morning it was back along the jogging path to the Margit Bridge and then left to Pest. It was the low-lying side of the city, often flooded before the Danube had been banked and restrained. Buda on the other side was hilly, topped on the south by the *citadella*. From a distance, the citadel looked medieval but it dated only from the nineteenth century. The medieval part of the city was actually the Royal Palace complex in Buda, on a lower hill across from the Chain Bridge. The first impression of the city was reinforced on this second visit. Everything was gray and the shops were still closed. It had been hard to change the shop hours, even in Germany. The weekend was sacred and nothing could move Europeans to change that.

The city was not beautiful, but it wasn't ugly either. The air quality was surprisingly good. The limestone of the massive circular nave of St. Steven's Cathedral was a dirty gray, suggesting that it had not always been so. The general impression was of a city down-at-the-heels. The plaster on many buildings had chipped off, revealing the bricks beneath. A few buildings had been restored—banks in particular—but most were suffering from decades of neglect. There was no overt poverty, no old women selling clothes on street corners, but little evidence of spirit either. People made their purposeful way in the streets without taking notice of their surroundings, or of each other.

The bookstores were still closed and, even assuming there would be anything in English, they would have to wait for Monday. After *Bajcsy Zsilinszky ut* I turned west and came out at the river again near the Chain Bridge. The promenade to the south would be pleasant in the summer, and even in this raw weather it was nice to be on the waterfront. After three-quarters of a mile there was the *Erzsebet* Bridge, across from the citadel. This seemed to be a tourist area, with boutiques selling folk dress and souvenirs. There were also a few restaurants, including the *Apostolok* that offered traditional Hungarian fare. I wandered into the Paris Arcades and found the small Hungarian history in English, and then northeast along the mile and a-half of *Rakoczi ut* to the *Blaha Lujza Ter*.

The language was impenetrable and even Farsi, with its familiar script and heavily-Arabic lexicon, seemed more manageable than this utterly foreign system of sounds, even with its Latin alphabet. It was another mile and a half to *Nyugati* Station, a massive art-deco building, and then back the same way I had come to the Paris Arcades. Everything was closed. But the *Apostolok* was open and a pork chop and country sausage with braised red cabbage and mashed potatoes and a couple of glasses of red wine was good and inexpensive. A Big Mac cost 274 forints, or about $1.65, and these entrees were only about twice that.

The municipal vehicles looked oddly familiar. In Pakistan we had received twenty East German military trucks for the Mine Dog program. They were left over from the Gulf War and we wondered how we would find spare parts for them. The Afghans cannibalized a few before discovering that they were standard Soviet-bloc issue and were abundant across the border in Uzbekistan. The same models were here in Budapest, used as garbage trucks. And there were other connections to the Middle East and Muslim world. During the Nasser years Egypt had been heavily dependent on the Eastern Bloc, exporting wine and leather goods to pay for arms. And a whole generation of musicians, technicians, and engineers had studied in Moscow, Budapest, Belgrade, and Sofia. In Egypt there were still unrepentant Nasserists who pined away for the palmy old days of nonalignment and socialist solidarity. Egyptians were probably better off these days, although the gap between the rich and poor had widened. But now there was no alternative to America and the market. Some found that hard to accept.

At the little zoo on Margit Island people stopped and admired the piglets, black and white in coloring, but miniature. They must have been from a pigmy breed because even the adults were ugly little brutes, with a heavy, underslung fold of flesh beneath the chin. In the hotel that night a couple sat at the bar accompanied by a huge dog. It looked like a poodle, but must have been three feet high at the shoulder. They even took it into the restaurant with them. Here, then, at least three conventional profanities were indulged: "wine, music, and hounds." Both pigs and dogs were unclean in Islam and Westerners' enthusiasm for them were as difficult for a Muslim to understand as the public freedom allowed to Western women. It showed what a marriage of convenience the Egyptian connection with the Eastern Bloc must have been, although it was before the rise of Islamism.

The next day would be Buda. But the weather didn't look promising outside the hotel. It had rained heavily the night before and the thermometer at the main entrance showed the temperature to be just above zero. A light snow was falling as I set out along the jogging path. This time at Margit Bridge it was right instead of left. Over the water the wind picked up and blew bitterly cold into my exposed ear, and I imagined its uninterrupted path over the eight time zones of the steppes before reaching us here in Hungary. On the

Buda side everything was closed and it looked gray and dismal. There were a few stands set up in a market area and a few old women selling carrot sticks and radishes in plastic bags. Near the riverfront there was a brick building with the characteristic leaden Turkish dome that had probably once been a bath. But, for the most part, the city on this raw Sunday morning was deserted. The day was clearly going to be going to be wet and miserable, so I walked only half a mile or so before turning back.

Back at the hotel it was warm—too warm—in the room and I spent the middle part of the day reading in the common room. I had brought along Anthony Cave Brown's *Treason in the Blood*, the story of St. John and Kim Philby. The early part contained some jarring notes and there seemed to be a credulous acceptance of the importance of too many westerners in the "mysterious" East, T. E. Lawrence chief among them. I wondered if the same credulity didn't apply to Kim Philby. In the murky world of espionage and counterespionage, who knew who did what, or whether anything was really done at all. There was probably no question that his treason led to scores or maybe even hundreds of deaths. But the portrait that emerged of Philby was unattractive and it was difficult to see the source of his self-assurance. The treason at least seemed understandable after the early neglect by his parents, followed by exile at the age of nine from his grandmother and the only home he had ever known. St. John Philby was a legitimate, if insufferable, eccentric. But from this account it was difficult to see Kim as anything but a pathetic victim of his father's brutishness and neglect.

Back in the room, the hotel advertised premium cable service and it was the usual international fare including three local Hungarian channels, several German channels, the BBC, Skynews, the French *arte* channel, one Italian, one Russian, the Cartoon Network, EuroSport and two American channels, the NBC Superchannel and CNN. In spite of their best effort, the American offerings succeeded in being, well, just American. NBC was apparently having difficulty because they had solicited letters from their audience and aired the responses in periodic plugs: "Your channel is so much a part of our daily lives that if it were discontinued we would seriously consider terminating our cable service." The sports events were often weeks-old, and it was hard to understand how anyone but an American could enjoy the puerile antics of Conan O'Brien.

CNN had added a stable of newsreaders of both sexes and several ethnic groups. But they were still provincials, innocents abroad. The content of news programs was largely the same on every channel, but the tone made the BBC more believable than CNN. There was an earnestness about CNN and a tendency to intrude editorially into such "content" as there was that seemed to lessen their credibility. American broadcast exports to the rest of the world amounted to $6 billion in 1996. But unless they changed, it seemed certain that the locals would catch up. It was like the immediate postwar years when it was the fashion in Italian movies to have an American car. Vittorio Gassman drove a Studebaker in one Fellini film. Now, European cars were the status symbols.

Aggressive marketing by the Americans was, paradoxically, expected to make local programmers improve the quality of their own offerings. The best of the locals were already rated higher than the imports. In Egypt the local channels showed Romanian and Polish films, not to mention the Czechs whose offerings in the sixties—*Closely Watched Trains* came to mind—filled "art" theaters. There was a certain amount of eyewash in these European offerings, the combination of existential drift and bare flesh purporting to constitute serious art. But there had to be a middle ground between the latest American bit of mayhem and the extinction of the local film industries. For dinner the breast of duck was a little slice of America, maybe California cuisine, the small pieces of meat surrounded by watercress and little else. It was not the hearty fare that I had become used to.

The next morning it was still overcast. But the thermometer outside showed five degrees Centigrade and there was no rain. So I walked to the Margit Bridge, this time through the center of the island, and again turned right towards Buda. Half a mile ahead, the stairs across from the Chain Bridge wound up to the Royal Palace complex. The Gothic Matthias Church stood just behind the Fisherman's Bastion, a white, limestone complex of crenelated walls and turrets that overlooked the Danube. It was in excellent condition and in fact dated only from the late nineteenth century.

The church itself was huge, with a steeple that stood several hundred feet high. Inside, the decor was unlike anything I had seen before: pink and mauve and mustard and light-blue whorls, hearts, chevrons, and herringbones. The colors were light pastel and the patterns looked like something on the face cards in a poker deck. It was odd, unlike anything recognizable from the East or the West: not geometric like Islamic art, not gilt like the Byzantine, and like nothing resembling Western liturgical art. Hungary was Roman Catholic in this no-man's-land bordering Islam and Orthodox Christianity. But in the sixteenth and seventeenth centuries it had effectively spent two centuries years out of the European mainstream. Maybe that had something to do with it.

There was a special section devoted to artifacts, including the royal crown of Hungary. This *did* look Byzantine, at first glance a relatively simple pair of gold bands crisscrossed at the top over a gold band around the temples. But on a closer look the whole was inlaid with precious stones and painted with miniatures—of "God the Father," "Jesus Christ the Son of God," and apostles, saints, kings, and heroes. The exhibit was well laid out, with texts in Hungarian, German, and English, and photographs and explanations of each of the miniatures. The little gold cross on the top sat at an odd angle, and there was a plausible explanation for that, although I forget what it was. The rest of the museum contained vestments and other liturgical gear.

Two hundred yards to the south was the Castle Palace complex. Inside, the museum was a testament to the capacity of the old command economy to fund collective endeavors. It was beautifully laid out with texts in Hungarian, German, and English, and the price of admission, 200 forints (about $1.25) seemed to be within the reach of everyone. A group of Hasidic Jews from America argued good-naturedly but persistently over qualification for student admission. The Jews in Hungary had probably been mostly Ashkenazim, the Sephardic Jews having arrived and departed with the Turks. There was still the old Jewish quarter and synagogue, although most Hungarian Jews had been sent to the death camps during the war. There was even a tour that centered on Jewish Budapest. There was also an exhibit on Aquincum, a frontier town and the Roman capital of Pannonia Inferior on the Danube. At its height, early in the third century AD, it had 50,000 inhabitants. The exhibit had the usual Roman artifacts, statuary, wall paintings, and mosaics. Most interesting was the exhibit on medieval Budapest that showed the development of the two cities from the end of the Roman through the Turkish periods.

I had used the Turks as the hook on which to hang my interest in Hungary, and there were a few pictures of baths and minarets when the city was Ottoman. But in the flesh there was almost nothing left from the Turkish period, and their yoke had apparently lain fairly lightly on Hungarian necks. One reason may have been distance. By the time Ottoman armies reached Hungary in their yearly campaigns against Vienna it was always autumn, and, whatever the outcome, they would soon have to retreat before winter set in. No, Hungary was in Europe not the East, although there was an insistence on its Europeanness that suggested that Hungarians themselves weren't sure about their identity.

The strongest influence seemed to come from Austria in the shotgun marriage that was the Austro-Hungarian Empire. Hungary became a partner after the Turks were driven out in 1686. But it was difficult to say what a Hungarian really was. There had been movements into Hungary of Slavs from the north and the south, of Germans and Ashkenazi Jews from Moravia, the Ukraine, Poland, Lithuania, and Galicia. The Jews had been the leaders of the forces of modernization in the nineteenth century, chiefly of financial and commercial enterprises. But there had been persistent nationality problems as a result of the expansion and then contraction of Hungary over the years, and many ethnic Hungarians still lived in Transylvania, or Romania.

From 1848 onward developments in Hungary mirrored the rest of Eastern Europe, with revolution and a brief expansion of democratic ideals, followed by repression and continuing serfdom. In the First World War Hungary had chosen the side of the Central Powers, and the peace that followed brought truncation of the country and confinement to its present borders. Then there was revolution again, the first Soviet Hungary, counter-revolution, widespread emigration, and fascism. The Second World War was another alliance with the losing side, and Hungarian "fast-moving units" mounted on bicycles had invaded the Soviet Union alongside the Germans. After the war Soviet Hungary settled in again, this time for a longer stay. The losses from the war were catastrophic, and probably the greatest inflation in history set in, with banknotes denominated in the quadrillions. But intellectual life revived, relative stability returned, and Hungary settled down into its existence as the happiest barrack in the Soviet camp.

The revolution in 1956 failed but it had resulted in a Hungarian solution that was less repressive than in other satellites. After the collapse of the Soviet Union, Hungary was an early convert to democratization and the market economy. The *Brief History of Hungary* gave a taste of recent intellectual currents, having been updated after the end of communism. But it still referred to categories like "lumpenproletariat" and "petty bourgeoisie" as if they had the same scientific basis as phyla in the animal kingdom. It referred to "the bleak soot-gray of classical capitalism, of the original accumulation of capital"—this in an Eastern Europe ravaged by decades of communist pollution. It was anachronistic, but gave a sense of an attitude that probably still prevailed beneath the surface change, the New York Bagels and Pizza Huts.

It was impossible to form much of an impression of the country in four days. The area around the Royal Palace was full of tour groups and the little shops and restaurants were touristy, with peasant fare and the help in bright blue folk dresses and smocks. It was also hard to know who this "folk" were, with all the movements of populations that had taken place over the centuries. The huge bronze hunting-scene in the middle of the complex probably represented what Hungary must once have been: rural, serf-ridden, medieval, and poor, anything but colorful. One hunter held a trophy wolf by the tail and the other displayed a stag. There was a brace of huge hunting dogs, their jaws pendulous and slavering, like the animal in the restaurant in the Ramada. The Hungarian crown had preserved the hunting proclivities of its steppe forebears, and the "huntsmen, kennelmen, whippers-in, falconers, austringers, and keepers preserving bison, deer, beaver, and hares . . ." constituted almost a class by themselves as they served royalty.

The restaurant at the Citadella, a mile to the south and up a steep series of stairs, was expensive by Hungarian standards. But the wild boar stew with mushrooms and dumplings was good. The citadel itself was relatively new, also dating from the nineteenth century. That was odd, since it was the highest place in Buda and dominated the Royal Complex to the north. Surely, something stood in its place before then. The citadel completed the visit to Budapest.

It had hardly been a visit to Hungary and I had seen nothing of the countryside. The flight back to Cairo was on Monday and I had half a day to see the bookstores. They looked interesting, but almost everything was in Hungarian and German and there was very little in English or French. I didn't see anything by Niebuhr. I did see several individuals who looked like intellectuals. With workers and peasants they had made up the population of Hungary during the Soviet period. But the old categories seemed to have broken down along with everything else, and it was hard to judge which of the joggers on the island had been representatives of the bourgeoisie. But then, jogging was probably, by definition, a bourgeois occupation.

The flight was at four o'clock and when I reached the airport at about three there was still an exit seat with extra leg-room, even though all the other passengers had checked in. It sounded like they were a tour group and, sure-enough, everyone else on the flight was on a package to Hurghada. For some reason that was how everyone—the Egyptians included—spelled the Arabic of *Ghardaqa*. At three thirty the management announced that there were "technical problems" and the flight would be delayed until seven o'clock. They thought. Maybe there would be space on the *Malev* flight at eleven o'clock. Or maybe we would have to wait for *Egypt Air* the next day. It was interesting how everyone accepted the delay with resignation, even humor. That must have been the result of fifty years of Soviet conditioning.

While we waited I chatted with an American MBA student from Case Western University doing a year abroad in Hungary, and a classmate, a Hungarian student who was very Americanized. The classmate wore a Dallas Cowboys ball cap turned backward and every other word seemed to be "fuck." They agreed that it was different studying in Hungary. Students didn't ask questions but tended to accept whatever the professor said as gospel. The Hungarian didn't really know what had happened in 1956 other than that Kadar was the result. I mentioned the difficulty of the language and he confessed that his Hungarian grammar was weak. There were post-position modifiers like in Urdu, so that you were always thinking ahead. Or was it behind?

While we waited they gave us a chit for a soft drink, which several of us turned into a pint of lager. But we had hardly taken a sip before they announced that we should board: the flight *would* leave at seven o'clock, after all. There were no Egyptians on the flight. The inflight magazine included a love story set in Europe, by Morsi Saad ed-Din, the current dean of Egyptian letters, and it was another reminder of the old connection with the Soviet Bloc. Mohammed Hassenein Heykal had rhapsodized about his trips to Eastern Europe and the Soviet Union as Nasser's Minister of Information. As far as he was concerned, nothing good had happened in Egypt since Nasser departed the scene.

It was wrong-headed but, perhaps, understandable as Egypt became a kleptocracy like every other developing country. But there was always the suspicion of sour grapes. The disenchantment of the old elites with the new was not so much with privilege itself, as with the fact that they were no longer its beneficiaries. And, anyway, intellectuals always knew better than everyone else.

16

The Seminar

The plane came in low over what remained of the first cataract and swung out over Lake Nasser before returning and landing to the north. Moqbel was there to meet me and we drove the five kilometers to the old Aswan exchange building, turning away from the city that was twenty kilometers in the other direction. At the exchange there were red carpets on the walkway, and the flame trees outside the little building were in full bloom. It was a typical Upper Egyptian summer morning, hot but dry, and held the promise—or threat—of more where that had come from. On the wall outside the entrance was a banner announcing the seminar, and the local television station actually turned up in midmorning to film the proceedings. Moqbel showed me around, as an example of what *sa'idis* could do with a little prompting and when they put their minds to it. The venue was a bargain. There was no charge for the facility, and a club down the street catered breakfast and lunch at eleven pounds, or about $3.25 a head. One of the most lasting legacies of the British in Egypt was a fondness for clubs and every syndicate or society seemed to have one.

The general manager was there to greet us and we expressed our satisfaction with what he had done. He was originally from Fayoum and I wondered what had brought him to Aswan since Egyptians were notorious homebodies. It was one reason why the company had trouble finding staff for Upper Egypt. The obligatory coffee and tea were served while we waited for the rest of the attendees to arrive. The vice chairman for Upper Egypt was scheduled to come by train from Assiut and he should have arrived by seven o'clock that morning. But it turned out that he had fallen ill the night before and wouldn't be attending. The central department chief, or CDC, was coming from Sohag by car and had left about six o'clock. That should have gotten him there by the nine o'clock starting time. But flat tires had delayed him and he didn't arrive until nearly ten. Meanwhile tea boys circulated with cardboard trays of the sweetened carbohydrates— *kunafa*, *basbusa*, and little twisted pastries—that were the bane of the Egyptian constitution. The boys were dark and thin, undoubtedly Nubian, and dressed in the ill-fitting and ill-matching pants and shirts that served as the uniform of the poor in Egypt. Both had faces that only a mother could love.

The month before I had been in Luxor for a marketing presentation to the employees of Upper Egypt, still an outpost of Christianity in the country. When the Muslims arrived in Egypt in the middle of the seventh century the Copts were at first cooperative, having been treated like second-class citizens by the Byzantines. But with increasing persecution and pressure to convert many left for Upper Egypt and the area still had a disproportionately Christian population. So it was no surprise that the presentation had been in the Coptic Orthodox Holy Bible's Friends Association Orphanage House. Amal, the firebrand Muslima, in her own words "surrounded with Maria and Jesus and Baba Shenudah," lectured on marketing and customer service, utterly foreign concepts to the Telecom Egypt employees: "Why do we need customers?" the employees said, "They need us."

We had been assisted by Tadros (Theodore) and Boulis (Paul), graduates of the orphanage. The exchange general manager was Eng. Romani, which in Arabic meant "Greek" and not "Roman" since the Byzantine Greeks were widely known as Romaeans. The fifty staff were the usual Egyptian mixture, except for one finely-chiseled little man who looked like the mummy of Ramses II. It all seemed innocent and ecumenical until you realized that the Copts and Muslims were periodically at each others' throats. Nineteen Copts had been killed in Kouseh the month before in clashes with Muslims.

This time I was in Aswan to show the flag in the "Finance for non-Financial Managers" seminar we put on for the employees of the 2nd zone in Upper Egypt. It included every exchange from Assiut to Aswan, and there were some storied names among them: Qift, the origin of the word "Copt" some said, and the village where Flinders Petrie found his expert excavators; Kalabsha, south of Aswan on Lake Nasser and the site of a relocated Ptolemaic temple; not to mention Edfu, Esna, Karnak, and Luxor. Moqbel had been there several weeks before looking for a venue for the seminar and had persuaded the general manager to refurbish the old *central Sad al-'Ali*, or the High Dam exchange building.

It dated from the 1960s when the Russians were building the dam. But a modern facility had replaced the old one and the exchange was now empty. The equipment was also gone, with the exception of a test room. The test room was still manned by two engineers, for what purpose no one seemed to know. But the general manager, showing commendable initiative, had cleaned up the place and had done it in ten days' time. The switch rooms were painted and turned into classrooms, most of the paint was scraped off the windows, the toilets now flushed, and air-conditioners had been installed in the classrooms. The A/Cs were important since at eight fifteen that morning—seven fifteen sun time—it was already 95° Fahrenheit. At the noon prayer break it was well over 100°. And this was only May. In July and August it would be insufferable without air conditioning.

We waited until ten o'clock and then began. I gave a little opening address, saying I had last been in Aswan with an ARENTO delegation in 1984 and how pleased I was to be here again. I stressed the importance of timely and accurate financial information to the future of this new shareholding company. Then Moqbel took over, and it was vintage Moqbel, armed as he was with the multiple file folders that he had labeled *sleeds*, or slides, in Arabic. He had ten fat binders with Microsoft Project slides, Excel spread sheets, and Word documents. They were his record of years of patient work in venues like this. It was where most of the work of Telecom Egypt took place, often in places that were far from the relative sophistication of Cairo or Alexandria.

The attendees were the usual Upper Egyptian mix. Of the thirty-five in the room there were a few Africans, Nilotic and looking like they came from southern Sudan. Others were dark but without African features, including the little man I had seen the month before in Luxor who looked like Ramses II. Still others had complexions that ranged from light brown to white. At the lightest end of the spectrum was engineer Binyamin, a man who could have been a Greek or a Turk. All three of the young men who were being groomed to take over for Moqbel were Copts. One, a graduate of the Faculty of English at Assiut University, cornered me and asked whether the Telecom Egypt chart of accounts was arranged according to a decimal, a binary, or a progressive system. I parried, suggesting that it was probably a combination of the three. Satisfied that he had brought the conundrum to my attention, he slipped away.

Moqbel ran these sessions by dint of personality. Where some taught by example, inviting responses from the attendees, he drove the subjects down their throats. In that respect he differed from Farouk, our other training superstar. Physically, the men were as different as two men could be. Farouk was not much over five feet tall. He was also overweight and nearly as wide as he was high. When he and the similarly-shaped general manager of costing in Telecom Egypt met, tenderly exchanging kisses, it was like the collision of two billiard balls on a green baize table. He also had a heart condition that wouldn't allow him to walk up a flight of stairs without serious discomfort.

But arrived at the venue Farouk was a consummate teacher. He was a former professor of accounting at the Sadat Academy of Management Science and, in spite of the lack of a PhD, he soon became "Dr. Farouk" in Telecom Egypt. It was in recognition of his knowledge and, more importantly, his ability to communicate that knowledge to his public-sector client. Farouk had not been a professor for nothing and he was an excellent trainer. He was not really a lecturer, although when on a subject that he himself had developed, he could be long-winded. But he was a natural teacher, a gift given to few enough in any culture, and he brought his students along *with* him, regularly involving the class in his lectures. In that process, Arabic was an ally: in the right hands, or the right tongue, the rhythms and syntax of the language lent themselves to very effective pedagogy and Farouk was a master pedagogue in the best sense of the word. He regularly sprinkled familiar sayings, pious nostrums, and questions in his lectures to ensure that the students were with him every step of the way.

He later had open-heart surgery and was on the shelf for several months. When he came back for a visit he had walked the five kilometers to the office from the east bank of the Nile. Before the operation, he could hardly take a step without pain. Walking was now part of his daily regimen. He seemed frail, having lost twenty pounds and an angry red scar disappeared around the second button of his shirt. But he could now comfortably walk up stairs and would soon be back in full-throated control of a classroom.

Moqbel was different. He said he had to be tough with the students, and he was probably right. All Egyptians have opinions and, in the right setting, they are only too ready to express them. This was that kind of setting, with an all-Egyptian group, the discussion conducted in Arabic, and dealing with a contentious issue: the inability of the commercial units to provide timely information to the headquarters finance department. So Moqbel had to use all the arts of his trade—rhetorical flourishes, sarcasm, and occasional humor—to get his points across. As a last resort, he simply shouted them down. But his greatest art was that he had done his homework. He knew what he was talking about and he ran the class like a martinet. But it was *his* way, and it worked. He was always thoroughly prepared and I learned a few lessons from him about organization.

I frequently had to caution him about the hours he put in, and told him that we would not allow him to work himself to exhaustion. He had a family—a wife and two teen-aged sons—and he owed them a part of his time. When I first met his wife and mentioned in passing that we were very happy with Moqbel, she had replied "so am I." It was a nice thing to have said. His only shortcoming was that he sometimes seemed happier identifying a problem than finding a solution, and it became a kind of standing joke between us: *ma feesh mashakil. Fi forus al-amal bass.* There are no problems, only opportunities.

He enjoyed the same respect and affection in Telecom Egypt as Farouk. The "*ya ikhwan*"—or "oh brothers"—with which he addressed the students truly expressed the relationship. He was one of the family. He also had the right stuff, but for another reason: his father had been the central department chief for Alexandria in the old company. Those were the days when there was only one telex machine in the city and when Nasser came to town his father kept it at home just to be in touch. Moqbel grew up helping with the paperwork of ARETO, the precursor to ARENTO, which was the predecessor to Telecom Egypt. His value in the Arab world was soon known and PALTEL offered him triple his salary, but he stayed in Egypt. He knew the chain of command and always reported these offers to me, of which there were many. He wanted my advice. Selfishly, I didn't want to lose him. But with a company the size of Telecom Egypt he would probably be better off in the long run remaining at home.

For all of his toughness, however, he was constitutionally frail. He was a big man, about six-feet three and must have weighed close to 250 pounds but these daily sessions took a toll on him. He would stand the whole time, giving as good as he got. The exchanges often became heated and when the general manager called from Cairo to check on the progress of the seminar, Moqbel held up his mobile phone so that she could hear the din. That was another characteristic of Egypt, although a recent one. Most attendees were carrying mobile phones. They rang throughout the seminar and the ring tones—a tune by Scott Joplin, a ditty from the notebook of Anna Magdalena Bach, even Jingle Bells—filled the classroom. It was useless telling people to turn them off. At an earlier conference in Cairo during an address by Vinton Cerf, one of the fathers of the Internet, the moderator tried to be tough with the abusers of mobile phones, saying that he would throw them out. But still the phones rang.

For Moqbel, there was never a question of stopping until the last question had been answered or the last objection entertained. But at the end of the day he was limping, either because of soreness in his leg or maybe something more serious. He said he had an intestinal problem and would occasionally bring me pictures of polyps taken by sigmoidoscope. Finally, when he had wrung the last objection out of the last civil servant, he thanked them all and we adjourned to the restaurant at the Basma Hotel for the closing banquet. It was a buffet and the thirty-five grew to forty-five with the drivers and tea boys. That was the Egyptian way. They descended like locusts on the food, and soon were carrying away plates groaning with salads, bread, meat, chicken, fish, rice, potatoes, pasta, and vegetables. Then there was dessert. The hotel manager had to call a halt in mid-meal because they had exhausted the spread. If buffet were an Olympic event Egypt would win the gold medal, hands down.

Afterwards, there were several hours before the flight to Cairo and Moqbel and I rested in his hotel room, he praying and I reading, alternately discussing Egyptian history and the present state of affairs in the country. He was aptly named—Moqbel meant "coming" or "next"—and he really was the future of Egypt, computer literate in all the Microsoft applications in Arabic, familiar with the challenges of privatization, an expert in international accounting standards, a bridge between the old and the new. He was also fortunate to travel with. The last time the flight from Upper Egypt had been delayed for several hours. Moqbel said it never happened to him, and so it was this time. Egypt Air was on schedule—leaving Aswan and arriving in Cairo after a stop in Luxor. Saber was waiting for us and by the time we had delivered Moqbel with his bag of gifts—*karkaday*, Aswan peanuts, and *dum* fruit—and dropped me in Zamalek, it was well after midnight. I had first seen Saber that morning at five thirty for the flight to Aswan so it had been a long day for him as well. But the seminar was one of the things we did that seemed to be worthwhile. Most of the credit belonged to Moqbel.

17

Lake Nasser

We were sitting in the restaurant as the *Kasr Ibrim* made its deliberate way south, as deliberately as *muhami* Ramadan chose his words and the bits of breakfast on his plate. In the background the sound system played the stately little *sicilienne* from the incidental music to *Pelleas and Melisande* by Fauré. The Lake Nasser cruise was the counterpoint to the Nile cruises, as leisurely and unhurried as the others were frenetic. The Nile cruises made their way between Luxor and Aswan, through the green of the cultivated strip on either side of the river. There was almost too much to see: Philae, and Kom Ombo, Edfu, Esna, and finally the extravagance of Luxor, Karnak, and the monuments and tombs on the west bank. Here, the *Kasr Ibrim* would steam through Egyptian Nubia to Abu Simbel. The cultivated strip was gone, swallowed up in the largest man-made lake in the world. There was almost nothing left to see but sand and water.

That allowed plenty of time for leisure and talk, and *muhami* Ramadan filled it with tales of revolutionary Egypt:

> I was the lawyer for Mohammed Neguib and many of his *collegios*. Heykal said that Neguib took $3 million from America to, you know, turn the revolution.

He spoke expansively with his hands and made a kind of turning gesture with his open palm. Both his English and Arabic—he used the two interchangeably—were delivered in a careful, measured monotone. I was talking with Abdel Halim Ramadan, *muhami*, or lawyer, to the great and advocate of lost causes in Egypt. Mohammed Neguib had been the titular head of the young officers after the revolution. In fact, he was the regent for Prince Ahmed Fu'ad before the republic was proclaimed in 1954 and Nasser became president. Heykal was Mohammed Hassanein Heykal, the journalist and author. Abdel Halim Ramadan continued:

> But Neguib didn't take the $3 million. It was Nasser who took the $3 million. You can read it all in a book called *The Game of Nations* by Miles Copeland. What I tell you has all been written. I will not tell you what was said between me and my clients. But this has all been written. The Americans had $3 million and they wanted to give it as a gift, but the American ambassador refused.
>
> Do you want me to be like the Turkish ambassador? he said. When the Egyptian national anthem was played and Nasser entered the Opera House the Turkish ambassador refused to stand. The next day he was sent away.
>
> So, you know, the CIA gave the money to Miles Copeland and he gave the money to Hassan Izzat who was a friend of Nasser.

He paused and smiled a weary smile that said he had seen it all. It was bemused and benignant and long-suffering. He was dressed in the gray suit that served as a uniform, although he would sometimes remove the coat during the heat of the day. He was short and bald, without a trace even of eyebrows. His complexion was sallow. He was seventy-four, he said, and had taken the cruise to recharge his batteries and write his memoirs. He went on:

> But it was not the whole $3 million. Because Miles Copeland had a party the day before and he didn't have change, you know, to pay for the sweets from Groppi. So he paid $10 to the man from Groppi. And so, it was $3 million minus $10.

He paused again, while the triviality of the $10 to Groppi registered. Then he continued:

> I brought a case against Heykal in the High Criminal Court of Giza. Then they said that the case should be dropped. I said NO. And I called Mohammed Neguib on the telephone and told him it would be better if he came with me to the High Criminal Court the next day and in his own words refuse to drop the case.

He turned to his breakfast. He had mixed the contents of the buffet together on the same plate: coco bits, rice crispies, yogurt, minced fruit, sausage. Then he continued.

> So, you know, Neguib said to me 'Come to my villa tomorrow at nine o'clock and we will have breakfast and then go to the High Criminal Court of Giza.' So after breakfast we went and all the court came out to greet him and, with his own hand, Mohammed Neguib signed the document.

He paused again and smiled that long-suffering smile.

> I have been a terrorist all my life, with my pen. When I returned to Egypt on September 13, 1981, I had 1,536 clients to defend, including Baba Shenouda. I also defended Khaled Islambouli.

The days of the cruise passed slowly and, unlike the Nile cruises, we were on our own most of the time. But in the four days and 200 miles from the High Dam to Abu Simbel, there were still a few monuments to be seen, rescued by UNESCO. In *A Thousand Miles up the Nile*, published in 1877, Amelia Edwards had described fourteen temples as well as grottoes, tombs, and other ruins, that lay between Philae and Abu Simbel. She had seen them all and was instrumental in supporting early efforts in Egyptology and archaeology. But it almost seemed that if you blinked you would miss them in those 200 miles.

The horizon was bounded by low sand hills, occasionally formed into perfect natural pyramids. It was easy to see why the pyramid shape was adopted by the ancient Egyptians for their tombs. It was also clear why they chose the sun as their chief god. Further north it was the moon, with its brilliance and changeability, that seemed the most noticeable celestial phenomenon. Here, it was the sun. The sun was a tyrant, dominating the day from its rising to the setting. It was only the 26th of March when we boarded the *Kasr Ibrim*, but it was already well over a hundred degrees Fahrenheit in Aswan.

The brochure describing the cruise had been hard to resist. We were interested in relaxing and it suggested we would do little else: So we had flown Egypt Air to Aswan with a stop in Luxor. Aswan was a relief after the bustle of Luxor. There, the massacre was still in peoples' minds, although the tourists were beginning to come back. The inhabitants of Luxor were confirmed rogues and scoundrels, corrupted by years of preying on foreigners. Here in Aswan they seemed less predatory. After arrival we collected our bags and agreed on twenty pounds, or about six dollars, for a taxi to the hotel, twelve miles away. Even the opening gambit of thirty pounds seemed fair. The cab was a Peugeot 504 station wagon, the village taxi of Upper Egypt. After ten miles we bumped over the cobblestones of the causeway on the old dam to the east bank of the river. To the right lay the island of Agilkia and the reconstructed temples of Philae, "the pearl of Egypt." To the left was what remained of the First Cataract.

The cataracts were outcroppings of Precambrian volcanic basement material, and there were six of them between Aswan and Khartoum. They were rocky and convoluted and made navigation impossible except at high water. But here only a small remnant remained above the water. The river broadened out between Aswan and the second cataract, just north of the Sudanese border at Wadi Halfa. It would be uninterrupted smooth sailing for the *Kasr Ibrim*.

The old dam had been built in 1902 and raised twice afterwards, the last time in 1934. The earlier work was dwarfed by the High Dam. But it had features that the new structure lacked, including spillways to allow the silt to pass through to the river on the other side. That was a major problem with the new dam, not only because of the buildup of silt beneath the lake but also because the 3 percent of Egypt that was cultivated was now deprived of the richness of the black earth of Ethiopia. Over 90 percent of the river's flow in Egypt came from the Blue Nile and Ethiopia.

Most of the water in the White Nile, coming from the lakes of central Africa, was lost in the *sudd* or great swamp of southern Sudan. Artificial fertilizers were now necessary to make up for the loss of the silt. There had been other harmful ecological effects of the dam, including the general rise in the water table and leaching of salts to the surface, the death of the sardine industry at the mouth of the Delta, and coastal erosion as the deposits disappeared. The old dam also had locks that allowed boats to pass, and there was an abandoned mule parked at the western end of the causeway.

The little town of Aswan seemed quiet and sleepy. The driver, Ahmed, pointed out the telephone exchange after I told him I was a consultant to *Shirkat Masriya lil Itissalat*, or Telecom Egypt. We had reservations at the Oberoi and we waited at the quay while the Pharaonic-prowed ferry slipped across from Elephantine Island. Inside the hotel the decor was a copy of the Mena House Oberoi at Giza. After lunch we began our serious relaxation.

In the evening we paid a visit to the new Nubian museum. It was supposed to be very good and it was, well laid-out with exhibits labeled in English and Arabic. The English texts were understandable, clearly written by a native English-speaker. The only problem was that the exhibits didn't seem to follow any chronological order and after a while I gave up trying to understand the relationship between the prehistoric era, the A-Group, the C-Group (there was no B-Group), the Kerma culture, the Napatan period, the Meroitic period, and the Ballana culture. There were a few Pharaonic exhibits. But this museum was more about anthropology than Egyptology, fuller of palettes, flint knives, and red pottery than hieroglyphs. Afterwards, the man in a horse-drawn *tonga* demanded thirty pounds for the five-minute ride back to the hotel. So, maybe the cabbies in Aswan were just as rascally as those in Luxor after all.

The next day, we were to board the ship sometime in the morning. We didn't know where or at what time. The general manager of the Oberoi called the travel agent but the office was closed on a Friday. However he learned that the *Kasr Ibrim* was berthed at the port area on the west side of Lake Nasser. So, at nine o'clock the ferry took us back across to the quay where Ahmed was waiting. The journey was the reverse of the previous afternoon: over the cobblestones of the old dam, past Philae and the First Cataract, before turning south towards the causeway of the High Dam. There we encountered the first unpleasantness of the day: the guard at the entrance insisted we pay the tourist fee to see the dam. Ahmed argued that we were only going to the boat on the other side. But the man in the booth simply turned his back and said nothing. He was sloppily dressed, not in uniform and needed a shave. Words wouldn't move him. If we wanted to go on we would have to pay the twenty pounds. So we did and entered the dual carriageway at the top of the High Dam. This was not like the old dam: it was the difference between driving on a country lane and a turnpike.

At the end of the causeway, and the entrance to the dock area, there was another booth with several guards and a young lieutenant in black uniform. And another bit of unpleasantness. The lieutenant said we could go no further, even though we saw another taxi 150 yards away, unloading at the end of what appeared to be a large shed. It was, in fact, the customs warehouse for traffic coming from the Sudan and ran the length of the pier. The *Kasr Ibrim* was nowhere to be seen, although we assumed it was on the other side of the shed. Ahmed had no luck with the lieutenant so I asked what the problem was. The answer was that we could go no further.

I said there was another taxi that had just done what we wanted to do, but this had no effect. So I asked the lieutenant if this was the way Egypt treated tourists, the key to its most important industry. We had come from abroad and had encountered nothing but problems with people of his kind. We had tickets to the boat but would have to walk the last 150 yards with our heavy bags. Was that the impression he wanted to leave? But he only smirked and repeated that the taxi could go no further.

Meanwhile, the other taxi had completed unloading and arrived at the booth. So we paid Ahmed, transferred the bags to the second Peugeot 504, and rode grandly to the end of the pier. We still couldn't see the ship but the new driver, Eissam, said it was behind the building at the river below. He took the two large bags and set off. As we rounded the end of the shed, the *Kasr Ibrim* came into view. From a distance, lying against the bank of the river, it looked like a Mississippi paddle steamer. There were four decks. The mooring lines played out to the shore and the umbilicus carrying power and telephone lines lay connected at the stern. At the top of the quay we paid Eissam and were delivered into the hands of the maritime crew. Then we descended the slope, crossed a rickety gangway and were aboard. Our adventure had begun.

The ship was about the size of a destroyer, three hundred feet long by maybe fifty feet wide. The staterooms were small but nicely appointed, and the cabinets were all wood or wood veneer. But it was in the little bath that the neatness and compactness of the nautical tradition was displayed: the fixtures were sparkling and substantial stainless steel, without a piece of plastic in sight. The tile was black-and-white checked and spotless. There were even washcloths, unusual in Egyptian hotel bathrooms.

Indirectly, the reason for our cruise lay in the exploding population of Egypt. In 1882, at the time of 'Arabi's revolt, there had been only about six million Egyptians. After the coming of the powers the population had grown rapidly. Whatever could be said about British highhandedness, their stewardship had been broadly beneficial. Egyptians didn't like to admit it, but the British had regulated the finances, improved irrigation, introduced a little education, and checked the most egregious excesses of the Macedonian khedives. The European bondholders may have been behind the intervention and Evelyn Baring, Lord Cromer, may have been insufferable. But the result had been general economic well-being and a population explosion.

In 1902 with the building of the first dam, the population had already grown to some nine million. In 1937 it was almost sixteen million. By 1956, it had grown to nearly twenty-five million and something clearly had to be done. Egypt had always exported food, but was now in danger of becoming a net importer. The cultivated area had increased with each of several improvements to the dam, but an upper limit had been reached. The old dam was unable to store water from one year to the next and 30 billion cubic meters were lost every year, flowing unused into the Mediterranean. There was also the need for electric power to create jobs for the *shebab*, the youth who were entering the labor market in increasing numbers every year.

The young officers of the revolution approached the problem in a straightforward military way. With the exception of displacing a few Nubians this wasn't social engineering, although other regimes in the continent of Africa weren't above that, with often-genocidal results. It was just hydrology and a new, higher dam was needed. In the heady days after the revolution, anything seemed possible. So when America backed out over Eastern-bloc arms and the Baghdad Pact, the Soviets stepped in. Over the eight years from 1960 to the inauguration of the dam in 1968, there had been a massive construction project in Egypt. It was one of the reasons why there had been 20,000 Russians in Egypt when Sadat threw them out in July of 1972. There had been more Russians in Egypt in 1972 than Americans in 1999. Individually they were just as big and pink as we were, but they didn't have any money.

The numbers describing the High Dam were impressive: 360 meters long, 980 meters broad at the base and forty meters high at the crown. It was earth-fill, with the total volume of the fill calculated at seventeen times that of the pyramid of Cheops at Giza. The level of the water was raised by sixty-three meters to 180 meters above sea level and the lake behind the dam was capable of storing 157 billion cubic meters. After allowance for evaporation, silting and a safety margin, that left eighty billion cubic meters to be divided between Egypt and the Sudan. Most importantly, it allowed water to be stored from one year to the next. And the turbines doubled the amount of electricity available in 1970.

But there were other results, not all of them positive. Massive dam projects in the developing world were now being reexamined because of adverse ecological effects. Here, greater salinity of the soil, an increase in the incidence of Bilharzia, and the loss of the natural fertilizing effects of the silt were all anticipated and steps were belatedly underway in Egypt to address them. Drainage projects now attempted to deal with the rising water table and the fertilizer residues. After an initial rise in rates of infection from Bilharzia—the schistosomes bore into human skin through the medium of standing water—the scourge was now diminishing. The infection leads to the swelling of abdominal organs, and the unnatural shape of the bellies of some *fellaheen* may be attributed to the disease. But you didn't have to be a *fellah* to be infected. Abdel Halim Hafez, one of the most beloved of Egyptian balladeers, died of Bilharzia in 1978.

But the most immediate impact would be the threat to the monuments, temples, and archaeological records of Nubia. The High Dam would create the lake later named after Colonel Nasser and it would extend 300 miles into Sudanese Nubia. The cultivated strip—most of it laid down in recent geological time—would disappear and with it an entire Nubian culture based on communal ownership of date palms and water wheels. The living, it was thought, could be accommodated further north, and many Nubians were resettled near Kom Ombo. But the dead would disappear forever. Beginning with the publication of a report by the Egyptian Antiquities Organization in June of 1955 the monuments became the object of a massive international rescue campaign. The report called attention to the threat of the lake and was widely distributed internationally. This initial appeal brought only a limited response.

However, also in 1955, UNESCO assisted in the creation of the Documentation and Study Center for the History of the Art and Civilization of Ancient Egypt, located in Cairo. The work of the center over the next several years included the contributions of Egyptian and foreign scholars, architects, and Egyptologists. It was an important precursor to the international effort that followed. At its general conference in Montevideo in 1954, UNESCO had already decided that the threat of the High Dam called for a response. But it wasn't until 1958, and the appointment of Saroite Okacha as Minister of Culture and National Guidance, that the program really took off. Okacha was an Egyptian but the name, having passed through the twin filters of colloquial Arabic and French, looked almost Japanese, something like Sadako Ogata, head of UNHCR. An English transliteration would be something like *Tharwat 'Akasha*, Tharwat being a fairly common Egyptian name. But since the Egyptians didn't normally pronounce the "th," it became an "s" and, hence, Sarwat. The French had spelled it "Saroite." *'Akasha* meant spider in Arabic.

Okacha had struck up a relationship with James Rorimer, Director of the Metropolitan Museum of Art in New York and with Mme. Desroches-Noblecourt of the Louvre. This ultimately bore fruit. Through them Okacha contacted René Maheu, Assistant Director-General of UNESCO and, at a stopover in the Cairo airport in January, 1959 the deal was struck: UNESCO would help to save the Nubian monuments. The Executive Board ratified the decision later in the month and the international rescue campaign was launched. The story is told in *Temples and Tombs of ANCIENT NUBIA, The International Rescue Campaign at Abu Simbel, Philae and Other Sites*. By the time it was completed in 1980, Argentina, Austria, Belgium, Canada, Czechoslovakia, Finland, France, West Germany, the GDR, Ghana, Hungary, India, Italy, the Netherlands, Poland, Denmark, Norway, Sweden, Spain, Switzerland, the UK, the United States, the USSR, and Yugoslavia would all assist Egypt in the excavation and preservation effort.

The most dramatic efforts were the moving of the temples of Abu Simbel and Philae to higher ground, although Philae was threatened not by the new but by the old dam. But there were countless other, less visible efforts, including the excavation and recording of sites that could not be moved and would be inundated by the lake. Much of the campaign was a race against time and the rising waters. Work on the High Dam was inaugurated in January of 1960 and the dismantling and transfer of temples began almost immediately thereafter. From the summer of 1960 through 1965, the temples of Debod and Taffa, the kiosk of Qertassi, the temples at Kalabsha, Beit el-Wali and Wadi es-Sebua, the tomb of Penout, the temples of Dendur, Dakka, Maharraqa, Aksha, Buhen, Suhen and, finally, Abu Simbel all received attention. The movement of the temples of Philae to the island of Agilkia was begun in 1962, the same year that excavations were completed in Sudanese Nubia. The evacuation of the Nubian population began in the spring of 1964. By 1965 the work in Egyptian Nubia was complete. The stage was set.

The first day of the cruise would be lunch, followed by a visit to the temple of Kalabsha, the hemi-speos of Beit el-Wali, and the kiosk of Kertassi. So, at one o'clock we went down to the restaurant and found we had assigned seats. At our table were a Canadian couple, an English lady, and *muhami* Ramadan. The Canadians were teachers at an international school in Cairo and it was their first assignment abroad. They were emphatically *not* Americans. The lady was a Yorkshirewoman and inveterate traveler who had begun her peregrinations as a child, cycling over the moors with her parents. It seemed that she hadn't stopped in sixty years, and there was hardly a place in Europe or Asia that she hadn't seen. She traveled alone, her husband not yet having exhausted the delights of the British Isles. Dr. Ramadan was, as usual, expansive:

> Edward VII was a man of honor. There was, you know Mrs. Simpson. He could have had Mrs. Simpson and kept the crown. But he preferred to take Mrs. Simpson and give up the crown. He was a man of honor. There is no honor left today. Every year I traveled for three months: to America, you know, to Chicago and New York. Then to London and Munich and Milano.

In the afternoon we gathered, the English and French speakers in separate groups, and embarked in the motor-launches for the fifteen-minute ride to the first of the temples.

What we now understand about the Nubian monuments is relatively recent knowledge. When Richard Lepsius and the Prussian expedition to Egypt and Nubia set out from Philae in November of 1843, many of these temples were being seen for the first time through the eyes of an "Egyptologist." Lepsius was the embodiment of the term. Champollion's grammar had advanced the study of the language of the ancient Egyptians, but Lepsius was the man who put the first tentative principles of Champollion into practice, correcting, correlating, and expanding the knowledge of the hieroglyphs. His brief description of the temples in *Egypt, Ethiopia and the Peninsula of Sinai* reads like just another dry recitation of remote facts—Pharaohs, gods, and texts—until you realize that he was identifying them, by name, provenance, and purpose, for the first time. The work of Lepsius was an extraordinary exercise in practical scholarship. The twelve immense volumes of the Prussian expedition, published in 1858 as the *Denkmäler aus Aegyptien und Aethiopien*, are probably the greatest work of Egyptology ever produced.

Lepsius confirmed Champollion's opinion that most of the temples of Nubia were Ptolemaic and Roman restorations of earlier buildings, most built by pharaohs of 18th and 19th dynasties (1550–1196 BC). Kalabsha was

Greco-Roman, having been built by Augustus Caesar in thirty AD on the ruins of earlier Ptolemaic structures. It was dedicated to Mandoulis, a local Nubian god. Next to Philae, it was the largest complex in Egyptian Nubia. It had originally been located thirty miles south of Aswan on the west bank of the river and had been under water for most of the year after the building of the first dam. Not everything that was threatened by the High Dam had been intact, and the rescue operation would atone for earlier sins as well.

Kalabsha had once been famous for the vivid colors on its walls, but they had disappeared, washed away in over sixty years of inundations. In 1960 the German Federal Republic offered to defray the costs of dismantling the temple and re-erecting it on a new site. The offer was accepted and over the two years 1962–63, more than sixteen-thousand stones were carefully disassembled, catalogued, and transported to the new site at Khor Ingi where they were reassembled. The firm of Hochtief AG—later the contractor for the airport of Jidda where its compound became a kind of Sodom and Gomorrah in the peninsula—was selected for the work. In the course of dismantling the temple, a Ptolemaic gate was discovered and was later presented as a gift to the Federal Republic. It was now in the Berlin Museum.

We listened as the English-speaking guide walked us through the forecourt, hypostyle halls, and inner sanctuaries. It was difficult to understand the purpose of these structures. They were religious buildings, but what were the beliefs of their congregations? And who were the congregations? The graffiti on the walls answered some of the questions and leant these imposing edifices a human touch. Most of the prayers and names scribbled on the walls appeared to come from the nearby Roman garrison town of Talmis. Nubia had always been a kind of disputed land, an avenue into Egypt for the products and people of Africa, as well as a buffer against their depredations. Who, among the garrison, banished to this remotest corner of the empire, did not pine away for the forests of his native Gaul or Spain or Bosnia? How strong was their belief in this Nubian god, Mandoulis? Or were they simply lapsed or fallen-away pagans?

A later group were not lapsed, and they were the Coptic Christians who turned the temple into a church in the sixth century. Christianity came late to Nubia and it was not until 537 that the Emperor Justinian closed the last pagan temple at Philae. The final triumph of Islam was also delayed in this out-of-the-way province. The Arab armies of Amr ibn el-'As conquered Egypt in 640 and the Islamization of the north proceeded apace. But Nubia proved a tougher nut to crack and, following an agreement with the Arabs, the area entered a kind of golden age. Christian Nubia became a great power in its own right and at one point in the tenth century controlled Upper Egypt as far as Akhmim, 265 miles north of Aswan. With power came trade and prosperity and Nubia controlled the traffic in ivory, ebony, and slaves. The decline began in the twelfth century when the Nubians mistakenly backed the reigning Fatimids in Egypt against the Ayyubids of Salah ed-Din.

The Fatimids lost and Salah ed-Din's brother, Turan Shah, marched south as far as Qasr Ibrim, 200 miles south of Aswan. After that, Nubia settled into a kind of peace with the Kurds in the north. But increasing pressure from Muslim tribes in the western desert, as well as incursions by the Mamluks, the Circassian military caste in Egypt, spelled the beginning of the end. By the time Selim the Grim invaded the northern Sudan in 1517, Nubia was primarily Muslim. There followed a long period of eclipse before it reentered history in the nineteenth century with Gordon, the Mahdi, and Kitchener.

The architecture of these Roman temples was Egyptian in the same way that institutional architecture in Europe and America was Roman nearly two millennia after the fall of Rome. The halls and sanctuaries retained the old simplicity, but the capitals of the columns became more ornate. Here at Kalabsha alternating clusters of dates and grapes, papyrus, and lotus flowers replaced the simple fronds of the originals. It was the same with the sacred language. From the relatively simple catalogue of phonograms and ideograms, the number of hieroglyphic characters saw a dramatic increase as the language wrestled with the increasing complexity of Egyptian life, first as a Greek dependency and then as a province of Rome. The apotheosis of the syncretic style was probably the temple of Dendera, near Qena, where the monumental gateway of Domitian and Trajan leads to the most elaborately decorated complex of its kind in Egypt.

Christianity, however, broke the stylistic and theological spell. With the triumph of the new dispensation in lower Nubia Kalabsha became a church. Coptic graffiti on the pylon celebrated the fact, although later additions had been cleared away early in the twentieth century. But it was in the little hemi-speos of Beit el-Wali behind the temple that Christianity asserted itself more bluntly. Originally a temple of Amon-Re and built by Ramesses II, the panels on the sides of the entrance hall showed prisoners—thick-lipped Africans and bearded northerners—taken in military campaigns, as well as scenes of tribute being offered by subject peoples. But the Arabic name—Beit el-Wali, or "House of the Holy Man"—referred to its later use as a church. Remnants of the arches of the little basilica-shaped church stood out clearly against the sides and back wall. They would probably have been barrel-vaulted and surmounted by domes. Finally, we saw the freestanding Greco-Roman kiosk of Qertassi. It originally lay twenty-seven miles south of Aswan, but was transferred to the vicinity of the High Dam by the Egyptian Antiquities Organization in 1960.

After wandering over the site where we saw prehistoric petroglyphs of animals scratched in the stone, we were transported back to the Kasr Ibrim by the same motor-launches that had brought us. There, said the program, we would enjoy "dinner and overnight aboard."

The schedule called for the ship to be underway the next morning at seven AM. By six o'clock preparations were well advanced for the departure. On a destroyer the evolution would involve mainly the firemen, radar operators, and deck hands, maybe half the ship's company. Here, the tasks were compressed. First, the motor launches were winched up to their berths on the stern. The engines would already have been brought on stream and power to the shore terminated. The captain, or *rai's*, handled most tasks on the bridge and a few seamen—or were they lakemen?—in blue sailors' suits tended the lines. It all took place silently and the hundred or-so guests would awaken in the morning to find the vessel underway.

The *Kasr Ibrim* was moored horizontally to the rock jetty. Using the engines to maneuver, the *rai's* swung the stern around so that it lay perpendicular to the shore before the last line was cast off at seven ten. Then, using the engines and the rudder, he turned the ship into the channel. Slowly, as the vessel gathered speed, the wake was churned into froth and the first channel buoy slipped by. Our journey to the south had begun. The second day would be a long day of steaming and dreaming before we arrived at Wadi el-Seboua that night.

The ship was topside-weight critical, not designed to operate in heavy weather. I thought of the stories of overloaded ferries on the great lakes of Africa that had capsized in sudden squalls, with the loss of all aboard. But there were probably no squalls to interrupt the succession of rainless days on Lake Nasser. Here, the average rainfall was less than two inches a year. With its shallow draught the *Kasr Ibrim* would nose up to the shore and rest while we climbed like ants over the occasional monument. There were four decks above the main deck, the first two consisting of staterooms and the upper two of an outdoor restaurant and sun deck. The main restaurant was below-decks where the waterline lay halfway up the glass of the portholes.

The ship was built to operate on the river, like the gunboats that had helped to defeat the Dervishes in 1898. They had been manufactured in London, disassembled, and shipped in pieces to Alexandria. From there, the were sent by riverboat and rail to railhead at Koseh, fifty miles south of Wadi Halfa and the Sudanese border. There they were reassembled:

> The earliest freight which the railway carried to Koseh was the first of the new stern-wheel gunboats. Train after train arrived

with its load of steel or iron, or with the cumbrous sections of the hull, and a warship in pieces . . . An improvised dockyard . . . was established, and the work—complicated as a Chinese puzzle—proceeded swiftly. . . . Their decks were protected by steel plates . . . Their armament was formidable . . . Every modern improvement was added . . . Yet with all this they drew only thirty-nine inches of water.

Churchill told the story. He was attached to the cavalry, the 21st Lancers, but he called it "The River War" and it had been primarily that. The *Kasr Ibrim* already seemed lost in the fastness of the sand and water. But we had flown from Cairo to Aswan in an hour and a-half. It took the Egyptian army much longer. Beginning in 1896, the army had floated or crawled on its belly for 1,500 miles from Cairo to Omdurman over a period of two and a-half years, from March of that year to September, 1898.

Here, the bridge was on the third deck, forward of the swimming pool and I visited the *ra'is* on the first day out of Aswan. The engine-order telegraph and wheel were small devices on a console and the captain sat in a comfortable chair, manipulating the two. In fact, there was little to manipulate when we were underway. The lake was six miles wide at its narrowest and we stayed in the middle of the channel. The course appeared to be at first due south, before we turned to southwest by south later in the day. Our speed was about fifteen knots. There was a Raytheon radar antenna on the mast, but it didn't appear to be used. The *ra'is* seemed to be sailing by the seat of his *gallabiya*. He was a *sa'idi* from Esna and, like most *sa'idis*, he spent the long days sipping tea and chatting with his cronies.

Our progress was regular and the pace placid, a contrast to the previous tumult in this part of the river. In his *Contributions to the Geography of Egypt*, John Ball separated the Nile valley into five regions from south to north: the Lake Plateau Region, the Sudd Region, the Central Sudan Region, the Cataract Region, and the Egyptian Region. We were now in the Cataract Region. It extended from the Sixth Cataract just north of Khartoum to Aswan, a distance of 1,145 miles along the river, but only about 600 miles as the crow flies. It was a region of hilly desert, interrupted along its course by outcrops of the hard, crystalline rocks that formed the cataracts. Before the High Dam, it differed from the other regions to the north and south. In the others, the Nile bed was rising due to the deposition of silt. Here, the action of the seventy-six billion tons of silt-laden water that tumbled through the cataracts in an average year acted, by erosion, to lower the bed of the river.

At a fall of 1 in 6,440, the slope was steeper than that of the other regions, and this contributed to the scouring action. Ball estimated that the bed of the river in this region had fallen by twenty-six feet over the past 3,800 years. But the High Dam had changed the dynamics of the river, at least in the northern reaches. The scouring still took place to the south, and the Second Cataract was still intact. But from the Sudanese border to Aswan the High Dam now ensured that the action was one of deposition. The thin layer of Nile mud that had allowed the Nubians to husband their palms and vegetables was gone, and the suspended silt was now gathering beneath us as we made our way south. It was estimated that in a century the volume of silt will amount to 5 percent of the lake's volume. In 500 years it will have displaced just over one-fifth of the total capacity of the reservoir.

At lunchtime we crossed the Tropic of Cancer, twenty-three degrees fifty minutes north latitude, and were rewarded with a certificate signed by "The Management." On this day, the 28th of March, the sun would have just crossed the Equator in its apparent course between the tropics, so it was still low in the sky. But it was already hot, well over a hundred degrees at noon. There was no ceremony to interrupt the buffet. In fact, there was little to interrupt our leisure on this cruise, none of the dress-up nights or pantomimes of the Nile cruises. It was uninterrupted sun and sand, punctuated only by an occasional flock of egrets, their white plumage flashing low over the water in the distance.

At the table, Dr. Ramadan was pensive. Then, without apparent transition, he asked: "

> Where do you live?"
>
> We live at 31 Ahmed Heshmat Street in Zamalek."
>
> Ah, 31 Ahmed Heshmat Basha Street. That was the villa of Salah Salem.

This was interesting.

> Fi su'al." (I have question)
>
> Ittafaddul." (Please, go ahead)

Salah Salem, after whom the road to the Cairo airport is named, was a member of the Revolutionary Command Council. I had heard that he was a tough guy. I asked about the story of his threat to put God in jail. But muhami Ramadan put it right.

> No, it was not Salah Salem or his brother Gamal Salem. There were eleven, you know, Mohammed Neguib, and Nasser, and Zacharia Mohei Eddin, and Salah Salem and Gamal Salem . . . and Sadat, but he was not important. His brother, Mohammed

> Asmat as-Sadat, was my driver. There is another book, you may read it in Arabic: *Al-Amaliqa wa al-Aqzam as-Sab'a* (The Seven Giants and Midgets). In it you will find forty pages about Abdel Halim Ramadan.
>
> The man you are talking about is Hamza al-Bassiuny. His father was very religious, you know, and all his children were named after relatives of the Prophet. There was a son called al-Abbas al-Bassiuny, after the uncle of the Prophet. And the name of Hamza was actually *al-*Hamza al-Bassiuny, named after another uncle of the Prophet.

He emphasized the definite article.

> His sisters were Fatima, and . . . and . . . and . . . But al-Hamza al-Bassiuny did not care about religion. He was in charge of the military prison. So when they talked about Islam he said: 'Bring your God down here and I will put HIM in jail.'

In the afternoon the ship suddenly changed course and speed. We had arrived in the vicinity of the second series of monuments, those of Wadi el-Seboua. The captain maneuvered the Kasr Ibrim into an alcove on the west bank hardly wider than the ship itself and the sailors clambered over the rocks to find a purchase for the mooring lines. We came to rest at 4:45, although the temples would have to wait for tomorrow. At 6:11 the sun set in a saddle of the hills to the west and the serious photographers lined the top deck for a shot. At the moment of tangency between the orange ball and the horizon it became apparent how the cartouche shape mimicked this confluence of sun and earth. The cartouches became elongated as texts grew and the need for space increased. Dinner that night was in the outside restaurant on the third deck. The moon was nearly full, it being the eleventh of *Zhu el-Higga*, and the moonlight made for a rare scene.

The third day would be busy. First, after breakfast, there would be the Temples of Wadi el-Seboua, Maharraqa, and Dakka. Like many of the Nubian temples, they had been submerged for most of the year, even before the High Dam. So the colors were gone, washed out to the same dun-color of the sandstone in the surrounding hills. The temples ranged from Dakka to Wadi el-Seboua, sixty to a hundred miles south of Aswan. They were all removed to a higher site about two and a-half miles to the west of the original site of el-Seboua. There, an earlier temple had been built by Amenophis III before being enlarged by Ramesses II. A second and larger temple had been built by Ramesses II between the years thirty-five and fifty of his reign, and so from 1255 to 1240 BC. It was this larger temple that had been moved.

The move was financed by the United States, although the work itself was carried out over the years 1962–65 by the Egyptian Antiquities Organization. The entry to the temple was through a line of sphinxes, a reminder of the skill of Egyptian artists in capturing the shape of animals. The conventions of Pharaonic human representation—a combination of profile and frontal view with distortion of members such as the hands and feet—would not have passed Renaissance ideals of anatomy. But the animals, seen here in the haunches of these recumbent man-lions, all self-contained muscle waiting to spring, were nearly perfect. The temple consisted of pylons, courts, and a hypostyle hall. As usual here, it had later been converted into a Coptic church. In the sanctuary, Ramesses II is seen making an offering to—of all people—the Apostle Peter.

The temples of Maharraqa and Dakka were also dismantled and resited near the temple of Wadi el-Seboua by the Egyptian Antiquities Organization. The work took place over the same 1962–65 period. Maharraqa, originally about eighty miles south of Aswan, had marked the northern boundary of the Meroites, an early Sudanese dynasty. An Italian expedition excavated a Meroitic cemetery at the original site and found texts in the still-undeciphered language. Dakka had originally been built by the Meroitic King Ergamenes in the third century BC, before being enlarged by Ptolemy IV in the same century. According to Amelia Edwards, the sculptures were "atrocious," the style "the Ptolemaic out-Ptolemied." Even in the third century BC things weren't like they used to be. They probably never were.

The launches took us back to the Kasr Ibrim by language group. At eleven o'clock we were underway again, now sailing approximately southwest by south, at a compass heading of perhaps 220 degrees. In the early afternoon, having reached Korosko, we came around to a heading of northwest by north to reach the sites of the temples of Amada and el-Derr and the tomb of Penout. They were also on the west bank and we reached them, as usual, by motor launch.

The 18th-dynasty temple of Amada had been raised 180 feet to a new location, a mile and a-half from the original site. The methods used to move these Nubian temples had run the gamut from the painstaking disassembly and reassembly of Kalabsha to the radical surgery of Abu Simbel. Amada provided an unusual challenge: the colors and sculpted decoration were mostly intact and dismantling the structure would have subjected them to flaking and cracking. At least part of it would have to be moved in one piece. So the French at Amada had done it—characteristically—their own way: they bound together the naos, the enclosed portion of the temple, with a combination of horizontal and vertical cables, concrete beams, and jacks, lest the move compromise its structural integrity. Then, they moved it as a unit, on rails, from the old to the new site. The transfer of the "Temple on Rails" was accomplished in three months, from January to March 1965. Re-erection of the pronaos began in July and the work was completed with the faithful reproduction of the incidental surroundings from the original site. The colors survived the transfer.

After Amada we saw the rock-cut hemi-speos of el-Derr, built by Ramesses II in the second half of his reign and dedicated to the rising sun. This was re-sited in 1964 by the Egyptian Antiquities Organization. The colors were also vivid, contrasting sharply with the sandstone of the surroundings. After el-Derr, we walked the 150 yards to the tomb of Penout, the Deputy of Lower Nubia under Ramesses IV. It had also been rock-cut, originally near the town of 'Aniba ten miles to the south and was re-sited by the Egyptians in a grotto here near Amada. The tomb contained an intact judgment scene where the heart of the deceased was weighed against Ma'at, the Egyptian god of order. The hieroglyphs were crude.

On the way back to the launches one of the guards found a scorpion and was tormenting it with a stick. The scorpion was large, maybe four inches long. It curved its back and struck repeatedly at the stick. The guards were unobtrusive, appearing only when the *Kasr Ibrim* tied up and accompanying us on our forays to the sites. They were dressed in civilian clothes but there was no mistaking their purpose. Rather than the omnipresent Kalashnikovs they carried HKs, a stubby German automatic weapon about the size of the Uzi. We had hardly given a thought to our safety in this remote area, but the Egyptian government was taking no chances after Luxor. Supplies for the temple guards were brought by Toyota from Upper Egypt.

In the afternoon, we came around again to southwest by south before passing the site of Qasr Ibrim. We paused only long enough for a view and a lecture on deck from our guide. It had originally been the Roman fortress and town of Primus and an archaeological site of some importance in the later period of Nubia, with Meroitic, Greek, Coptic, Nubian, and Arabic influences. The finds included intact papyrus, parchment, and paper in addition to rock inscriptions. The time frame extended from the Roman occupation, around 22 BC, through 1528 AD, when Suleiman the Magnificent installed a Bosnian regiment in the town. It sat high above the lake, although during this high water the lake lapped at the lower parts of the site. In a photo taken in 1987, the water-level was several hundred-feet lower. The site was still so fragile that tourists were not allowed to land.

The night passed quietly, notable only for a sit-down dinner instead of the usual buffet. We were due to arrive at Abu Simbel about noon the next day. But first there was Toshka, and at midmorning the next day the outlet appeared several miles away to the west. The Toshka project was a latter-day effort by the government to relieve the pressure on the Nile Valley and the need for jobs for the *shebab*. The area above the High Dam had once been fertile and had, in fact, been the granary of Rome. Why not irrigate it with excess water from the lake and make the desert bloom? The infrastructure would attract millions of people away from the overpopulated Nile Valley and kill several birds with one stone. And it would be Mubarak's showpiece, the legacy of this latest pharaoh.

But it had all been tried before, with indifferent results. Land reclamation in Egypt had never worked very well and the shebab were not interested in a few feddans of agricultural land, even if it had. What about the years when there would be no excess water? And nobody wanted to move to Toshka. The joke making its way around Cairo illustrated Mubarak's conundrum. A man had opened a new coffee shop and hung three portraits on the wall. He was asked by a patron who they were:

Who is that on the left?

That is Gamal 'Abdel-Nasser, the hero of the Revolution.

And who is the one in the middle?

That is Anwar al-Sadat, the hero of the October War.

And who is the third one?

That's Hosni Mubarak, the father of Ala' Mubarak, my partner in the shop.

There was nothing left for heroes these days but the dismal science and the market.

At about eleven o'clock several of us gathered at the highest point on the ship, the sundeck under the radar antenna, to watch the arrival at Abu Simbel. As we approached, the outline and then the details of the familiar hill with the colossi appeared ahead and to the west. The scene was among the best-known of the David Roberts prints and the rescue of the monuments was the most famous of the efforts of UNESCO. The temples hadn't even been known to Europe before Burckhardt reported them in 1813. They were opened in 1817 by the former circus strongman, Belzoni. At noon we moored to the bank under the temples, the scene magnificent except for the concrete box the Antiquities Organization was building just above the landing area. Unfinished concrete pillars with reinforcing rod sticking awkwardly into the air spoiled what should have been a grand arrival.

It was hot at noon and our tour of the temples was scheduled for three o'clock. Then, when we went ashore and stood at the feet of the four, sixty-foot statues of Ramesses II we realized just how colossal they were. Our guide described the details of this extraordinary monument to a single man. But his family was there too, with Queen Nofretari, his mother, and Prince Amenhirkhopshef near the first colossus. The Princesses Bent'ana, Nebettawy, and Esenofre were near the second. The Queen and Princess Beketmut and Prince Ri'amsese stood by the third, and Princess Meryatamun, Queen Muttuya, and Princess Nofretari were near the last colossus to the north. The smaller temple was dedicated to the goddess Hathor and Queen Nofretari. Who said this man was only thinking about himself?

The ditty about fools' names and fools' faces came to mind as we took in the immensity of the statues. But the graffiti, objectionable in another context, added a touch of humanity to the scene. It wasn't like Meda'in Saleh, the Nabataean tombs north of Medina, where Saudis had spray painted their names over the monuments. Here, there were records of passersby over the previous 2,700 years. Lepsius had discovered Greek inscriptions left by the mercenaries of Psammeticus I who came here in the seventh century BC. He also found Phoenician inscriptions. And there were later testaments to travelers and soldiers, including "Hall R. E. 1897." He was with Kitchener's expedition, probably an engineer attached to the railway staff. The expedition had reached the vicinity of Abu Simbel in April of 1896, but there were another 600 miles and seventeen months to go before they reached Omdurman. And high up on the wall, above the right shoulder of the most southerly colossus, appeared the name "LESSEPS." It was certainly Ferdinand Marie de Lesseps, the French diplomat and builder of the Suez Canal.

The interior of the temples was the usual catalogue of reliefs of the king, gods, and goddesses, offerings, and scenes of victory, especially that of Ramesses II over a Hittite army at Qadesh on the Orontes. They were ranged in the great hall, a second pillared hall, followed by a vestibule and finally a sanctuary, the holy of holies. There, four statues were cut from the rock: Amun of Thebes, Ramesses as a god, and the gods of the two other cult centers in Egypt, Ra-Harakhte of Heliopolis and Ptah-Tatenen of Memphis. Twice a year, on February 21 and October 21, the sun would penetrate to the holy of holies. After the move, the dates had slipped to February 22 and October 22. It was another example of the engineering sophistication of the ancient Egyptians, although the significance of the dates is not known.

Another technological marvel, as remarkable in its own way, was the scene inside the concrete dome that had been erected over the re-sited temple. Entrance was through a small door to the right of the colossi and we soon passed from the scene of a remote Nubian temple into a high-tech world like something out of a James Bond film. In fact, parts of "The Spy who Loved Me" had been filmed under the dome. With a span of nearly two hundred feet and a height of nearly ninety, the dome covered the Great Temple and carried the weight of the artificial hill constructed above it. Outside the dome everything was yellow sandstone. Inside it was cold, gray, indifferent concrete. Concrete was probably the most familiar building material in Egypt, but this was concrete of a different order: no cold joints, no exposed reinforcing bar, no honeycombs, no forming lumber left in the finished surface. This was first-rate construction. There were the spines of the supports poured over the internal pillars and roofs of the temple, then the shell itself towering over the empty space above the supporting structure. It was like the inside of a cathedral. A walkway circled the dome at a height of about fifty feet, from which a passage led to an exit high up in the middle of the artificial hill in the back.

Outside in the sunlight we reflected on what we had seen. The salvage operation at Abu Simbel was the most controversial of the Nubian campaign. The method finally adopted—the "cutting scheme"—where the temple would be sawn into massive blocks and removed to a new site 213 feet above the old—had been described as "butchery" by purists. But everything, from the building of the cofferdam to restrain the rising waters, to the dismantling and strengthening of the blocks, the cutting and lifting process, storage, followed by reerection, then the building of the domes and finally the sculpting of the area, had been carried out without visible damage to the temple.

There were lines in the colossi themselves, evidence of the cuts, although they were otherwise as Roberts had seen them in November of 1838. And on closer inspection, the artificial hill into which the temples were built—or, actually reassembled around the facades—looked like a giant, three-dimensional jigsaw puzzle. The operation had lasted from April of 1964 to September of 1968 when, with great fanfare, the new temples were inaugurated. It had involved more than 1,700 workers with their families and support staff, and meant that a small community of thousands had lived at the site. The rescue effort was an example of what the international community could accomplish, when challenged and well organized.

There were several hours of daylight left and we used them to good effect. Armies of visitors suddenly appeared over the hill to the left of the monuments and then, just as suddenly, they disappeared. They must have been on the Nile cruises, flown in and out of Abu Simbel in an afternoon. After the last group left, the temples were deserted and we wore a path over the gangplank to the plateau at the feet of the colossi. The water beneath us was green with what seemed to be algae. But the effluents seemed nonexistent:

we had seen no factories or communities emptying their sewage into the lake, and the contributions of the Kasr Ibrim or the Eugenie, her sister ship, would have been negligible in the great expanse of water. It was puzzling.

We had technically completed the tour but the management saved the best for last: outside dinner by candlelight followed by a sound-and-light show. The elements conspired together in a final apotheosis. As the sun set the moon was already above the horizon, nearly at the full. Then, halfway through dinner, lights bathed the temple face and the triumphal march from *Aida* boomed over invisible speakers. There was no stentorian accompaniment, no word-painting, to spoil the scene. It was just the moon, the music, and the temples. Afterward, we made a final tour. The place really was ours—there was no one else there—and we walked through the empty temples, taking in details we had missed that afternoon. It was almost magical.

The next morning the spell was broken. It was all logistics and by seven o'clock we had packed, fed, and walked over the hill to the area where a bus would collect us for the ride to the airport. A note from the travel agent suggested that we reconfirm the tickets but there had been no telephones for the past five days and we had abandoned ourselves to the organizing abilities of Egypt Air. The airport was full of *khawagas*—where had they come from?—and we waited while several flights boarded and left. Then it was the turn of those of us with orange boarding passes. The flight was full and a Dutch couple sat with their children in their laps. But no one seemed to care. In Aswan, the airport was even fuller of foreigners and there was no place to sit. It looked like tourism was back in Upper Egypt.

In Cairo, we arrived at the old domestic airport. For twenty-five pounds a taxi driver agreed to deliver us to Zamalek. It was another Peugeot 504 station-wagon. There were pictures of Christ and the Virgin Mary on the dashboard, but his name was Mohammed. So, the taxi was owned by a Christian and driven by a Muslim.

All Egyptians were one, he said.

18

Siwa

Siwa was the fifth of the great oases in the Western Desert of Egypt and the most difficult to reach. Where the others—Bahriya, Farafra, Dakhla, and Kharga—swung in a great arc south of Cairo and were accessible from the Nile Valley, Siwa was more isolated could really only be reached from the Mediterranean coast. The map did show tracks to Siwa leading north of west from Bahriya and slightly south of west from Cairo through the Qattara Depression, but they were not used and today everyone took the metalled road south from Mersa Matrouh. The oases were probably all part of the same system, but Siwa was somehow different. Its isolation had led to the preservation of its own language, a Berber dialect, and a hostility to outsiders that had not entirely dissipated. President Mubarak had been there earlier in the year to open a mineral-water bottling plant and, like everywhere else in Egypt, jobs and development seemed to be everyone's preoccupation in the oasis.

Siwa had also been the site of the Oracle of Amun, one of seven famous oracles in the ancient world and the only one outside of Greece. Croesus had consulted it in 550 BC and twenty-five years later the army of Cambyses was lost somewhere between Kharga and Siwa on its way to destroy the oracle, against which he bore a personal grudge. Alexander the Great, a great believer in oracles, consulted it in 331 BC after being crowned Pharaoh in Memphis. Arrian says that Alexander refused to reveal what he learned but afterwards considered himself a son of Amun and expressed his desire to be buried there. A Greek archaeologist had recently announced the discovery of Alexander's tomb at Siwa, but after causing a brief stir in the academic world, the discovery seemed to have been discredited.

As with the earlier trip to the other oases, our guide was Ahmed Fakhry. The volumes on Bahriya and Farafra, Dakhla and Kharga were out of print. But for some reason the one on Siwa was not and was available in every bookshop in town. Like the other volumes, it was as much a labor of love as a record of the history and geography of the oasis. If we absorbed half of its enthusiasm we would be keen visitors, and we had no reason not to be. We had arranged to spend the first night in Alexandria and meet the managing director of one of the project subcontractors for dinner. He seemed particularly anxious to see us, calling several times in the week before to remind us of the date. He even called me in the office on the afternoon we were to leave to confirm that we were coming. It was the long weekend of the *Eid el-Adha*, and we expected half the population of Cairo to be on the road to Alexandria. But, surprisingly, there was very little traffic and it took just under three hours, door to door from the apartment to the Palestine Hotel. The Palestine was under new ownership, not the old Egyptian Hotels Corporation of our first stay in Egypt. The new management combined with the old spectacular setting, including the gardens adjoining the Montaza Palace, made it the best hotel in Alexandria.

We called when we arrived and arranged to meet him at eight o'clock at his apartment. He thought we might like to see his collection of pottery. We were late and he had obviously been waiting when he met us at the door, bowing in a formal, slightly awkward way to Martha. Then he asked where we would like to start. He was a collector of pottery, and of much else besides, and over the next hour we were led, slightly dumbfounded, from room to room. There was hardly a free inch on the floor for another carpet or display cabinet, or on the walls for another painting or etching. The living room was heavily Syrian, the furniture the boxy and uncomfortable mother-of-pearl inlay style. But this was no time to quibble. It was not meant to be lived in but to be seen. There were display cases with shards of old Islamic pottery, mounted Iznik tiles on the walls, Persian and Caucasian carpets on the floors, more display cases of Bohemian crystal, an entire *qibla* or prayer niche on one wall, a collection of old *shishas* or waterpipes, and a plate of chocolate-covered dates to which we were invited to help ourselves.

And that was just the living room. He explained the provenance and cost of acquisition of each painting, most of them Egyptian. But there were many by European artists in the several hundred in the collection, including original lithographs by Toulouse-Lautrec and Picasso. An antique Chippendale set and a Buddhist wooden shrine opened to a gilded scene in the dining room. Even the little foyer between the dining room and the kitchen was packed with artifacts, more pottery, tiles, and crystal. We paused for a soft drink in the kitchen, the glasses laid out on a tray awaiting our arrival. He explained that the cook was in the hospital, otherwise he would have offered us dinner as well. Even here, the most functional room in the apartment, the walls were papered in paintings and etchings.

And on it went. The bedrooms were packed with antiques and nudes, including the guest bedroom where, he hoped, we would stay on our next visit. The bathrooms displayed more etchings and we had to move aside the towels to achieve the full effect. The tour ended in his inner sanctum, the study, simple and English with a large campaign chest-of-drawers and a Chippendale bookshelf that covered one entire wall. The video and audio systems were very modern and his collection of operas was arranged alphabetically beneath the twenty-seven inch television set. His favorite was *Turandot*.

We sat in the study and slowly digested what we had seen. This was not an apartment, but a museum, and we had just been given a private tour by its courtly curator, buyer, and artistic director. We were struck at how meticulously everything was arranged, even though the impulse seemed to be collection for its own sake. Some people collect the books or paintings that interest them, and the passion seems to be for particular pieces or periods. Here the passion seemed to be for *collection* itself, although among these hundreds of paintings, carpets, books, etchings, pieces of furniture, pottery, tiles, and crystal there must have been some that were his favorites. He didn't go out often in the evenings, he said, obviously preferring his own company and that of his pieces to what was offered by society at large.

Together, we knew enough about what we saw to ask a few questions and appear genuinely impressed. But it was more than appearance. We may not have liked Bohemian crystal or Damascus inlay, but what he had assembled was a phenomenon that had to be appreciated in its entirety. It was oddly Egyptian, probably uncatalogued and uninsured. That was astonishing since there were individual pieces probably worth tens of thousands of dollars. There were two trusted servants who cleaned the house twice a week and accidental breakage must have been his greatest concern. The *bawwab* who accompanied us to the eleventh floor in the elevator was the guarantor that no unauthorized person would be admitted and that nothing would be taken.

Much of it had been acquired from two existing collections, and the prices of some of the individual items had been very low. But the investment was still considerable. He was the managing director of a computer software company, with a masters degree in mathematics and a PhD in computer science. Like many local contractors he had been swimming in the wake of USAID for years, a pilot fish after the sharks, picking up lucrative scraps like the contracts awarded to automate the systems of local organizations. We tried not to remember that foreign aid was once described as taking money from poor people in rich countries and giving it to rich people in poor countries. But his car was an older Fiat, and he obviously didn't favor the Mercedes 500s of other subcontractors whose passion was for conspicuous consumption and deferential lackeys. His consumption was determinedly inconspicuous.

We left for the restaurant in his car. He drove with the same awkward, retiring manner with which he greeted us, a little alarming in the chaotic Alexandria traffic. Dinner was good but not great, which was just as well since our appetite for the superlative that night had been exhausted. We arrived back at the Palestine well after midnight, later than we had planned. This would delay our departure the next morning. But the evening had been worth it. As we left he had presented Martha with a small portrait by a local artist, nicely framed. In one respect, the museum was the worst possible preparation for a visit to rural Egypt, although we had never felt that the two couldn't coexist before. But Siwa was different and we would have another, more emotional experience before we arrived in the oasis. Together, the two would almost spoil it for us.

The drive from Alexandria was a hint of the larger Mediterranean world that grew stronger the farther we moved west. Fig trees lined the road and beyond the ridge to the north we caught an occasional glimpse of the flat turquoise blue of the sea. The hills to the south were of brilliant white limestone and they had been quarried mechanically, cut into blocks, leaving large rambling walls fifty feet high, where the machinery couldn't approach any closer. This gave them a monumental, designed look and we could almost imagine them to be the remains of Pharaonic or Roman buildings. The impression was strengthened when we passed *Bourg el-Arab*, a real monument but sitting up very prominently like the limestone blocks to the south of the road.

The north coast had been undeveloped during our first stay in Egypt, for security reasons it was said. But now tourist villages—*qurya*s in Arabic—lined the road and billboards announced them at regular intervals: White Village, Diplomats Village, Santa Monica, and many others. The developments were mostly small, detached houses built in the shed style, and they marched by the thousands over the dunes. The question now was whether the infrastructure, particularly the sewage systems, could handle the numbers without damage to the beautiful white-sand beaches and crystal-clear water. Some Egyptians said that it was already too late.

A hundred kilometers from Alexandria a sign announced El-Alamein and we turned off the main road to a small siding that ran parallel to the south. There was a museum on the right and to the left, unrecognizable from the road, the Allied cemetery. It was unimpressive for one of the most important battles of the Second World War, but seemed somehow appropriate as part of the rolling, featureless terrain over which the conflict had taken place. Rommel's forces, outnumbered in every important measure—aircraft, tanks and men—had been stopped there in June of 1942. Still, so confident had everyone been of his victory that Mussolini had his white charger flown into Derna on the Libyan coast in preparation for a triumphal entry into Cairo. The approach had brought about "the Flap" at British headquarters in Cairo and July 1st was known as Ash Wednesday, with smoke from burning files darkening the sky over Garden City. Plans were made for the evacuation of women and children to Palestine and South Africa. But Rommel had been halted, to the chagrin of most Egyptians who were prepared to welcome him as a liberator.

Cairo had glittered through the first three years of the war, suffering none of the privations of London, and everyone recognized that the flap was only a bad case of jitters. The gaiety soon returned and the buildup to Montgomery's eventual victory in October began in earnest. Everyone talked about the demoralization of the British troops, and the incompetence of their commanders. Nobody liked Montgomery very much, but everyone agreed that it was about time the British had someone as nasty as Rommel, not the succession of decent nonentities who had been in command until then. By the time he attacked Montgomery had overwhelming superiority, bringing the full might of the British Empire to bear against an enemy that was overstretched, poorly supplied, and largely ignored in favor of the drama building at Stalingrad. In the autumn of 1942 there were 225 German divisions in Russia, fifty of them armored. Rommel had four German divisions in Egypt, two of them Panzers.

So overwhelming were the odds in Montgomery's favor that his job was simply to avoid a mistake, and in that he succeeded. The casualty figures revealed an intense, but short, battle before Rommel broke off and began his long retreat to the west. The Allied cemetery contained about 4,000 graves, with another 9,000 memorialized but buried elsewhere. The Italian and German cemeteries contained a combined 9,000. The little Greek memorial listed 480. The numbers were miniscule by comparison with other battles of the twentieth century, and would have been only a few hours' casualties on the Western Front during the First World War.

But wandering among the headstones was still a moving experience. The gardens were beautifully manicured in a country where hardly anything was well-kept anymore. There were Britishers, New Zealanders, Australians, Greeks, Poles, South Africans, and black Africans. Many of the headstones had testimonials, most of them the standard recourse in grief, such as "Greater love hath no man than he give his life for his fellows'" or "I have fought a good fight, I have finished my course," or "Some corner of a foreign field forever England." But some of them were touchingly personal: "He was only a boy, but he was brave like a man;" or "Mac, you made a woman happy." Among the most moving was the single headstone: "11 soldiers of the 1939–1945 War, known unto God." Only one was defiant: "A cruel and futile war robbed us of our dearest one. The price was too great." The average age seemed to be the late-twenties, and there were troopers in their midthirties. We thought that this little memorial to a little battle might somehow serve as a testament to all the forgotten and unmourned dead in the war, to the tens of thousands of civilians—men, women, and children—in Dresden or Coventry or Tokyo, vaporized or incinerated in firestorms that consumed everyone so that none was left to mourn. The German and Italian memorials were ten kilometers to the west and we decided to see them on the return trip.

So we pressed on the remaining 185 kilometers to Mersa Matrouh, the recently-planted fig orchards on the left competing with the new tourist villages on the right. It was now early afternoon and we decided that we would not try to reach Siwa that night. Mersa Matrouh seemed good-sized as we approached it, before descending a little ridge, over the railroad tracks to what became the main street. But in reality it was a one-horse town with the sleepy indifference of rural Egypt. There were traffic policemen at every intersection, but their main function seemed to be to ratify the chaos that everywhere prevailed.

The guidebook said that the best hotel in town "and perhaps in Egypt" was the *Beau Site*, and we found it at the west end of the town. Since it was early in the season there were rooms available and we settled down for the evening. The clientele was cosmopolitan—French, American, Egyptian, and Italian—and we might have been in almost any tourist hotel in the eastern Mediterranean. We turned in early. We wanted to get an early start for Siwa the next morning.

Mersa Matrouh—"the forgotten anchorage?"—in Arabic, or Paraetonium to the Greeks, had always been the gateway to the oracle from the Mediterranean. The road today couldn't be too different from that in ancient times. The map showed that it extended slightly west of south, to within fifty miles of the Libyan border. It had been first paved for the visit of King Fuad in 1928 and was supposed to be very good. It was, well maintained with only a short rough part for the last thirty miles into Siwa.

At first, the desert was unlike anything we had seen in Egypt, rough, red-brown sand and gravel dotted with low scrub. It looked like the southwestern United States, or pictures of the Tunisian desert taken during the war. Herds of camels—dark and shaggy, not the sleek white Sudanese animals we saw around Cairo—appeared periodically, with many foals in evidence, all legs and trotting timidly behind their mothers. Some of the females were still pregnant and the view in cross-section was startling, with two feet of abdomen extending on either side of the two skinny legs and the swiveled head and neck.

Eventually the scrub and gravel disappeared and the red-brown turned to the more familiar yellow. There was an almost-imperceptible rise and fall as the nothingness stretched away to the horizon in every direction. It was then that we realized how isolated Siwa was and how risky it had once been to go there. The oasis was about fifty miles wide from east to west and the likelihood of reaching some part of it was good, using nothing more than the sun as an aid to navigation. But there were problems of water—it was said that Alexander ran out after two days and was saved only by his godlike status—and sudden sandstorms from the south, like the one that buried Cambyses and his army. And what we would cover in just under three hours had been a seven-day journey by camel. They had been seven days of utter desolation.

A few miles from the oasis, interesting sandstone formations began to appear, naturally sculpted out of the plain over which we had traveled for the past hour. We had begun at sea level and climbed gradually to about 200 meters before beginning our descent. Siwa was an average of eighteen meters below sea level and the final drop down the escarpment was sharp but not long. The colors ranged ahead of us were typical of these oases: the blue-green of date palms and an almost silvery tinge of the olives. Ahmed Fakhry reported that there were 240,000 date palms and 25,000 olive trees in Siwa, planted on 1,300 feddans or just over the same number of acres.

As we reached the flat the most noticeable features were not the trees but the three or four large sandstone formations that stood up starkly out of the valley floor and we passed one as we entered the little town. We had reservations at the government rest-house, the *Arous el-Waha* or "Bridegroom of the Oasis." We passed it on our left and crept through the center of town, a foot deep in water in front of the police station, before returning and checking in. They had no record of the reservation but thought they might have a room—"in an hour"—if we were patient. The thickset desk clerk did not appear to be from Siwa, and he spent most of his time in the adjoining office watching television. There was no one else there.

So we went back to the first of the sandstone formations we had seen to have a look around. According to the map in the lobby of the rest house, it was *Jebel al-Mawta*, or the "Hill of the Dead," and there were tombs cut in the rock at several levels before we reached the top. There were also gun positions, sandbagged but abandoned, near the summit. From the top, there was a commanding view of the oasis. To the west, standing up starkly out of the green, was another tall sandstone formation. In front of us was the irregular outline of the old town, now crumbling and abandoned. To the east was the temple of Amun. Beyond the temple was a lake, given the surrounding deposits probably heavily saline. The tombs were small, some single and others with multiple cubicles cut for individual bodies. We didn't see the larger ones that at one time contained paintings like those we had seen in Bahriya. Most of them had been vandalized, with German soldiers carving out whole scenes for a few piasters during the war. Back at the hotel a room was available although there was the usual problem with the plumbing in the oases. There wasn't much water pressure and the shower didn't drain.

It was still early in the afternoon so we decided to see what we could while there was daylight. We were directed to the temple of Amun by the owner of the East-West restaurant who, in a rare bit of entrepreneurship, had printed a map of the oasis on the back of his take-out menu. Even more impressive there were no English misspellings in the key. We drove through the dusty little town until we entered a grove of date palms. After passing a public bath area, we came to a single, standing panel of reliefs on a recent masonry support. It was the Temple of *Umm 'Ubaydah* and the second temple of Amun in the oasis. The reliefs showed two lines of deities, all that was left of a larger wall destroyed first by an earthquake in 1811 and then by a governor who dynamited it in 1897 to reuse the stone for the police station. Several other large blocks with reliefs lay fallen around the single wall.

There wasn't much to see at *Umm 'Ubaydah* but several hundred yards beyond was the main temple itself. Entrance was through the a small gate, the scene dominated by the mosque whose plain minaret was still standing. The buildings in the little village were typical of the oasis: mud brick, but hard like concrete since the soil was saline, and in some places large chunks of salt appeared very white in the walls. Rain was still the greatest enemy of the buildings, and over the years many had simply melted away in the infrequent showers. The headers and jambs were of palm logs. The overall impression was one of desolation, like the ruins of Der'iya outside Riyadh in Saudi Arabia. There, we had been in Qasim, the heart of Wahhabi Najd and not a friendly place. Here in Siwa the inhabitants seemed about as unfriendly and they seemed to barely tolerate outsiders. The impression was reinforced in the little village near the center of town.

The temple itself was in a corner of the enclosure, which was maybe a hundred yards square. The temple walls, regular and chiseled in basalt, looked out of place in this warren of mud-brick. Much of the brick had been cleared away by Ahmed Fakhry and the walls were being repaired by a German team. This last bit of information came from the guide who hung around the village and made himself useful to the occasional visitor. He was one of the few in the oasis who seemed to be friendly. The temple was from the 26th dynasty (664–525 BC) to which additions were later made. It consisted of two halls and a sanctuary, the original entrance of a simple, cornice style to which fluted Doric columns were later added. In the sanctuary there were inscriptions of a king and deities high up on the walls, now barely legible. The entrances to the three rooms were being repaired and a metal post supported the header in each. The interior of the temple was roped off and inaccessible because of the work. After a decent interval, we left.

Back at the hotel the reception area was empty although the television blared from the adjoining alcove. It was still light so I took a turn around the town, but it was deserted on this afternoon before the feast. I looked for some of the famous Siwa olives but found none. I did buy a bag of dried dates, not identifiable by any of Ahmed Fakhry's categories. In one side street I was interrogated in Arabic by a little female Siwan about ten years old:

"Are you a Christian?

Yes.

Being a Muslim is better, and do you know why?

Why?

Because Muslims go to heaven and Christians go to hell."

With this helpful bit of information I returned to the hotel. Dinner was large cubes of beef, eggplant slices, and rice. The staff were trained in the old Egyptian Hotels Corporation style, the waiter pouring the mineral water with a graceful turn of the wrist and departing with a slight pirouette. The *'isha'* prayer, very loud with the speaker barely fifty yards across the road, was oddly disconcerting, the amplified *muezzin* wavering between several nearby scales in discordant fractions of tones as if he were utterly tone-deaf.

We were awakened the next morning before dawn by the same voice, just as loud but more insistent than the night before. The morning call to prayer can be beautiful, and prayer *is* sometimes better than sleep. But not on this particular morning or with this particular *muezzin*, and on the first day of the Feast, he went on and on for at least fifteen minutes. There was no set number for the iterations on this day, and they must have been in the hundreds:

Ash shadu an la illaha il Ullah

Ash shadu an la illaha il Ullah . . .

Ash shadu an la illaha il Ullah . . . wa sadaqa wa'da wa nasr 'abda wa hazem il ahzab wahida.

To the fmiliar "I testify there is no God but God" he added "He hath fulfilled his promise and made victorious His servant and prevailed singlehandedly over the hostile factions." It was not an auspicious beginning to the day.

But we were in Siwa so we might as well see what we could. The old town, deserted and very prominent on a hill in the middle of the new, was in ruins but the jagged shapes were interesting against the skyline. I asked directions from an unfriendly African on the way to the top. The population of the oasis had once been Berber with a later sprinkling of Arabs and African slaves from the Sudan. This man was not a mixture but looked like a pure central African. From the summit there was a good view of the oasis but the impression of Qasim was, if anything, stronger here. Even the animals seemed cloistered in the miserable little hovels that clustered around the base of the hill. The streets were almost deserted. Fortunately, I had bought gas earlier that morning because the single station in town was now closed and the pumps locked.

Back at the hotel we decided that we had done Siwa. We had undoubtedly not done it justice, and there were many things of interest that we hadn't seen. As a matter of fact, a Swiss anthropologist was here at the time, a sponsor of exhibitions of Siwan culture in Europe. In the hotel lobby was a poster of women wearing the spectacular Siwan jewelry, advertising an exhibition in Finland. The anthropologist's van was parked in the lot next to the rest house and her dog snarled at me through the window on each my forays into the town. But we were not anthropologists and something—maybe it was the season—made us feel unwelcome here. Like Alexander, we came, saw the oracle, and departed.

The drive back to Mersa Matrouh was the three hours of featureless sand in reverse. They were able to accommodate us again at the Beau Site and we spent an hour at the beach in the early afternoon. In the evening we drove to *Aguiba*, supposedly the most beautiful beach on the north coast, and it was. It lay at the foot of a sandstone promontory, maybe 200 feet high, and the levels of stratification ranging in color from beige to gold were very striking against the aquamarine colors of the water. The beach itself was a long, narrow inlet, and the water was successively translucent, turquoise, and then royal blue. Everything seemed very Mediterranean, with the limestone hills, neatly-tended olive and fig orchards, and the ground recently turned over between the trees. Even the people seemed different. We might have been somewhere in Greece.

Dinner was at an Italian restaurant in town and the menu was another in our collection of Egyptian menu stories. It had obviously been transliterated from Italian into Arabic, and then from Arabic into English and was an interesting study in the metamorphosis of words as they passed through the three languages. Our favorite was "Kaput Shino," not a bad rendering of the intermediate Arabic from the original "cappuccino." Here the problem was transliteration, not translation like the mixed grill we had seen on the menu in Alexandria as "Different liver, kidneys, testicles, and throat parts."

The next day it was back along the Mediterranean to El-Alamain. The German and Italian monuments were across the highway, north of the battlefield, and they were as moving in their own way as the expanse of the the Allied cemetery. Both were large structures, more ossuaries than cemeteries, the German looking very medieval and Teutonic. Cairo was seven hours from Mersa Matrouh and it was only when we were a hundred kilometers and an hour from home that we realized that we had left our passports at the Beau Site. There was no question of going back that day, and I briefly thought about flying up the next weekend. But the hotel had an office in Nasr City and a weekly messenger service, and we found the office and the passports there several days later. So it was a satisfactory ending to an odd experience.

A little like the visit itself.

19

George Herbert Walker Bush

It was a fundraising dinner for the Future Foundation at the Semiramis Hotel in Cairo and the featured speaker was the former president George H. W. Bush. Gamal Mubarak was the head of the foundation and the organization was dedicated to the provision of affordable housing for the poor. Gamal gave the opening address in barely-accented American English. He referred to his mother only as "Suzanne Mubarak" and spoke of her untiring efforts in aid of the poor in Egypt, a woman "whose sense of maternity extends to the whole country." The address consisted of little more than platitudes but there was something about this family that set them apart from most of the other ruling families in the region.

They seemed to be decent people, even with the regime's tough anti-Islamist measures, tens of thousands in jail on the mere suspicion of fundamentalist sympathy, the stage-managed democracy and lack of a designated successor. Not even Nasser or Sadat had operated without a vice president and everyone's fear was that Gamal was being groomed to take over, like Assad was doing with his sons in Syria. Gamal was smart and progressive, but the other son, Ala', was considered by Egyptians to be little more than a *bakshish* collector, a Mr. Ten-percent.

The audience consisted of the commercial upper crust of Egypt, many of whom I saw at Chamber of Commerce functions. There were about a hundred tables with an average of ten at a table and, at 500 pounds a head, it meant about 500,000 pounds for the foundation. There were a few *hijabs* in evidence but most of the women were stylishly dressed with the usual display of diamonds the size of hazelnuts. Everyone spent the first half-hour circulating among the tables and greeting everyone else: here the head of the National Bank of Egypt, over there the owner of one of the cellphone franchises. There was a great deal of embracing and kissing in the air. Like most Egyptians the men smoked heavily and many smoked cigars throughout the meal. After the master of ceremonies asked everyone to be seated it took another ten minutes for the hubbub to die down. And many—especially the women—carried on their conversations during the address by Bush, not paying the slightest attention to him.

My seat was at a back table and when I arrived there was only the director of a marine transport firm in Alexandria I had seen at other functions. Several others arrived later, a man who looked Slavic with his very Egyptian wife and then a retired general and two younger men who nodded and smiled pleasantly. The table was near the doors to the kitchen and we had a close-up view of how a hotel serves over a thousand guests at a banquet. A kind of meal captain, like a football coach on the sidelines, pointed the waiters in the right direction, patting them on the back as they poured in a continuous stream from the kitchen, some to the left, some to the right, and some straight ahead. The food came promptly and it was hot.

When Bush was introduced he was the same man remembered from Desert Storm days, aw-shucks humble and oddly inarticulate. I thought of Ann Richards crack about him as a man born with a silver foot in his mouth. Even tonight his remarks were the kind of thing that must have given his handlers nightmares. Christ, what was he going to say *next*? His entourage included Brent Scowcroft, the former national security advisor from Utah. Bush tossed out a few jokes about speakers who went on too long and then told the story of John Kennedy addressing a Chamber of Commerce luncheon: "If I weren't president," Kennedy had said, "I would be buying stock." "If you weren't president," said someone in the audience, "*I* would be buying stock too." That got a good laugh. After a few minutes the Egyptians were getting into it. They weren't used to stump speeches, but this was going to be fun.

Bush told the story of being made a member of the Order of the Garter "by the Queen of England." He said it as if we didn't know they had a queen over there. But when he got home to his little house in America, his wife Barbara—"the mother of governors"—had simply said "George, make the coffee!" He barked out the punch-line. There was polite laughter but this was verging on sacred ground with an Egyptian audience. They took their gender roles seriously. The women put up with the paunches and the cigars as long as they could wear those hazelnuts. The joke making the rounds in Cairo was that in the Arab World the woman walked three feet behind the man, and in Europe she was even with him. In America she walked three feet ahead.

The former president—although we learned from the master of ceremonies that a president was always a president—was having a good time being unemployed, watching his kids grow up. And yes, people were saying that George, the governor of Texas, was leading in the Republican polls. He was even favored to beat the Democratic nominee. But *he*, the father, was the first one to admit that polls had a way of turning around. That got a laugh too. With one son as governor of Texas—with the second-largest population in the country—and a second son the governor of Florida—the fourth-largest—he was the head of a dynasty. One American in four answered to a Bush. He wasn't sure that he liked the idea of the family having to put up with the intrusive American press, a constant theme of the evening. But hey, it had happened only once before in American history with the Adams, and he was looking forward to seeing if it wouldn't happen again.

At the beginning of his remarks he had used the old Groucho Marx line: "What did you talk about? . . . We talked about thirty minutes." That was his limit, he said. But he finished after twenty-eight, and he was doing the counting. Most of it was a rehash of events in the world in 1998, nothing that a casual reader of an international newspaper wouldn't know. He spent about half the time on the Middle East and, over and over again, stressed the strength of the Egyptian-American relationship. He spoke of his admiration for the role that President Mubarak—"your dad," he said, in Gamal's direction—had played in the peace process. But everyone was really just waiting for the question and answer period. It didn't take much imagination to guess what the questions would be.

He said at the outset that he reserved the right not to respond: "If I don't like the question, hell no, I'm not going to answer it." So he passed over Monica Lewinsky and any criticism of the Clinton administration: "Hey, I had my chance and lost and now he is the President. *And I'm not going to criticize my President.*" That got a round of applause. He didn't know anything about the Copts in Egypt, but said there was an isolationist streak in the United States and we sometimes tended to preach to other people. Engagement, not preaching, was the answer to problems. He mentioned China as an example. And no, he didn't believe in the Pinochet decision: "Hell, Saddam Hussein said that *I* was a war criminal and Ramsey Clark, that *craaazy*—he drew out the syllable— former attorney general, went to Baghdad and supported him."

But he took on a few tough questions as well. Why hadn't he finished the job in Iraq? The answer was heated: "Hey, we built a coalition and we did the job. The job was to get *Sadd*um—he still put the accent on the first syllable—out of Kuwait. It was not to kill *Sadd*um Hussein. Or kill more of those scared, eighteen-year-old Iraqi kids than we had to." And now he was almost shouting: "If we had gone to Baghdad, it would have been without you and the Saudis and the Europeans. It would be a bunch of Yankees occupying Arab land. *And I just wasn't going to do that.*" This brought down the house. "Hey," he said, "Thatcher and Major are out of work and Mitterand is in heaven, I'm unemployed, and that guy is still in power. You figure it out." That brought down the house again.

Then, there was the perception that the United States was not evenhanded in its dealings with the Arabs and the Israelis. This was the real question everyone had come to ask that night. What did he think about it? He thought that if that perception was true we Americans should do something about it. Why did the Republicans seem to be more sympathetic to the Arabs than the Democrats? "Gosh," he said, "if that is the perception I guess I should be pleased." He didn't know why, although he thought it was worth looking into. But, of course, he knew why. Here was the man who, in one of the most extraordinary laments in the history of the American presidency, had said that he was "just one lonely guy trying to stand up against this powerful organization." He wasn't speaking, as leader of the sole remaining superpower, about the Russians or the Chinese or the North Koreans. He was talking about AIPAC, the American Israel Public Affairs Committee.

His administration's relations with Netanyahu had been stormy, he conceded, and everyone in the room knew that. Everyone also knew what Bush-Baker had done with the loan guarantees and of their opposition to the settlements. He made the right noises about Wye Plantation, but nobody in the room had much use for it. Why Wye? Especially since the price of Wye was the unwritten but apparently formal undertaking that the United States would never again put pressure on Israel. What Bush couldn't say was what everyone, even the Egyptians, thought they knew: the Democrats were the party of the Jews.

The reality was more complex. John Foster Dulles came as close to getting it right as anyone. In an address before the United Nations at the height of the Suez crisis in 1956, he had said that Americans had the closest ties of culture, history, and shared values with the British, the French, and the Israelis, "but this aggression will not stand." And it didn't. Tonight, everyone thought that it was light-years from Bush, Baker, and Scowcroft to Clinton, Albright, and Sandy Berger. But the settlements had continued their inexorable pace, regardless of who was in the White House. Nixon had said that he "didn't owe anything to these people" but in 1973, when faced with another defeat of American by Soviet arms—the scuttle in Vietnam was underway and the Indians had just routed the Pakistanis in one of the great tank battles in history—he had come through in a big way. Ronald Reagan, a Republican, had been the most instinctively pro-Israeli president since, well, since Lyndon Johnson. And Jimmy Carter, a Democrat, was the first president to give the Palestinian problem the attention it deserved.

In fact the Israeli hold on the West bank had been consolidated under a succession of presidents, Republican and Democrat alike. The settlements began as a violation of international law, of the 4th Geneva Convention. They had successively become "obstacles" to peace, and then "difficulties" in the way of a final settlement. The imbecility of the American position was demonstrated at Wye when—futilely, it seems—Madeline Albright had asked the Israelis for "a temporary time-out" in the building of settlements. Not a cessation of settlement activity but "a temporary time-out." The Egyptians, and the rest of the Arab World, had witnessed this utterly cynical process unfolding over the past twenty years and they were asking tonight, very politely, whether we Americans didn't see it too and whether we were going to do anything about it. They weren't asking us to make moral equivalents of Netanyahu and Saddam Hussein, but just, please, to recognize that both were in violation of the law and UN resolutions. At least Bush had tried.

When it was over, we waited outside the ballroom while the Bush entourage cleared out. We were held up by typical Egyptian security men—buzzed haircuts, little earphones, striped pants, plaid coats, checkered shirts, and patterned ties. I rode down the escalator next to Daniel Kurtzer, the American Ambassador in Cairo. I had earlier heard him respond to the same questions at another Chamber of Commerce function and while the Egyptians were unfailingly polite I don't think anyone in the room believed a word he said. He had started with a little Arabic and a *Goha* story and there was a titter of appreciation from the audience. But it would take more than simple-minded patronizing to satisfy the Egyptians.

In George H. W. Bush we had just seen an American original in action, with all the strengths and weaknesses of the type. For all of the occasional gaffes, there was something to be said for plain speaking.

20

Telecom 99

It was supposed to be the conference of the year, or the decade, or maybe even of the century. In the buildup to the event there was enough hyperbole to last for what little remained of the twentieth century. Bill Gates and Steve Jobs would be there and such lesser luminaries as William Kennard, head of the FCC, Edward Gertsner, the chairman of IBM, and the CEO's of every major telecommunications and information technology company in the world. But in the event, even more than hyperbole, we were served up mantras, hymns to the transforming power of communications, solemnly intoned by the purveyors of handsets, satellites, switches, routers, and most of all, solutions. Communications, we were told, would change everything we did, the way we lived, worked, loved, and played. The language was apocalyptic: we were in the midst of a revolution, long-distance was dying, and geography was dead.

But the last word may have been Gertsner's on the first day when he quoted the futurist who said: "There is no need to predict the future. The future is already here. It's just unevenly distributed." There had always been the haves and the have-nots. Now, there were the knows and the know-nots. Unfortunately, they were the same people. And wandering through the acres of glitter, the three-story exhibits, full-scale models of shuttles, satellites, and booster rockets, the galaxies of Swiss-misses passing out bonbons, the bewildering array of exhibitors with solutions to problems they didn't know existed, the attendees from Afghanistan, the Lao Republic, Burundi, Vietnam, Rwanda, and Sierra Leone must have felt that they were in a different world. They were all used to violence and revolution, but Kalashnikovs and a willingness to use them now weren't enough. The weapons in this revolution were different and they didn't even know what they looked like.

I decided to attend a week before the conference began and the travel agent couldn't find a hotel room in Geneva. In fact, there wasn't a room to be had within 150 kilometers of the city. The Telecom Egypt delegation had made reservations two years before. The population of Geneva was only about 180,000 but this event would double that. It was as if five million people suddenly descended on Manhattan. But there had to be a way. So I called Lausanne and then Bern and considered myself lucky to find a room in Bern, an hour and a-half away by train. But then, suddenly, there *was* a way and it all happened overnight, electronically: e-mail traffic from Cairo to New York to Geneva to New York and back to Cairo. Just like the futurists said. A friend of the brother of one of the project staff knew a banker in Nyon, just outside Geneva, and it seemed that he would be in Sharm el-Sheikh with his family for the week. So they offered me the use of their house for the duration of the conference. It was in the country, five kilometers from the train station, which was about twenty-five minutes from the conference center at the airport.

So I flew *Swissair* to Geneva via Zurich. The first leg was as smooth as a Swiss watch: quietly efficient, not the Teutonic thoroughness of *Lufthansa* or the officiousness of *KLM*. But in Zurich the Swiss displayed feet of clay just like everyone else. First, there was a forty-five minute delay and then it took ten minutes to board the first ten rows of the connecting flight to Geneva. But airborne it was all quiet efficiency again, and then an extraordinary scene appeared. To the left of the aircraft the Swiss Alps gradually deployed in a field like icebergs, standing above the flat, leaden sea of the cloud cover, individual jagged peaks and there seemed to be hundreds of them. Some were higher than others and the highest of all was Mt. Blanc. They lasted for about twenty minutes but, spectacular as the phenomenon seemed, they weren't *real* mountains, nothing like the 27,000 feet of Rakaposhi in the Karakorams, or even the 19,000 feet of Kilimanjaro. But then the in-flight magazine showed Mt. Blanc at at 4,807 meters, or 15,771 feet. It was a real mountain after all.

In Geneva Anne-Karin picked me up at the airport and as we left the parking lot she pointed out Palexpo where the conference would take place. It was a thirty-minute drive to Nyon and we soon settled into broken French, fragments and then partial sentences coming back from my fourteen months in West Africa. The house was in the country, five kilometers outside Nyon, in a little development called *en Closelet,* outside the village of *Cheserex,* on the road to *Crassier.* By the end of the week those three *C*'s would be engraved in my memory, and that of every cab driver in Nyon. The house was one of an attached three-story four-plex and was new and spotless. It was appointed with every convenience, from the espresso machine to the sensor that automatically turned on the downstairs lights in the morning. Philippe worked for UBS, Union Bank of Switzerland, and spent a part of his week in Zurich. That would probably qualify him as one of the gnomes of Zurich, but in the flesh he was decidedly un-gnome-like. In fact, that afternoon he was at a festival celebrated by the shepherds when they came down from the mountains with their flocks at the end of the summer. He would be fed all day and come home replete.

Dinner was veal with rice and *haricots* followed, in the French way, by the salad. Afterwards came the cheese. Philippe arrived about eight o'clock and we chatted about Switzerland and America. The next morning he drove me to the station for the eight ten train to the airport and we resumed our conversation on differences in the way of doing business in the two countries. He had spent a couple of years in New York and came equipped with cell phone, fax, and e-mail access. But it was all too cutthroat in America and, even though everyone was drawn into its technological orbit, some had reservations about where we all, willy-nilly, seemed to be headed.

After lodging, transportation was the chief concern at Telecom 99. Taxis were expensive and the daily ride from Cheserex to the Nyon station cost an average of twenty-six francs, or eighteen dollars. And that was just one way. The train wasn't much cheaper—about seventeen dollars for a one-way, second-class ticket to the airport, and twenty-nine dollars for a round trip. But there was a Telecom 99 special, a second-class pass for 152 francs—about $110—that allowed travel on all public transportation between Montreux and Geneva for the ten days of the conference. It would have been a bargain at twice the price. Gas was expensive at nearly four dollars a gallon and driving wasn't really an option, if only because of the hassle and parking. Besides, as the *VIA*, the railway magazine said, "*Voyage mains libres et qualite de vie au lieu de stress et embouteillages.*" Leave the driving to us.

The train was crowded that first morning. Added to the normal commuters were the Telecom people. We were mainly male, spoke a variety of languages, and came from a variety of destinations between Montreux and Geneva. But we were recognizable for our darker coloring and our uniform of dark suits, although we accessorized differently with a wide selection of clunky shoes, colored shirts, and patterned ties. At the airport we were funneled out the main exit to a waiting bus that would take us to Palexpo. It eventually made its way to the Exhibition Hall, half a-mile and twenty minutes away through heavy traffic before we realized that the Opening Forum was in the arena, only a few-hundred yards from where we had left the train.

The keynote address was by Yoshio Utsumi, the secretary general of the International Telecommunications Union, or ITU, and it included his "little joke" about the shot put and the marathon. The last big international event had been the world track and field championships that summer in

Lausanne, and Telecom 99 was also going to start like the shot put and end like the marathon. Or something like that. But the opening was really the showcase for the heavy hitters—the CEO's of Nortel, IBM, Ericsson, Lucent, NTT (Nippon Telephone and Telegraph, the largest telephone company in the world), and sundry ministers of telecommunications. We heard alarming prospects for the uninitiated or the unwired: "The era of the personal computer as we know it is over;" "The old industry is gone. All that's left is the inertia;" and "The refusal to join the networked world is not an option."

Gerstner was the most impressive of the westerners. He was short, compact, bemused, and looked slightly pugnacious. Speaking extemporaneously and pacing in front of the podium while digital pictures flashed on the big screen, he went on for half an-hour without once losing the thread of his argument. The Europeans spoke from the podium with prepared speeches. Gerstner spoke without notes, gesturing expansively with his hands, so much so that we noticed that he was missing half the index finger and a portion of the middle finger on his right hand. He got a laugh with the line: "There is e-mail, e-commerce, e-trade and e-news. Pretty soon people will be saying e-nough." But his was still a call to the networked world. He clearly didn't represent the old IBM where employees were sent home for wearing loafers: people shouldn't come to work in bedroom apparel. Gerstner was wearing loafers and the big screen showed that they had tassels.

The address of H.E. Mr. Jichuan Wu, minister of information from China, was eagerly awaited. He had recently spoken about investment in the Internet in China and we all waited to hear what that meant. But, I later learned, he didn't enlighten us much. Actually, I didn't have a headset—being relatively comfortable in French and Arabic, the other two languages most commonly used in these ITU events—and I missed the speech. I could only see it on the big screen, and noticed that his mouth remained closed most of the time. His lips made very few movements as he articulated the sounds in little staccato bursts. He looked like a bad ventriloquist. The Japanese head of NTT, Mr. Miyazu, had the same economy of speech and both were different from, say, the Australian whose mouth seemed to be wide open all the time. The Namibian minister was a white man—like most of the members of the Namibian rugby team in the World Cup—and had that unmistakable South African accent. The only Namibian I had seen before was the sprinter Frankie Fredericks. Then the minister from the Sudan launched into a long, flowery address, bringing the greetings of the Sudanese people to Mr. Utsumi. It was the kind of thing that made Middle East ITU conferences such a waste of time: all protocol and no substance.

But the message from the opening session was really what the big five said it was: open standards, high technology, low margins, high volume, customer focus, data transmission, Internet access, IP networks and, above all, speed. Mr. Utusmi put it best: the industry was changing so fast that some companies that would want booths at the next conference in 2003 didn't even exist today. And today was the last day to register. But, still, a little voice from somewhere was trying to make itself heard above the din: everyone was talking about transport, not content. The revolutionary effect of the first IT application, word processing, was that it allowed us to be more careful writers. Now, everyone was forgetting punctuation and capitals and venting in chat rooms. Technology meant that there was just more unedited garbage out there in the ozone, more space junk. The medium wasn't the message. The message was the message, and it always would be. But the voice sounded cranky and feeble.

The Development Summit

The next day was the opening of the Development Summit and the beginning of the real work of the conference. It may have been only a side-show of the trade show, but it was where the countries of the developing world would learn what lay in store for them. They were chosen by the ITU on the basis of GDP (low) and exposure to change (high). That meant countries as different as Afghanistan, Equatorial Guinea, and Kiribati with low GDPs, and Kyrgyzstan and Uzbekistan still adjusting to the breakup of the Soviet Union. There were about sixty countries in the Summit and three seats allocated for each. With a hundred seats available for visitors, the private sector, and the press, and that meant about three hundred seats in the hall. I sat in the back and looked over a sea of black heads, with the exception of the blonde bouffant of the lady from Kyrgyzstan. Most were from sub-Saharan Africa, although Asia—with the Lao Republic, Vietnam, and Mongolia—and the Pacific region—with Tuvalu, Tonga, and Western Samoa—were also there. There were thick rolls of fat around African necks, birdlike Asian heads standing up out of unfamiliar starched collars, and the massive frames of the Pacific islanders. Surprisingly, India, Pakistan, and the Philippines were there. Equally surprisingly, Egypt was not.

The keynote address by the minister of information from Zimbabwe almost derailed the proceedings before they began: the technology gap was a plot by the developed world to keep the developing world in thrall, and finance was the key to their exploitation. Fortunately, no one in the remaining five days of the summit took up the theme. There was admittedly a great deal of confusion and acknowledgment of vulnerability in a world where three-fourths of the planet's six billion people had never placed a telephone call. But everyone seemed to realize that, while life was basically unfair, railing against the inequity wasn't going to solve anything. There would have to be developing-world solutions to developing-world challenges and the best thing to do was to get on with it. In fact, on the last day the Ugandan delegate sheepishly confessed what he was reluctant to say in the open forum: his country was opening the market and doing just that.

The CEO of SwissCom offered the sensible perspective that telecommunications was a tool that could connect, but also disconnect people. Direct, face-to-face communication was always the preferred option. The second speaker, John Chambers of Cisco, seemed to be an anomaly in this summit. He was young and sleek and, like Gerstner, he paced the floor, punctuating the celebrity-laced video presentation with commentary. Maybe his hubris was understandable. Cisco had become the most profitable, fastest-growing company in history since its founding ten years earlier by a group of computer scientists from Stanford. Its market capitalization was already $222 billion, probably more than the combined GDPs of the countries in the room. But his name-dropping was annoying: Kofi Anan, Mr. Blair, Prime Minister Goh Chok Tong of Singapore, Prime Minister Mahathir of Malaysia, Mr. Clinton, President Jiang of China, Prime Minister Miyazaki of Japan. At least he got them right. At a presentation in Cairo the week before an American consultant—billed as one of the twenty-five most important people in the world—had solemnly intoned:

> Why I was there, and stood on the very spot where your President Sadat and Prime Minister Begin, signed the Camp David accords under the sponsorship of President Truman.

His credibility had instantly melted away.

This presentation was all about speed. Cisco had gone through seven major reorganizations in its short history, in response to the changing market. In the future it wasn't the strong that would survive, but the fast. Chambers had a southern accent and was sometimes hard to follow. His delivery was too fast and when he repeated the question he had posed to all the above luminaries—"Do you *git* it?"—I don't think anyone in the room *got* it. Then he made a demonstration of voice over the Internet with a subordinate. It was all "Jim" and "John" and folksy American chitchat. He left us with a couple of zingers: "In five years voice will be free" and "Circuits are dinosaurs." Then he was gone. Several Americans were seated next to me in the back of the room and it turned out they were from Cisco. They formed a kind of personal cheering section. When I suggested they tell their CEO he needed to slow down his delivery, they thanked me very much and said he already *had*, before they moved off at warp speed after their fast-disappearing leader. Surprisingly, the Zimbabwean thanked Mr. Chambers for his "wonderful presentation," so maybe he wasn't such an anomaly after all.

The midmorning session was on the "Centre of Excellence Concept," the softest of the several sessions we would sit through during the week. It was like training: how could you say anything *bad* about excellence or training. There was the usual screed about human resources being a company's most valuable asset, and the need to introduce gender sensitivity into the equation. The problem was in doing something meaningful about these exemplary ideas. The two afternoon sessions, "Settlements and Accounting rate Reform" and "Community Access," were anything but soft. They went to the heart of the developing world's conundrum: how to pay for access to telecom services for their rapidly growing but cash-strapped populations. Teledensity in the room probably averaged less than five per hundred, and in sub-Saharan Africa it was *point* 5 percent. The developed countries had traditionally subsidized the developing world's build-out by sending back a portion of the tariffs they collected for overseas calls. But in 1996 the FCC had announced that American subscribers were paying over $5 billion to other countries for inefficient services, and we weren't going to do it any more. Now, everyone seemed to be climbing on the bandwagon.

Accounting rates were officially "the accounting revenue division procedure." That meant, in a simple world, that countries would agree on a rate they would share on a fifty-fifty basis for traffic between them. If Egypt and the United States, for example, had agreed on an accounting rate of a dollar, each side would receive fifty cents for each minute of calls between the two countries. Since many more minutes originated in the United States than in Egypt—by a factor of about nine to one—Egypt was a net beneficiary of these "settlements." American companies—AT&T, MCI, Sprint, and WorldCom—paid the settlements to Egypt on a quarterly basis. The funds had been used to build new plant and connect new subscribers. Egypt had raised teledensity from 1 percent in 1980 to about 8 percent today, funded in part by settlements that represented about 25 percent of their gross revenues. It was the total of these amounts with the rest of the world that bothered the FCC. Their main objection was that the rates were not cost-based. They estimated that it cost only seventeen cents to terminate a call in Egypt.

There were proposals to change to more cost-based rates, or to a system of termination charges, or originator-keep-all, or to some other as-yet undefined arrangement. But a larger problem was that it was no longer a simple world and people were finding alternatives to the settlements system. Not only were there transit carriers and other intermediaries, but new companies were increasingly going *around* the system, costs or no costs, settlement rates or no settlement rates. That was the real danger. We would learn later in the week from one of these pirates how it was done. The choice for the developing world was stark: did they want a smaller percentage of something or a smaller percentage of nothing? And as traffic became a commodity like oil or pork-bellies, there would no longer even be percentages.

The second topic, community access was the old universal service dressed up in developing-world garb. Universal service—where every citizen had his or her own telephone—was really not an option in the developing world. Instead, each citizen should have *access* to telecommunications services within some agreed-upon radius from his or her village. It had already led to things like mobile telecenters in Africa and solar-powered wireless units helicoptered into remote areas of the Sahel. The mantra about information—it was "the key to open all doors"—drove this development and we accepted it unchallenged, leaving aside for the moment problems with computer availability and maintenance, not to mention illiteracy and the fact that for the majority information was available only in English. Most Africans came equipped with three languages: a tribal language, the *lingua franca* of the country, and either English or French. There was the joke that people who spoke three languages were called trilingual, those who spoke two languages were called bilingual, and those who spoke only one language were called Americans. It may have been true, but Americans had an enormous advantage. Even those people with a rudimentary knowledge of English were not very productive in the language.

Everyone seemed to accept the fact that the keys to community access were entrepreneurs. And it was then I realized that the three thousand private shops in Cairo alone, reselling telecommunications services in comfortable surroundings with polite, attentive staff, were not a problem but a solution. Telecom Egypt had tried to control them, with predictable results. Other countries spoke of their success with telecenters and, if entrepreneurs were the key to access, profits were the keys to the entrepreneurs. The first day ended with a discussion of "Teleapplications" and we heard another mantra: automation had played a major role in the industrial revolution and now it was playing a similar role in the information revolution. There would be a new paradigm in services like health care, with a centrally-located doctor examining a patient over the net. But there were details to be worked out, things like infrastructure, affordable tariffs, standards, licensing, and legal arrangements. A whole new world seemed to be opening before our eyes. But those in the room were not in the developing world for nothing. They were not dreamers and it was clear to everyone that the devil would be in the details.

The session ended promptly at five thirty. On the one day during the week when it did not the cameraman flashed a picture of a clock on the big screen. The conference employees were probably unionized. The summits were in the most remote hall of Palexpo, a thousand meters from the train station, a brisk ten-minute walk away. Then, it was ten-minute ride to the main train station in Geneva, the *Gare de Cornavain*. Even in mid-October it was still light at six o'clock, so there was time to see a little of the city on this first day. I was looking for books by Johann Ludwig—or John Lewis or Jean Louis—Burckhardt, the Swiss traveler. After Niebuhr, he was probably the most respected European traveler in the Arab World. He had died of dysentery in Cairo in 1817 and after several years of looking I had found his tomb in a little cemetery outside the *Bab Nasr*. I had bought his *Travels in Arabia* in London and the *Travels in Nubia* recently in Cairo. But I had only seen the *Travels in Syria and the Holy Land* once, years before when I didn't have the $2,000 asking price. And then there were *Notes on the Bedouins and the Wahhabis* and the *Arabic Proverbs*. Switzerland must surely be familiar with one of its most eminent sons. I would soon realize how provincial I was.

The map of the city showed the downtown centered on bridges over the Rhone, which emptied into Lake Geneva. The *Pont du Mont Blanc* seemed the most direct and it was a beautiful walk in the fading light, with swans gliding in the lee of the little island that supported the bridge. At an information kisok we located the likely area of bookstores and I headed towards the old city, up the hill on the south side of the lake. But it was getting dark, the shops seemed to be closing and I had the area staked out. So I retreated to the area below the station where I had seen several restaurants. The Swissair in-flight magazine said that we were entering the season of *La Chasse* and that game was now on the menu in Switzerland.

The restaurants were scattered over the area to the south of the station and most had their menus posted outside. The offerings were interesting: *Supreme de faisan roti*, or roast pheasant, *Civet de chevreuil aux airelles*, venison stew with blueberries, and *Salmis de sanglier*, wild-boar sausage. Most came with *speatzli* and *choux de Bruxelles*, or thick noodles and Brussels sprouts. To some tastes it was pretty heavy fare, and a Swiss girl at the conference wrinkled her nose when I told her what I was eating. But, with good bread and a carafe of wine, it was delicious and filling. It wasn't cheap. A meal like one of the above, with wine, maybe a simple green salad and coffee, came to about sixty francs, or just over forty dollars. It was twice the cost of the same kind of thing I had most recently in Paris.

The trains ran regularly to Nyon throughout the evening. Only once did I catch the milk-run—Chambesy, Les Tuileries, Genthod Bellevue,

Creux de Genthod, Versoix, Point Ceard, Mies, Tannay, Coppet, Founex, Caligny, Crans, Nyon—and even that took only half an hour. But by the time I had reached the station in Nyon, waited for a taxi, recited the three *C's*, and arrived at the house, it was after nine o'clock. That made for a very busy fourteen-hour day and I was ready to sleep.

More Development

The next day began with an address by H.E. Mme. Oulematou Ascofare Tamboura, the minister of communications from Mali. She was still madame *le* ministre, not madame *la* ministre, and if the new head of the French Academy (herself a woman) had anything to say about it, she would remain so. Her presentation was in that characteristic West African *patois* and, like most Africans, she was nothing if not frank. Development had been a disappointment, although a Tuareg revolt in the north and international isolation hadn't helped. Like most of those educated in the French system, she punctuated her delivery with little reminders to keep our attention: *"Mesdames et monsieurs . . ."* Her country consisted of over a million square kilometers of virtually nothing, Sahel and desert. The Sahel was an area of scrub with most of the original tree cover now gone, and it spread across the waist of Africa, from Mauritania on the Atlantic to the Sudan on the Red Sea. Technology could help in the deployment of the networks across this fastness and the ITU, of course, had a role to play in all of this, although it wasn't clear what that role would be. It seemed that the developing world hoped that the organization would act as a kind of buffer against the voracious appetites of the operators and vendors in the exhibit halls next door. If so, it was a feeble hope.

Mme. Tamboura was followed by an American who clearly had not been born in America. He started with a quote from Yogi Berra—the Egyptians would have understood Berra as a kind of American *Goha*, "humorous, absurd, and sometimes wise"—and his message was that we were obsessed with teledensity to the detriment of other important things, such as education, health, and the reduction of infant mortality. But "when all you have is a hammer, everything looks like a nail." It turned out that he was originally Ethiopian, but an American success story. Sleek and impeccably cravated, he had come back with something to sell to his old friends: *WorldSpace*, a satellite service that would help to "produce information affluence" and "reduce poverty and ignorance." *Afristar* had already been launched. Satellite technology was the answer in Africa. Running thousands of miles of copper cable across the continent was not. If we had questions we could visit the *WorldSpace* exhibit in Hall 7.

And so it went. The remaining days of the Development Summit would be variations of the two issues we covered on the first two days, availability and finance: how to bring telecommunications services to the developing world and how to pay for them. But the process had barely begun. Several vendors made presentations and they were, as might be expected, a hard-headed lot. Teledensity may have been a poor measure, but it was the best we had. They were interested in low costs and low prices to make their offerings commercially viable. IP networks could be "abundant, simple, cheap, and quick." The business of telecommunications was business and it could work in everyone's favor.

But the old paradigm died hard. The man from the Moroccan regulatory commission wanted fewer pitches from vendors! And the representative from Senegal wanted to discuss not technology but education and training: they were the keys to advancement. They were both right. Information was fuzzy but telecommunications was not. It was the pipe through which the information had to be poured. And with less than 5 percent of the world being connected, the information revolution was a pipe-dream for most. A Brazilian and a Colombian then reported impressive results in connecting rural areas, and a man from The Gambia wanted to know about the technologies they used and the rates of penetration they had achieved. But the answer was that they really didn't know. Technologies were for the companies to decide and percentages were unimportant. Then, there was another mantra from an American: *communication was a basic human right*, like speech and religion. But it seemed that the world had enough rights, and plenty of unfinished business in the ones we already had.

Wireless seemed to be the wave of the future. It had taken the telecommunications industry over a hundred years to wire the first billion customers, but only ten years to connect the first billion wireless customers. There were parts of Scandinavia where wireless penetration exceeded fixed and they looked forward to rates exceeding 100 percent in the not-too-distant future. In spite of fear of the health effects of pressing these little microwave ovens to their heads, the developing world was deploying them as fast as they could. It was probably appropriate that an Israeli should speak about mobile deployment, per capita usage in Israel being the highest in the world. The director general of the ministry of communications, a former colonel in the IDF, was the speaker and there was a measure of menace in his flat Hebrew-accented English. But he was one of us, and his remarks were the kind of no-nonsense commentary you would expect from a representative of the developed world. The Israelis had made a *mistake* in their regulatory arrangements, and was there another regulator in the region that would admit to a mistake? But his presence in the Development Forum was a reminder of an absurdity. With a per capita GDP of about $18,000 Israel already exceeded those of the southern-tier European countries and was approaching that of Great Britain. Yet it was the largest recipient in the world of American foreign aid. The federal government in the United States probably spent more on the average Israeli that it did on the average resident of inner-city America.

The forum closed precisely at five thirty and I hustled off to catch the 5:39 train to Geneva. It was a week of hustle, and we were like ants, pouring in steady stream along preordained paths. The exhibit halls in Palexpo were so full of feverish human beings that we had to go outside to catch a breath of fresh air. Between the halls were the paths we all trod with our briefcases and badges. There were the internal paths from hall to hall, then the brisk, bracing walk outside, the path to the pedestrian overpass to Hall 7, and then along its 500-meter length to the underground train station. If the stream was interrupted—like some giant thumb erasing a score or more of us—it quickly re-formed and flowed on as before. I ate as much as I wanted in the eight days and still lost a couple of pounds, so great was the sheer physical and mental activity of the conference.

This time I went across the Rhone and directly up the hill to *le Grande Rue* where I expected to find the bookstores. The cobblestones were slick after a light rain. I was looking for the *Librarie des Amateurs*, but it was closed. The hours were crazy: two to four, Tuesdays through Fridays. Imagine a telephone system available only two hours a day, four days a week. There were other shops and at one I found a *Geograhie de d'Anville* that looked interesting. But it wasn't Burckhardt. At a second shop we established who Burckhardt was: he was *not* Jacob Burckhardt the Renaissance scholar, but Jean Louis Burckhardt the Arabian traveler. The helpful clerk listened politely until we looked in a reference biography and found the right Burckhardt, with his own paragraph. But they had nothing by him. At a print shop down the street the lady's eyes went blank when I asked if she had anything by David Roberts, the Scot whose series on Spain, Egypt, and the Holy Land were classics. I began to wonder who was the provincial here. Dinner was more of *la chasse*, this time garnished with sautéed chestnuts and some really heavy speatzli. By the time I had retraced my steps to the train station, caught the milk run, waited for a taxi, recited the three *C's* and arrived at the house, I was spent. The next day would be more of the same.

Day Four

The exposition was huge. The floor plan, provided in the registration package and sponsored by Sun Microsystems ("The network is in the computer"), showed the arena and halls 0, 1, 2, 3, 4, 5, 7, and 8. For some reason there was no hall 6. The plan appeared to be drawn to scale and a later calculation showed over a million and a half square feet, or nearly forty acres of floor space. There were about 1,500 exhibitors. The most spectacular exhibits—those of Siemens, Nortel, Alcatel, and Lucent—were in hall 4. Telecom Egypt was in hall 7, the farthest from the entry hall, and the Egyptians complained about the lack of traffic. But they were next to the *vestiarie*, the cloakroom, and everybody who left luggage, and that was nearly everybody, had to pass by their booth. In the same hall 7 were Cisco and Microsoft, and that was pretty fast company.

The summits occupied the *Centre de Congres*, which was itself about the size of a football field. But still it was only one-fortieth of the total. And the Development Summit was only a quarter of that. Let's see, a quarter of one-fortieth: it was a measure of the importance of the developing world. But if the anxieties expressed in the Development Summit had not been confined to Conference Centre A they would have spilled out and filled the entire forty acres.

Wednesday was devoted to the "Internet in Developing Countries" and "Development Models." We heard a lecture by the head of UNCTAD on this new animal, this odd thing that had metamorphosed from a little academic network into a leviathan that would change human experience as we knew it. It was truly nature red in tooth and claw and survival of the fastest. But there was another, less threatening side to the monster: it was friendly, and held out the prospect that every citizen would have access to the new repository of wealth, information itself.

I had heard the mantra in Egypt, about the plan to connect all Egyptian children—that precious investment in the country's future—to the Internet. But half of them were illiterate and the other half were tapping out designs in the *Khan el-Khalili* or collecting garbage. The educational system was a disaster. But there was another, more urgent, problem. Most of the information on the Internet was in English, and most was useless anyway. To be useful to the citizens of Egypt information would have to be in a language that was understood by the majority of Egyptians. That was when the Indian representative spoke up and suggested that the ITU had a role to play in ensuring that there was local content on the Internet. It was an example of the limitations of multilateralism, where everything was the responsibility of everyone. In fact, the only guarantee of Indian content on the Internet was for Indians to put it there themselves. The other problem had to do with the search engines that would make the information useful to more of us. And then we realized that this monster was still in its infancy, not even an adolescent yet, just a massive baby threatening to eat us out of house and home. What we needed was some kind of technological leptin to reduce its appetite and make it more agile.

Speakers from Vietnam, Kenya, and Nepal detailed their experience in providing access. The Vietnamese secretary general of the Department of Posts and Telecommunications, was the keynote speaker, but he arrived half an hour late, complaining of Geneva's cold. There appeared to be some successes, and the Nepali delivered a lecture on the need for competition. A man from the ITU made the useful suggestion that the Internet was probably not a cyberbullet and could well be a distraction. He then tried to engage the audience in a discussion of several questions about deployment—level of access, cost, and the role of government. But the penchant of the moderator for endless circumlocution, with summaries of everything that had just been said, stifled any real discussion. There was one speaker, however, who would not be stilled. He was a British journalist headquartered in Dubai, and he spoke passionately about the past glories of the developing world: "Make Timbuktu again what it once was, a great center of intellectual development."

Unfortunately, it sounded patronizing, of the "some of my best friends are Africans" sort. Actually when the first European, René Caille, arrived in Timbuktu in 1828, ravaged by scurvy and blistered by the sun, he found almost nothing left to mark its incarnation as a seat of Islamic learning. This was an example of a European fantasy transformed and offered up as an ersatz African fantasy: "You were great once, time to be great again." It was an attractive thought, but the way was forward, not backward. There was hard work to be done on the problems of access and cost before the Internet would be the answer for Africa.

The afternoon sessions dealt with development models. But if there was a constant theme it was the need for transparent regulatory principles that encouraged development. There was some confusion about the word "regulation." In Egypt, the government was simultaneously introducing a regulator and *de*-regulating the sector. But the difference was only semantic. The regulator was supposed to preside over the deregulated sector as a kind of referee. It was in this sense that regulation was necessary: it established the ground rules so that everyone knew where they stood. There would be no participation by the private sector—and certainly none by foreign investors—unless there were clear rules for interconnection, technical standards, dispute-resolution mechanisms, a sound body of commercial law, and provisions for repatriating profits. The speakers ranged from the private sector in the United States and Belgium to representatives of government in Argentina, the Netherlands, and Thailand. The terms "stakeholder," "business principles," "local ownership," "affordable," "realistic," and "effective" were the buzzwords. Big was not necessarily better, and the session was brought to a close by a man from Alcatel Belgium who suggested that mega-projects could be a liability. Alcatel was busy implementing its own mega-project in Egypt, NILE (New Income from Local Exchanges) Vision, so maybe there were exceptions.

That night on television there was coverage of the conference. On the French channel there was also a gritty documentary on the American war in Vietnam, part of that French obsession with American traumas. The documentary was a reminder that it was a different America then—and a different information age—from what we saw today. It had been filmed in Hue during the Tet offensive and there were none of the massive, petroleum-fueled explosions that were the staple of every movie since Rambo. Instead, the air seemed to be filled with whizzing, deadly, random little bits of lead. The GI's were matter-of-fact, whether taking cover behind a tank, firing into a building, or dragging a wounded buddy out of the line of fire. The corpses had the heavy, gelatinous look of the beef carcasses carried through the streets of Cairo in motorized three-wheelers. The soldiers seemed heroic as they went about their deadly chores. It seemed light-years between Vietnam and Kosovo where no Americans had died.

Day Five

Thursday was the last day of the presentations since Friday would be devoted to working groups. The sessions covered "Internet Governance" and "The Future for Private Companies . . . in Developing Countries." The first was largely a guide to getting on the net. Access was not a foregone conclusion. There were things like "domain names" and "IP addresses" that determined who could and who couldn't participate. But, beyond these, there was only uncertainty: the Internet was "a seventh continent," but one with no governance. There we were again, adrift in this revolution with no link to established institutions or procedures. Governments were often as helpless as individuals, and questions of content, suitability, and conformity to societal norms were important. It seemed that there really was no way to control the Internet, and that was both its greatest opportunity as well as its greatest threat.

The afternoon session on the role of the private sector was really the climax of the week. It was the session Mr. Hamadoun Toure, the director of the telecommunications development bureau at the ITU, had chosen above all others to attend. He was from Chad, another landlocked, strife-torn nation in the Sahel and his words were a testament to another revolution that had already taken place, the Reagan revolution. Now, private answers to public problems were the normal reflex, even in the developing world. The people in the room were realists, they wanted trade not aid, partners not donors. But the idea was easier to articulate than to put into practice. Everyone, including the private companies that had paraded through the summit for the past four days, wanted the same thing: increased access on a profitable basis. It was just that no one knew how to make it happen on any meaningful scale. The business case had to be there. Even the variants of the BT (build and transfer) schemes had not been as profitable as expected. There were build, operate and transfer (BOT); build, transfer, and operate (BTO) build own, operate, and transfer (BOOT), concession contracts, and exclusive contracts.

Venezuela was a star. A consortium led by GTE had bought 40 percent of the monopoly telephone company in 1992 and the government had sold another 44 percent to the public beginning in 1996. The results were impressive: the network was now 66 percent digitized, penetration was nearly 20 percent, and the company was the second largest investor in the country. There were many rural telecenters, and employees were now among the 100,000 happy shareholders. The employees seemed to be the key. Even with a political revolution in the country, and a populist backlash over the lack of development during the past twenty years, there didn't seem to be a move to undo the telecom liberalization. Everyone wanted the recipe, as if the thing could be bottled and released elsewhere. But it required the will to think differently, to recognize a different way of doing business, to reward initiative and punish inertia. In spite of all the talk about the importance of the market, the civil servants who made up the bulk of the attendees in the hall were probably not ready for these things. And they knew it.

There were a few words of advice from the developed world. The Venezuelan experience was "fully applicable" elsewhere, and debt relief could be used creatively to foster development. Even with all the talk about data, switched voice would be around for a while, although investment decisions today should consider Internet protocol, or IP, networks. Good regulation was the key to foreign direct investment. It was probably appropriate that the final word should be about finance, just as it had opened the summit: "Any good deal can be financed, anywhere. The trick is to make it a good one." That was the challenge.

The Final Day

On the final day the conference broke into working groups. The group discussing "Settlement and Accounting Rate Reform" gathered in a small room above the forum hall. The moderator was the Jamaican ambassador in Geneva and he kept the often-freeform discussion on track. The settlements system was the way the developed and developing worlds had traditionally divided up the spoils. It was an emotional issue and the implicit threat was that the developed world, led by the United States, was going to turn off the spigot. To the representative from Ghana this was a matter of equity, of fairness, even of *morality*. And there were operators—one was represented in the room—that were going *around* the system to connect subscribers more cheaply, and that wasn't right. It was a kind of *sin*. Countries like Ghana were poor and they needed these subsidies from the wealthy countries just so they could stand still, much less narrow the growing technology gap.

That put the problem at its starkest and we danced around the issue for the rest of the session. If subsidies were needed, it was suggested, we should agree on what they should be. If not, let the market determine the best solution. The dividing line in the room was stark. The Pakistani delegate was outraged about the cheaters, about leaky PBXs, VSATs and other illegal channels into his network. He asked several questions, but didn't seem to pay much attention to the answers. Maybe his mind was elsewhere: the military coup in Pakistan had been announced the night before. The American representing a company from Los Angeles that had started out as a callback outfit five years before, was equally straightforward: he was sympathetic to Pakistani concerns, but his margins were small and he had to survive in the market. He bought capacity from the cheapest provider and if that meant going round the system, it was just too bad.

All the issues brought up in the summit were there in the smaller group: international agreements, costing methodologies, the changing environment, the role of the ITU, subsidies, the plight of the developing world. Surprisingly, at least one country fell on the wrong side of the divide. Uganda had decided that the best way to attract investment was to open the system, settlements or no settlements. And that is what they had done. If Uganda hadn't been overcharging in the first place, there would have been no market for callback. The Ugandan solution may not have been popular in the room, but it represented the future. The handwriting was on the wall: the issue was not whether the old system should disappear, but when. The only question was what would be left to fill the void. In fact, callback was the mildest form of the new predation. At least it fell within the settlement system. The real threat was from Internet voice and from companies like the one in Los Angeles. Again, the choice for the developing world, again, was stark: it could have a declining proportion of something or a declining proportion of nothing. It was their choice. But it was clear that the people from Ghana, Cuba, Guinea Bissau, India, and Pakistan were not yet convinced. In the John Chambers formulation, they didn't "git it."

The closing session was back in the main hall. It was largely a report from the working groups of their conclusions. We heard what the delegates had done with the Centre of Excellence Concept, Community Telecenters, and Accounting Rate Reform. A *rapporteur* dutifully detailed the conclusion of each. And then our heads were filled, for the last time, with notions of technological challenge, competitive prices, the Internet, paradigm changes, the need for dialogue, the Internet, the need for regulation, development challenges, and the Internet. It was not an optimistic group that exited Palexpo A into the yawning chasm outside.

Burckhardt and Home

The next day would be devoted to Burckhardt. I knew that he had been born in Lausanne in 1784. What I didn't know was that his family had moved to Basel shortly afterwards and it was there that he had grown to adulthood. After the French Revolution his father had been tried for his life by the revolutionary party in Basel and, according to the "Memoir" in *The Travels in Nubia,* Burckhardt was "a daily witness of the misery suffered under the republican French." There "he imbibed at a very early age, a detestation of their principles, a resolution never to bend under their yoke." He became an Anglophile and all his works were published in English. His journeys in the Near East were at the direction and expense of the London-based Association for Promoting the Discovery of the Interior Parts of Africa.

He sailed for the Levant in March, 1809 and spent two and a-half years in Syria, traveling to the interior of the country, improving his Arabic, and incidentally becoming the first European since Crusader times to see Petra. He arrived in Cairo in September of 1812, intending to join the yearly caravan to Timbuctu. It would go westward through Fezzan, the largest group of oases in the central Sahara, roughly 500 miles south of Tripoli. But the caravan was delayed and, with apologies to the Association, Burckhardt set out to the south, exploring Nubia as far as Dongola, and incidentally becoming the first European since Roman times to see the great temple at Abu Simbel. He reached the Red Sea at Suakin and crossed in a pilgrim ship to Jidda. In Ta'if he met the Pasha, Muhammed Ali, then prosecuting his war on the Wahabis. Burckhardt performed the pilgrimage rites, continued to Medina, before making his way back to Cairo in June of 1815 in poor health. He had contracted dysentery in Arabia and it eventually carried him off. He died in Cairo on the 15th of March, 1817 and was buried somewhere in the city. After several years of searching I found his tomb in one of the poorest areas of Cairo with its memorial of his brief span of thirty-three lunar years. What it didn't say was that there wasn't a name in the annals of European travelers in the Near East, unless it was Niebuhr, that was held in such reverence as that of Burckhardt.

Lausanne was only forty minutes to the east by train and I decided to see his birthplace for myself. Maybe there would even be a memorial. I had hurtled the five kilometers from Cheserex to Nyon every day for the past week by taxi. This morning I walked. Most of the houses were sturdy, independent dwellings, surrounded by arbors and gardens. The little village was closed and shuttered against the early-morning fog but on the other side it opened out into extensive fields. Most were planted in what looked like sugar beets. Just outside Nyon there was a sugar beet elevator and several carts, loaded to overflowing with the beets, parked nearby. Other fields were planted in maize. The stalks were short and the heads appeared to be stunted. But then corn, unlike the American version on the cob, was fed to animals in Europe. There were also fields planted in something with spiky purple flowers, and some in mustard.

Other fields—long, rolling swells of land between the lake and the mountains to the west—lay fallow. The fields sloped up gradually from the lake to the foot of the western range. Above Cheserex it looked to be heavily forested. Near Geneva, the cover was not so apparent and the range displayed itself nakedly in layers of limestone. The corn and sugar beets probably replaced what had once been forest, but there were still little islands of green in the swells. Halfway to Nyon I went down a dirt path to one cluster of trees and entered far enough to see that it was dense. The trees were mostly oak and birch, although there were a few evergreens. The undergrowth was thick and I half expected one of the objects of *la chasse*—a deer, a pheasant, or a wild boar—to explode from its hiding place. But nothing disturbed the quiet of the morning.

I was the only pedestrian on the road. The cars came and went at what appeared to be the normal European rate of speed. I could hear the high-pitched whine as they approached and then the reverse effect as they disappeared. This being Europe, there was no cloud of dust. I reached the outskirts of Nyon after an hour and it was another twenty minutes to the train station. The 10:08 for Lausanne was waiting on the siding. It was the milk run, only three cars, and we made our deliberate way through Pringins, Gland, Alleman, Morges, and Loney Preverenges towards Lausanne.

The morning mist had lifted and now the slopes—closer to the mountains the farther north we went—were covered with vineyards. At 10:52 we pulled into Lausanne.

The city lay in the hills to the west of the lake and it was difficult to see from the station where the old city might be. But I walked up a long sloping *Avenue Louis-Ruche0nnet* before turning to the right on the *Pl. Chauderon-Montbenon* to the *Rue de Geneve*. And then the medieval city appeared across the gorge, topped by the spires of the cathedral. The gorge was spanned by several bridges and I crossed by *Le Grand Pont* before resuming my climb. The streets were filled with people shopping in an outdoor market full of beautiful produce at ruinous prices. There were apples, Swiss chard, broccoli, tomatoes, new potatoes, and fresh chestnuts. As I walked the prim cobblestone streets in the crisp autumn air I thought of Burckhardt in dusty, refuse-filled Cairo and of his letter to the Association from that city, dated July 20, 1815:

> I hope that you have found Sir Joseph Banks in good health. That venerable and noble minded patron of science has written me a letter containing expressions which I could expect only from a parent. As such I revere him, and my gratitude towards him would alone be sufficient to induce me to pursue my task, even if so many other considerations of honor and duty did not concur in demanding from me every exertion of my faculties towards this object.

Banks was the botanist who accompanied Cook on his first voyage to the South Seas. He was a member of the committee of the Association. In a shop on the upper east side of Manhattan in 1988 I had found a pair of twenty-four-inch globes, one terrestrial and the other celestial, that had belonged to Banks. They were asking $85,000 for the pair.

At the cathedral a plaque said that it had been consecrated on October 20, 1275 by Pope Gregory X. But in 1536 during *"la Dispute de Lausanne"* the city had gone over to the Protestants. Stained glass windows lined the walls but the nave was otherwise unadorned. Over a hundred meters long by thirty meters wide, it was a massive, football-field sized testament to the spare power of Protestantism. I tried to remember Burckhardt's religious affiliation before he became al-Haji Ibrahim al-Mahdi Abdullah. I couldn't, but the Gothic entranceway of the madrasa and mausoleum of al-Nasir Mohammad in Fatimid Cairo must have reminded him of the Cathedral of Lausanne. It had been taken from a Crusader church in Acre and had the same pointed arch and provenance as this one, dating from 1296. Up the hill and behind the cathedral I found a bookshop that carried antiquarian books. But this was a Saturday and it was closed. There was no street name or number on the window, much less an e-mail address.

From the vantage point near the cathedral I looked over the old city below. It was a sea of steeply-peaked, red-tile roofs, irregular as they followed the pattern of the little streets or lanes. In that respect it resembled Fatimid Cairo. But I still wondered what brought these sober northern Europeans to the teeming, foetid East. For Burckhardt it seemed to be duty, duty, and more duty. He had a responsibility to the Association and, in spite of sickness, he would carry it out. But a letter from Cairo dated September 2, 1815 suggested that it was a trial:

> I shall leave Alexandria next week and return by way of Damietta to Cairo, where I hope to finish my journals. The worst effects of my fever were shewn in a depression and listlessness which seldom permitted me to take up the pen . . . I have laid it down as an invariable rule never to sacrifice security to time, however reluctantly I may submit to the privation of almost every means of instruction, and to the total want of rational society. The latter, which is but feebly felt in travelling, engrosses all one's leisure thoughts during the tediousness of a long protracted fixed residence in any part of these uncivilized countries.

His grave was in one of the poorest parts of Cairo, an area of cardboard shanties and little lopsided tombs. There, his labors had come to an end. There was no memorial to Burckhardt in Lausanne.

Sunday was the return flight to Cairo on Turkish Airlines through Istanbul. In the departure lounge at the airport I recognized the Kyrgyz lady with the blonde bouffant. The Turks were moving steadily eastward into the former Soviet Union, into old Russian Turkestan—Kyrgyzstan, Turkmenistan, Uzbekistan, Tajikistan, and Kazakhstan—and Enver's dream of pan-Turan looked like it might finally be realized, eighty years on. The flight left at four fifteen and this time, without the cloud cover, the Alps were snowless on the lower slopes. We turned left over Brindisi and landed in Istanbul from the west. The transit lounge was the usual Babel and, in addition to French, English, and Arabic it included Turkish, an unfamiliar language. But thanks to Ataturk the monitors were in the Latin script and I read Guyantep, Antalya and Ashkabad. The sign over the gate read *kapi*, or "government office," the word conjuring up centuries of Ottoman domination of the Arab World. The monitor showed an EgyptAir flight to Cairo, the same flight that was highjacked the following night. On board, the cover of the in-flight magazine featured a lake with a typical autumn scene, all golds and browns with fallen leaves. It was a reminder that Turkey had always been a kind of debatable land, a meeting place between the desert and the sewn, north and south, east and west.

I was now halfway back to Cairo and reflected on the events of the past week. In the taxi that afternoon the driver told me that he had worked during the week for Cisco. They, too, were staying in Nyon since it was cheaper than Geneva. That seemed an odd concern for the most profitable company in history, but maybe that was how they stayed that way. Cisco was one of the architects of the new information order. With their technical wizardry they would bring undoubted benefits to the world. However, in the headlong career toward the future everyone seemed to ignore the pioneering work of the past.

But it was reassuring to know that there was still some reverence for the old. I bought a copy of *The Sunday Times* in the airport and an article in the money section led with the title "Works of the world's great brains soar in value." There would be a sale of books that week at Christies, and almost all would be scientific. There would be first editions of Copernicus's *De Revolutionibus Orbium Coelestium* dating from 1543 and Galileo's *Sidereus Nuncius* from 1610. Newton, Einstein, Fleming, and Crick and Watson would also be represented. Individual prices up to half a million pounds were expected. And to be fair, Bill Gates was said to be interested in the history of science.

I didn't find anything by Burckhardt in Switzerland but I did buy the *Geographie de d'Anville*. One of the mantras offered up at the conference was that, with the advent of the Internet "geography was dead." I hoped not. Jean Baptiste Bourguignon d'Anville (1697–1782) had been the most important geographer of the eighteenth century, one of the giants on whose shoulders everyone who followed stood. Even in the mid-1960s in the Navy we had still depended on star sights to establish positions at sea. Now, GPS was built into mobile phones. But that was only a detail and the old principles of position-finding remained the same. The *d'Anville* was a two-volume compendium taken from his maps and containing "the origin, location, manners and customs of all the people of antiquity, and a description of each place in particular, accompanied by a listing of interesting events through the reign of Clovis, with the chronology in the margin." It had been printed in Paris in "M. DCCC. VII." The date was an anachronism, and it was only with Arabic numerals and the decimal point that we were able to deal in nanoseconds. But the book was still a recitation of the best knowledge available in 1807.

That was the same thing, after all, that we had just heard in Geneva in 1999.

21

The Zabbaleen

The word came from the Arabic word *zibala*, or "refuse, rubbish, garbage, sweepings." A *zabbal* was a street sweeper. *Zabbaleen* was the plural and it described to the people who collected and recycled garbage. With a population of fifteen million—and that was at night, not during the day when *fellaheen* from the outlying villages came into the city to sell their produce—Cairo generated a lot of garbage. It was said that the city produced 8,000 tons of solid waste a day. That worked out to just over half a kilo, or about a pound per person for each of the fifteen million. It was beyond the capacity of the *zabbaleen* to collect it all and much was left to decompose in side streets, abandoned lots, or on the tops of buildings. For years we drove by an empty lot in Dokki that was filled with refuse, rising in a solid mass to a height of about fifteen feet. When they took down the fence to build on the site, the compacted layers could be read like an archeological record of the last fifty years. We actually knew an English couple in the 1980s who were excavating near Mit Rahina and old Memphis, who said they learned more about the Pharaonic civilization from what people threw away than from what they kept.

Collecting garbage was more than a job. It was a way of life. The people who did it constituted a caste unto themselves and on a flight to Egypt I remembered chatting with a Maltese nun who came every summer to minister to the garbage collectors in Cairo. She tried to introduce small improvements into their lives, but it was difficult with people so poor. She spoke of little children, tired after their nightly rounds, sitting with their heads in her lap at midmorning and falling asleep. Most of the *zabbaleen* were Christians, although it was not an invariable rule. There had been a recent Egyptian attempt to describe their lives: Yousriya Loza Sawiris had written a paper, *Solid Waste Management, A Pilot Project in Cairo, Egypt*. It was published by the Harvard Institute for International Development.

Sawiris was a prominent Coptic name, and this concern for the *zabbaleen* seemed community-spirited. The patriarch of the Sawiris family had made a fortune in Egypt before the revolution, lost it all when Nasser came to power, and had left for Libya where he made a second fortune. He had come back after Sadat and was now working on his third. He was the principal owner of Orascom Telecom, a powerhouse in mobile telephony throughout Africa and the Levant.

The paper contained some important facts and figures. There were five garbage collection settlements: Mukattam, Isbet el-Nakhle, Mo'atamadia, Tara, and a composite south of the city made up of El-Baragiel, Ain es-Sera, and Helwan. Mukattam was the largest, with a population of 20,000 souls. The other four combined were only about half that many. Mukattam alone processed 2,500 tons of garbage a day. Together, the others processed a combined 3,000 tons. The word "processed" was important, because the zabbaleen didn't simply collect garbage, they recycled it. In fact, the effort was a classic community-based recycling effort. It was everything the developed world, generating its own prodigious amounts of waste, was now encouraging. The involvement of Harvard was not so much to encourage the activity as to document what was already taking place. Maybe we could learn something from the developing world for a change. But before we waxed lyrical about this ecological awareness, we should probably understand the costs.

Because there were costs of the recycling, on the environment and especially on the health of the *zabbaleen*. In terms of the environment, there were the problems of carbon dioxide from wet garbage, lead in the air from unregulated fires, and a general lack of sanitation. The air quality in Cairo was abysmal although, even on a bad day, it didn't seem as toxic as Delhi, Athens, or even Los Angeles. But the real villain was what you didn't see, mainly lead, smelted in countless little shops where batteries were recycled. Lead in the air was particularly damaging to developing children. Then, there was the plague of flies, dubbed by some the national bird of Egypt. Flies were carriers of disease, and they seemed to be everywhere. Egyptians were always amused at the effort of westerners to swat the flies. Even if you were successful, there were millions more where that one came from.

The worst effects of the pollution were on the health of the people, particularly children, who were involved in the recycling effort. The diseases associated with garbage were many, and the paper estimated their incidence among the *zabbaleen*: gastroenteritis and diarrhea (20 percent), chest inflammation and asthma (20 percent), virus due to flies (20 percent), ophthalmic diseases (15 percent), kidney failure and renal disease (10 percent), and food poisoning (5 percent). The greatest killer of children was tetanus, where the pathogen entered through an open cut in the skin. Most of the children were barefoot and they literally lived with their parents in the garbage. A recent vaccination law had reduced tetanus by half, but the other diseases were still endemic.

The *zabbaleen* were not the only sanitary workers in Cairo. There were other recyclers, brokers, and administrators, as well as junkmen, scavengers, and municipal sanitation departments that collected street waste. The junkmen took everything, from books and magazines to broken appliances. There were also municipal dumpsites, construction waste sites, and a "resource recovery industry" that included primary dealers, brokers, secondary dealers, and processors. This industry was probably what the *zabbaleen* dealt with when they had finished their own processing of the waste. But in terms of volumes, it was the *zabbaleen* who really counted.

In the 1980s the little lopsided donkey carts were the most visible sign of the recycling effort. They were generally driven by children, often little girls who looked like they hadn't yet reached puberty. In Ma'adi we saw them as we drove to work. They were probably from the Helwan settlement. But we didn't see much of them because they were gone by midmorning and so were we. Collection was generally a nocturnal activity, with sorting taking place in the settlement later in the day. The things they collected were many. The first was organic waste. This was another way of saying discarded food, and the *zabbaleen* ate what they could before feeding the rest to the pigs, their cash crop. Trichinosis among Copts was fairly common, and many now refused to eat the mortadella and other processed meats sold in shops like Morcos or Thomas. But well-cooked, the pork chops, filets, and roasts were a welcome source of variation in a Cairo diet.

A second category was plastics. After they had been separated and sold by the *zabbaleen* plastic bottles would be washed, granulated, and molded by others in the resource recovery industry. *Baraka* in Arabic meant "blessing, benediction," and it was literally that, being the most common brand of bottled water in Egypt. The PVC brought 1,300–1,500 pounds, or $380–$440, per ton. The money was considerable and there were some who said that, beneath their rags, the *zabbaleen* were wealthy. But that sounded like a rationalization for official indifference to their condition. Other categories included compost, paper, cardboard, glass, metals and fabrics, mainly cottons. Just like the PVC, each was passed up chain to others in the recycling industry. It all seemed very efficient, this reprocessing of what appeared to be about 70 percent of the daily volume of waste in Cairo. But what was missing behind the numbers was the human side of the story.

I had always wanted to see a couple of things that existed beneath the surface of our privileged life in Cairo: a slaughterhouse, and a *zabbaleen* settlement.

In spite of years of requests to see a slaughterhouse, the butcher in Zamalek had been firm in his refusal. It was not something I wanted to see, he said, and he was probably right. I had seen buffaloes slaughtered by the side of the road in Baluchistan and the sheer volume of offal was astonishing. I couldn't imagine what it must be like on an industrial scale and I never saw my third world abattoir. The *zabbaleen* were more accessible, if you knew where to look. But it wasn't until Laura spent the summer with us and did a project at a recycling center with the *zabbaleen*, that I had my chance.

We decided to see the recycling center on a weekend, and the drive to the Citadel was familiar. From there, we would follow a minibus from the center up the hill. It would not be the Mukattam I knew. That was *Salah Salem* to the turnoff, past the caves that had been used as ammunition dumps by the British during the war, then the crest and the beautiful little el-Guyushi mosque and, finally, a view of the Nile valley and the city spread out below. Instead, we took the unfamiliar autostrade and drove in a more southerly direction at the base of the mountain. After a mile, we turned off the autostrade into a very poor area, filled with refuse and pools of stagnant water. Beyond a short rise, we reached a little plateau and then began the ascent through typically poor Cairo neighborhood with potholed streets, pedestrian traffic, cars, and an occasional truck filling the road to overflowing.

After about half a mile the recycling center announced itself with a scene out of the *Inferno*, an open pit, maybe a quarter of a mile on a side, filled with a gray mass of refuse. There was no other color, just the gray, and smoke rose in individual fires scattered over the Stygian surface. Actually, there was no surface as such, since it was being worked by a backhoe, and bucketsful were being loaded onto a conveyor at the back. The belt carried the material to a large inverted "V" before falling again to the level of the trucks where it was loaded. It looked like the pit had been carved out of the mountainside, since there was a sheer wall along the back where the conveyor lay. The material was used as compost in land reclamation projects.

The center where Laura worked was inside the compound where the pit lay but separate from it. There, girls were working in various handicrafts, from paper-making to sewing. They were *zabbaleen* and most had had no schooling. The surroundings were neat and clean, and we would later appreciate how welcome this must have been to the girls. They were friendly and showed us how they worked. On the ground floor, they were making paper by macerating loose pages in a slurry of water, before spreading, pressing, drying, and cutting it to size. The final product was a coarse paper, very attractive and suitable for brochures, greeting cards, and wedding announcements. In the little gift shop it was priced like the specialty product it was. The "paperless office" promised by the personal computer revolution had, instead, produced a torrent of paper, and we later sent several years of accumulated project files to the Mukattam for recycling. The same kind of thing was done with cloth, and the product was a kind of mixed bag, like the rugs made from scraps in the United States.

This first visit was interesting but it was only a hors d'oeuvre. The real area of interest was up the hill, around the back of the pit, and there we would see where the girls lived. It would take place on the next weekend. Then, we drove past the recycling center and the compost pit and continued up the mountain. The Mukattam range sat maybe 1,500 feet above the valley floor, and was sheer on its western face. It had a storied past, and had served as a quarry for the limestone that was used to build the pyramids of Giza and Dahshur. Here, on the back side or eastern face, the rise was more gradual. In fact, it wasn't so much a face as a slope, passable to vehicular traffic, and the built-up area continued all the way to the top. The *zabbaleen* settlement wasn't long in announcing itself. First, there were telltale piles of segregated garbage: cardboard, the boxes collapsed and gathered together in stacks like cordwood; mounds of plastic Baraka bottles, paper in heaps, piles of scrap metal. And in the midst it all was the organic material, the wet garbage, along with the pigs, goats, dogs, cats, and human beings that consumed it.

But the garbage wasn't so much in separate piles as in separate houses, because the *zabbaleen* lived where they worked, or worked where they lived. A shop or housefront would be piled high with cardboard. Another, unfinished like so many buildings in Cairo, would be full to the ceiling with plastic bottles, tethered by their necks in smaller groups before being sent off to be washed, granulated, and molded into pellets. The pellets would be turned into the cheap plastic bowls and other implements we saw in the *sha'bi* markets. Still other buildings would be full to overflowing with paper: cheap books, magazines, newspapers, and loose leaves. Some of it would be turned into the specialty sheets we had seen the girls making below. But that was just a little cottage industry, and the real volumes were here, farther up the hill. And filling the air with its aroma was the organic stuff and the living things that were attracted to it. The wet garbage seemed to be everywhere, as pervasive as its odor, filling the buildings, the little yards in front, and spilling into the streets.

The first thing you noticed were the flies, attracted to the warm, moist medium as an ideal place to lay their eggs. They appeared in swarms, rising en masse as we drove by, before settling again after we had passed. They were vectors of disease, carrying the microbes from the garbage to the human hosts and back again in a continual cycle. They lighted on the faces of children, and there were so many that the children no longer even made the effort to brush them away. The flies sat on open sores, around mouths and, particularly, around the eyes. Ophthalmia, or conjunctivitis, once so noticeable to visitors to Egypt, was probably no longer the scourge it had been. How many blind reciters of the Qur'an had been made, courtesy of the flies? But still it was a public health problem and even a few blind children were too many.

There must have been rats, but they were nocturnal animals and furtive. They were also vectors of disease, carriers of the fleas that spread the bacterium *yersina pestis* that was responsible for the bubonic plague, or Black Death. Medieval Cairo was periodically visited by the plague and it was not uncommon for a quarter or a third of the population to be carried off. The bodies would be collected and buried outside the walls of the city until the bearers themselves became infected. Then, they lay in the streets where they fell, becoming themselves a source of corruption and pestilence. The rats weren't blamed, instead it was the minorities, the Copts and Jews, and there would be outbreaks of violence against these unfortuntes. Now, the plague was gone and so, it seemed, were the rats. In ten years in Cairo, one of the most densely populated cities in the world and an ideal medium for rats, I had seen only a handful. Actually, I saw more Egyptian mongoose than rats, and maybe that was the reason.

A second element in the food chain were the chickens, the roosters strutting through the heaps and the hens pecking at loose grains or scraps, occasionally darting in to collect a choice bit before one of the larger animals found it. The other animals were soiled by their contact with the garbage, but the chickens managed to preserve their dignity and their smooth, unruffled feathers. Next were the goats and sheep, ruminants and herbivores, and what were they doing here in this steaming, foetid mass? But even for the ruminants there were edible scraps, cuttings, greens, turnip ends, onionskins, corn silk, eggplant stumps. The Egyptians were a bean-eating people and they accompanied their messes with vegetables, all requiring paring, chopping, slicing, and dicing. The rejects went into the garbage and, so, up to the Mukattam. The Children of Israel may have decamped for the land of milk and honey, but they left behind the land of wheat, maize, beans, lentils, onions, garlic, marrows, okra, eggplant, cucumbers, and melons. The ruminants had plenty to occupy them in their leisurely browsing through the mass.

Next were the carnivores, and their attentions were anything but leisurely. Cats had been a part of Egypt since Pharaonic times and they found much to their taste in the mounds, particularly the remains of chicken and fish. Dogs prowled and snapped at anything that looked edible, bones, skins, and bits of fat. There was enough for everyone in this feast, but the dogs never seemed to believe it and while they ate they kept a watchful eye on their peers. Occasionally, one would charge a smaller dog and drive it away from a choice morsel, before returning to its own. They were typical Egyptian street dogs, beige in color with dark patches around the muzzle, looking like shepherds, but smaller. They were supposed to be full of rabies, although often not in the foaming-at-the-mouth stage. In Ma'adi in the 1980s the police shot dogs and left them where they fell. One lay under our kitchen window for a week, growing fatter until the pressure of the gases burst the envelope, followed by collapse and escape of the liquid contents. We finally persuaded the *bawwab* to bury it, but it was just the kind of silly thing a foreigner would do. He probably tossed the carcass in an open pier hole at a nearby building site.

Last in the food chain were the omnivores, the pigs and people. The pigs weren't cute little pink things or the thousand-pound Poland China animals we saw in encyclopedias. They were ugly brutes, looking like the wild boars we had seen rooting through the garbage heaps behind the Islamic University in Islamabad. They were small, the adults looking like they weighed maybe seventy-five pounds, and they came in several colors: white, gray, or black, and I saw an occasional black bristle on a pork roast from Thomas.

But the most striking were the redheads. These were not smooth animals, but were covered in coarse hair. The hair itself was not evenly distributed, but appeared in tufts with spaces between the individual strands. For some reason, the red ones stood out, with their ugly snouts and the long, individual auburn hairs running the length of their backs. The pigs rooted methodically through the piles, paying no attention to the other animals. They were ideally made for their task, with jaws that could snap the femur of a cow. Pigs could be dangerous to humans, although these probably lived in peace with their fellow omnivores. When they weren't roaming the streets they were kept in pens somewhere near the settlement. Muslim dislike of pigs was more than dietary fastidiousness. They had a kind of shuddering horror of them, and Christian indulgence of these animals, as well as their use of alcohol, were probably more responsible for the sectarian divide than their alleged polytheism.

Finally, at the top of the chain, were the humans. Like the others, they lived and worked in the garbage. All of them, men, women, and children, were involved in the business. In the 1990s, small Toyotas had replaced the donkey carts. That meant a different kind of pollution and the need for capital investment as well as running costs, gas, oil, and maintenance. It also meant that men had replaced the children, at least as drivers, and we would see them in the morning in Dokki as they completed their rounds. What looked like large mesh drop-cloths would be tied up around smaller bags, and the huge bundles would be loaded on the Toyotas. There were still children involved, mainly boys, and they would bring smaller bags to the central collection area. "Smaller" was a relative term and I never saw a child who wasn't, like the Toyotas, overloaded. Then, groaning with the weight, the little trucks would set off for the Mukattam. The toll on shock absorbers and leaf springs, not to mention human shoulders, and backs, must have been terrific.

In the settlement the Toyotas would be unloaded and the women and older girls would set to work sorting the mass into the familiar piles: organic, plastic, cardboard, paper, metal, and cloth. There couldn't have been much room for hygiene in this work. You wondered how they escaped the garbage in the hours when they weren't working in it, and the answer was that they probably couldn't. They weren't like the little boys who worked in the automobile repair shops, whose clothes were black and stiffened with motor oil. At the end of the day, the boys changed clothes. Here, they were deeply soiled with organic waste, and the odors must have permeated everything they wore. That is what made the girls in the recycling center stand out, the neatness and cleanliness of the surroundings, and of themselves. The women sat when they could and clusters of them would be chatting as they worked.

The smaller children had not yet been drafted into the workforce. They stood, barefoot and often half-naked, attended only by the flies, or played with what passed for toys they found in the heaps. They could look forward to matriculation, but only into the ranks of the older children, as garbage boys or truck drivers, or sorters. The girls would probably marry only truck drivers or sorters and so the cycle would continue. Somehow, amid the garbage, they were born, grew up, married, made love, gave birth, raised families, died, and were buried. It was the same with the other animals in the chain, and all of them—flies, chickens, geese, sheep, goats, cats, dogs, pigs, and people—lived together in this crazy commune based on trash.

It was called a "settlement" because the people had been "settled" here. There was talk of "settling" them somewhere else, beyond the city where they would still be out of sight. The proposed site seemed to be near Qatamayia, still on the Mukattam but farther south, where the new country club and golf course had recently been built. It was a world-class facility, with undulating fairways, water hazards, and large smooth greens. The move outside the city would have other consequences, not all of them good for the *zabbaleen*, including greater commute time and increased running costs for the Toyotas. The concern about visibility was odd, though. We were in our eighth year in Cairo and we had to go out of our way to see the settlement. Tourists didn't see the garbage collectors, unless it was early in the morning when they made on their rounds, and they certainly didn't see where they lived. The congressional delegations that passed through Cairo on a regular basis were probably not taken up the Mukattam. The reality was that, for all of their ecological service to the city, the *zabbaleen* were an embarrassment.

Several weeks later we went up to see the churches cut out of the rock at the top of the Mukattam. We went up the same way, bouncing past the recycling center and the compost pit, then the settlement itself. Beyond the settlement the road improved. After about half a-mile a gate announced the sacred precincts and we were admitted after a short inquiry as to our interest. We said we just wanted to see the place. Nestled into an area just below the summit and the microwave towers, it covered several acres and was as quiet and clean as the settlement below was noisy and filthy. To the right was a little reception center where booklets on Egyptian Christianity and these churches were sold. To the left and on the cliff face biblical scenes had been carved into the limestone. Texts in Arabic identified each. Below, and hewn out of the same limestone, were a series of small churches and chapels. They looked new although, given the antiquity of Egyptian Christianity and settlement on the Mukattam, it would be surprising if the site weren't very old. In the foreground a European artist—someone said he was Polish—was working with a pneumatic hammer on a large sculpture.

At the far end of the site were two more grotto-like churches and a large amphitheater, also cut out of the rock. Inside the amphitheater it was cool and looked like it would hold several hundred people. Back outside, the sun was bright, the effect increased by the reflected glare off the limestone walls. Occasionally, another car would arrive and disgorge its contents of nicely-dressed families who strolled through the grounds. The scene, with its quiet, almost monastic air, disturbed only by the pneumatic hammer of the Pole, the unhurried pace of the visitors, and especially the cleanliness, were in stark contrast with the settlement below. Was this a kind of parish for the *zabbaleen*, a place they could come for quiet and reflection, away from the filth of their everyday lives? Or were they equally unwelcome here? The question remained unanswered.

A short postscript will complete the story of the *zabbaleen* and their swine. The Egyptian authorities, always suspicious of this Christian predilection for pigs and with an instinctive horror of the animals themselves, used the pretext of fears over the spread of H_1N_1 influenza to call for the culling of swine in April of 2009. The fact that the two phenomena were unrelated made no difference to the bureaucrats. The result was probably predictable: much organic waste, previously consumed by the pigs, is now left to rot in Cairo neighborhoods. And the lives of the garbage collectors who were their owners have been made more difficult still.

22

The City

People said that Cairo was like Calcutta, you either loved it you or hated it. There was no middle ground. There was probably more reason to hate than to love it. After a long absence the city reintroduced itself with the chaotic traffic on the airport road and the knot in the pit of your stomach. The knot came from the air quality, or lack thereof. The per-capita distribution of cars in Egypt was probably no greater than in other developing countries, but they seemed to be concentrated in Cairo where, on a given day, nearly a third of the country's population could be found. They burned leaded gas, maintenance was poor and, along with the power plants and little lead smelters to the south, cars were a major contributing factor to the toxic cloud that enveloped the city. Even public transportation, on which most of Cairo's poor depended, was a factor and until more buses were converted to natural gas they would continue to make their own contribution to the miasma.

Air quality was only the most noticeable thing, and a returning visitor would soon experience again the noise, the press of people, the decaying buildings, and the dust. Dust was the bane of our lives in Cairo. The streetsweepers didn't collect trash so much as dust, and what they swept into little mounds and scooped into their trolleys would soon be replaced by more dust. It had been that way for thousands of years. Dust was everywhere, on the streets and in the houses. It covered the leaves of the broad-leafed trees, the rubber trees and banyans. The most noticeable change after an occasional rain was that the leaves in the trees were now clean. They would remain that way for a week or so before taking on again their familiar gray-green hue.

But there were reasons to love the city as well. It was one of the world's major metropolises, and a return to Cairo after living elsewhere in the Middle East was a reminder of the fact. Jidda and Amman were as clean, neat and efficient as Cairo was dirty, chaotic, and hopelessly inefficient. In Amman most taxis were new and the meters actually worked. The roads were paved, the civil works were built to western standard, and in the office there was the prospect of accomplishing something. Jidda was much the same. But there was very little to *do* in Amman or Jidda. Cairo on the other hand was a cornucopia, a horn of plenty for the initiate, and the view from our twenty-eighth story apartment in Zamalek was an invitation to its riches. In reality it was several worlds at once.

Immediately below and to the east, on Ahmed Maher Street, were the embassies that backed onto the river. They were older buildings situated in large leafy grounds planted with bougainvilleas, frangipanis, acacias, jacarandas, and flame trees. They were as gracious as the new concrete boxes going up around the city were not, and they conjured up visions of a quieter and more refined era. Staffing the Zamalek houses in that era would have been Nubian *sufragis*, drivers, maids, and cooks, old family retainers who knew their place, and that place wasn't all bad. The sufragis came from the Ghayt en-Nubi neighborhood that lay beyond the old Opera House. But beneath the surface contentment there had probably lurked simmering resentments. Old timers at Telecom Egypt remembered a time when you couldn't appear in a *gallabiya* on Qasr en-Nil Street. On the same street you heard only English or French, Greek or Italian. When the Cairo mob—and it was hard to imagine such a thing on the eve of the twenty-first century—burned down most of European Cairo in 1952, they targeted shops with signs in Latin script, emblems of the oppressors.

Today, in the foreground to the south, was the tall circular stricture surmounted by a needle and known as the Cairo Tower or, more colloquially, as *wa'ef rusfel* or "Roosevelt's erection." This was a reference not to Teddy or Franklin D. but to Kermit Roosevelt, a CIA operative in the region during the 1950's. Roosevelt was behind the attempt to curry favor with Nasser by means of a gift of $3 million, given by Miles Copeland to a close Nasser associate. In spite of his reputation as a firebrand and demagogue, Nasser had a sense of humor, and he reportedly took the money but wondered what to do with it. After rejecting the idea of a giant sphinx with a thumb to its nose and twinkling fingers as lacking in subtlety, he used it to build the tower. It would be seen by every American operative from his room in the Nile Hilton, just across the river to the east, a standing reminder of the futility of offering bribes in post-revolution Egypt. Whatever the intent, the top of the tower offered a nice view of the city, although it was not as good as ours from the twenty-eighth floor.

Another reminder of the recent past was the Gezira Club, visible from a window to the southwest. It had been another oasis of privilege, to which native Egyptians were not admitted. The little cemetery for foreigners in the middle of the grounds was a reminder of the men, women, and children who hadn't survived the rigors of colonial service in Egypt. But the cemetery was another oddity in the late twentieth century and few people—certainly not the Egyptians—paid much attention to it. The Gezira Club was now emphatically Egyptian. The racetrack was still there, running like a girdle around the grounds, but badly gone to seed. They still ran races in the 1980s but the amounts bet at the track were derisory, a few pounds at a time. We occasionally played golf on the nine-hole course, but couples strolling over the fairways made it not only annoying but dangerous. You could kill someone with a golf ball. Now, the club was so packed on the weekends that drivers sat for hours outside on Gezira Street, waiting to be admitted.

Zamalek itself, to the south of the Gezira Club, and especially the area around 26th July Street, was another area with a storied past. It had been the neighborhood of European embassies after they were moved from Ezbekiyya, and of the shops that catered to the people who staffed them. To some extent, they still did. Thomas was still there on 26th July Street, still offering its deli selection of pork and wines, and a few tables where the Francophones could sit and talk. There was still an occasional restaurant like Don Quichotte, and the butchers, fishmongers, grocers, and booksellers whose clientele was primarily foreign. But Zamalek was changing as well. The store on the corner of 26th July and Barazil streets once belonged to the Greek greengrocer who supplied the *khawagas* with their everyday needs. Now it sold cheap shoes. Supermarkets had recently sprung up in Cairo, driving the smaller fry out of business. The supermarkets were an improvement if measured by convenience, cleanliness, and price, and their immediate success was an indication that the shopping public thought so too.

But the most visible sign of the change in Zamalek was 26th July Street itself, which was now elevated. An ugly concrete bridge ran from Bulaq on the east bank of the Nile to Mohandessin on the west, literally eclipsing the street that had once defined European Cairo. It represented another latter-day phenomenon in the city, the flyover, designed to ease the flow of traffic. It briefly did, but at the cost of the pedestrian scale of the city. People still parked under the bridge and walked on the street below, but it just wasn't the same thing.

The embassies, the Gezira Club, and Zamalek represented the recent past, but there was more to see from our vantage point on the twenty-eighth floor. Beyond the embassies was the river itself, the mighty Nile nearing the end of its 4,000-mile journey to the Mediterranean from the lakes of Central Africa. Actually, the Nile looked anything but mighty here, probably because we were seeing only half of it. Zamalek was on Gezira, a long sausage-shaped island that divided the river, and the other half lay behind us, across from Imbaba. In the distance beyond the Nile lay the Mukattam, the range of hills to the east, and the two were reminders of a remote past. But before you reached the Mukattam there were remnants of a kind of middle past. On the east bank of the river, south of the twin towers of the World Trade Center, was Bulaq, the old port of Cairo. It was where visitors coming upriver to the city once disembarked, as Pietro della Valle had done in 1616. There had still been an overland journey of a mile to the Fatimid metropolis, *al-Qahira*, the City of the Victorious. It was through the Ezbekiyya, an area that was later built up around the *birket* or lake of the same name, and della Valle had camped near Bulaq for the night.

But closer at hand than *al-Qahira* was the shallow dome and needle-like Ottoman minaret of the sixteenth-century mosque of Sinan Pasha. Sinan was an anomaly among the tyrants of Cairo, and his mosque was a Turkish oddity among the masterpieces of the Mamluk city. He was an Albanian and not a slave, the conquerer of the Yemen, and twice governor of Cairo. He eventually became viceroy of Egypt like Mohammed Ali, another Albanian or Macedonian who would follow 250 years later. His mosque lay among the little foundries, metalworking shops, and automobile repair shops that now made up Bulaq. The grounds were leafy and green and, in spite of the general decay of the buildings, it was an oasis of quiet amid the din and clutter.

Upriver from Bulaq were the Nile Hilton and the Egyptian Museum. As recently as the 1970s the Hilton had been the only decent hotel in Cairo, and aircrews had to book months in advance to be assured of rooms. It was still the doyen—or was it the dowager—of five-star Cairo hotels, where the old hands came to see and to be seen, although the code switching was even fiercer now in the patio restaurant behind the Marriott. The Hilton still saw its share of academics, journalists, and other literati, often dressed in safari jackets, although it wasn't clear what big game they were pursuing. Now, Cairo was awash in five-star hotels. In addition to the old palace that had been turned into the Marriott, there were the Ramses Hilton, the two Sheratons, the Semiramis, the Conrad, and the Four Seasons, all on the river and all within a couple of miles of one-another. These were the major establishments, and didn't include lesser fry like the el-Burg, the Pyramisa, and Shepheard's. The last was a storied name in the city, the original also having been burned down by the mob in 1952. The Swiss had taken over the New Shepheard's from the Egyptian Hotels Corporation, but it was still a little down at the heels. My most lasting memory of New Shepheard's was the sight of a mongoose streaking across the floor and into a planter box next to the bar.

When it was completed the Egyptian Museum had been pronounced an architectural abomination by Flinders Petrie. The lighting was still poor and the labels on the exhibits were often undecipherable. But no one could argue with the contents. If nothing else, there was the Tutankhamun exhibit on the third floor. An interesting annex to the museum complex was the library to the left of the main building. There could be found a trove of printed works, everything from sixteenth-century European histories of the world to records of the synagogues of Egypt. A morning in the library would be followed by a *shawerma* and a beer at the Hilton. The Stellas were cold but the meat still came in the old, bland *shami* loaf, not the *baladi* loaves featured by the other big hotels. At the Marriott there was now a *forn* and a fat *fellaha* to attend it, and the bread came to the table so hot that steam still hissed from little fissures in the pockets.

Along with the *baladi* bread, the major changes in Egypt from the 1980s to the 1990s were the availability of good, ready-made men's shirts, and the plague of *shishas,* or waterpipes, in the better establishments. In the eighties the only good shirts had been tailor-made, except that the long-staple cotton was exported and you couldn't find decent material in the shops on Gumhuriyya Street. But in the nineties Egyptian factories made shirts out of long-staple cotton to European design and offered them at shops like Daniel Hector, New Man, and Mobaco. At ninety pounds they would have been a bargain at twice the price. Old men had always smoked waterpipes in the little tea shops, but now they were the rage in all the big hotels and even women indulged. It was not unusual to see a girl in Levi's and hijab smoking a *shisha*. The habit later spread to Jordan and Palestine.

The view from the twenty-eighth story was dominated by the Nile, and the bridges that spanned the river were were a record of the architectural changes that had taken place in the city. It was spectacular at night when the scene was ablaze with light. To the north, and just within view, was the Imbaba bridge. It was a railroad bridge and so really didn't count. But further south were the structures that carried vehicular and pedestrian traffic over the river that increasingly came to bisect the city. The first was the 26th July bridge where the old, graceful ground-level structure was being dismantled. It was now almost gone, replaced by an extension of the concrete ribbon that ran above the street. The new bridge was modern, nondescript, and functional, except that there were cold joints in the concrete and forming lumber was still visible underneath. Seven hundred yards further south was the 6th October bridge, also modern and functional and also exhibiting little flaws in the work. These two bridges were built to carry the increasingly chaotic traffic between Dokki, Agouza, and Mohandessin on the west and Bulaq, Ezbekiyya, and the downtown on the east, and no concession had been made to aesthetics. The engineers could barely keep up with the growth in traffic. But the bridges brought other advantages and under the huge structures poor Cairenes often took shelter, or slept, or urinated, or all three, leaving telltale streaks on the walls.

Another seven hundred yards to the south was the Tahrir bridge, a throwback to earlier era. It lay at ground level and carried traffic from the Gala bridge in the west, over the island of Gezira to Tahrir Square in the east. There were traffic signals at several points along the way, and it was definitely not the high road. The span was supported by graceful arches like the bridges over the Seine, and at either end lay the recumbent lions the nineteenth-century architect had seen fit to post as sentinels. Their bland gaze had witnessed a tumultuous century in Egyptian history. Another mile to the south was the Gama'a bridge. It carried traffic from the vicinity of Cairo University, past the Israeli embassy, to the island of Rhoda on the east. The university and the embassy were an unlikely combination, but for the politically-active the proximity was fortuitous. It facilitated demonstrations and they sometimes blocked the way, requiring crossing at a bridge further north or south. Finally, just in view another mile to the south, was the Giza bridge. It was supposedly a "swing" bridge, but I never saw it swung.

To the east of the bridges, but short of the medieval city, lay the modern commercial center of Cairo. The area was actually fairly small, a rough quadrangle bordered on the west by Ramses Street, on the east by Gumhuriyya Street, on the north by 26th July Street and on the south by Tahrir Street. Altogether it was about a fifth of a square-mile in extent. But packed into the quadrangle were restaurants, publishers, bookbinders, banks, shoe stores, haberdashers, jewelers, confectioners, and booksellers. A tour of the bookstores constituted a regular weekend routine. The best of the lot in the '90s was the reinvigorated Orientaliste on Qasr en-Nil Street, just off Talat Harb. It had not always been so welcoming. The shop was originally owned by a Jew who was forced to leave in one of the periodic upheavals that had convulsed the region after 1948. He had been succeeded by his Egyptian partner who inherited the large inventory of fine old books, David Roberts lithographs, artwork, and maps.

On the few occasions in the eighties when the partner appeared in the shop he sat as if stuffed and mounted amid the artifacts. He would not exhibit his goods, he would not reduce the prices, and he would not show much interest in customers. To be fair, I think he'd had a stroke, but his commercial sense was abysmal. After his death the shop was sold to a group that included Hassan Kamy, the tenor. Kamy's wife ran it with a marketing sense as sure as the previous owner's had been deficient. She computerized the inventory and allowed access, behind a false wall, to the basement below, where the stock was much greater than what appeared above ground. She also advertised in the glossy magazines and newspapers and, most importantly, maintained the same prices after devaluation. And she took credit cards.

Where the prices had once been astronomical, they were now affordable, less than you would pay in London for the same items, probably because the pervasive damp and humidity had compromised the bindings of some of the books. I found treasures on a weekly basis: the large, beautifully-detailed 1811 French Expedition map of the city, an 1819 edition of Burckhardt's *Travels in Nubia,* and an 1848 Roberts lithograph of "Cairo Looking West." Those were just the big-ticket items, but there were countless others as well, offerings by Richard Burton, Richard Lepsius, Flinders Petrie, Edward Robinson, St. John Philby, Winston Churchill, Slatin Pasha, Gertrude Bell, and Sheikh Abd er-Rahman el-Jabarti. The last was author of the nine-volume *Merveilles ou Chroniques,* translated into French from the original Arabic by a group of beys and effendis. It was a firsthand, eyewitness account of Egyptian history by an Egyptian, or what passed for an Egyptian in those fractious, foreign-dominated times. This set had been printed on cheap paper and was cheaply bound. But it was not expensive to have it rebound in leather and it became a kind of encyclopedia of eighteenth-century Egypt.

In the eighties I had used another bookbinder on Sherif Street and, if you could put up with wait, the price was right. A complete, sixteen-volume reprint of Burton's *Arabian Nights* in leather and good cloth had cost the equivalent of ninety dollars, or just over five dollars a volume. But, Anwar, the little man who ran the shop, had gone to meet his maker and now the backlog was even greater. At the Orientaliste they offered to send the Jabarti to their own binder, and it was back in a couple of weeks. The price was still right. But the story of the Orientaliste had not run its course. There was apparently a dispute among the new owners because, suddenly one day in January of 2000, the shop closed. A guard sitting in a lawn chair on the sidewalk outside said—in true Egyptian fashion—that it would open again in a week. The week turned into a month, and then into June. June turned into September and, when I last visited Cairo in December of 2001, the guard was still there in his lawn chair and the shop was still closed.

Beyond the Orientaliste was Talat Harb Square, and another remnant of European Cairo. The buildings on the corner of Qasr en-Nil and Talat Harb streets would not have been out of place in Paris or Brussels. In fact, if your eye was drawn upward from the level of the sidewalk, this part of Cairo had many graceful facades. Unfortunately, behind the facades lay ruinous interiors and inefficient cage elevators that had a habit of stopping between floors. If you were lucky there was a *bawwab* who, for a few piasters, would expertly manipulate the controls. But there was another problem, and it was that this part of the city was laid out radially, like Paris. That meant, in the first few months, that you never knew where you were. Streets were not parallel, and you often wound up miles from where you wanted to be. Eventually, you came to know the city, but it was like learning Egyptian Arabic: there were no rules, you just had to know it. Asking directions was a mistake because no self-respecting Egyptian would admit that he didn't know the answer, and they often didn't. Bad directions were worse than no directions at all.

A second bookshop on a morning's rounds might be the Readers Corner on Abdel Khaliq Tharwat Street. I never bought anything there. That was because none of the old books that lined the upper shelves was for sale. The store was owned by Armenians and they weren't interested in selling anything but the newspapers, reprints, and newer books on the lower shelves. But it was worth a stop, just to see if they had changed their minds. They never did. Then, it was on to the Anglo Egyptian Bookstore on Sharif Street. Anglo Egyptian carried mostly new books. But not all new was bad and there were many recent titles of interest. I once scoured Cairo for Alan Gardiner's *Egyptian Grammar* making the rounds of most of the bookstores. But it was at Anglo Egyptian that I found the answer. The man at the front desk said they used to sell it for 150 pounds, although they hadn't carried it in years. It was out of print but he told me where to find several others on the same subject. His memory was even more remarkable when he showed me his identity card: he had been born in 1902, and so was then ninety-three years old. His longevity was amazing in a country where carbohydrates were the national drug and heart disease or adult-onset diabetes carried off most of the population by the age of fifty-five.

Then, it was back past the square at the intersection of Emad ed-Din and and Qasr en-Nil streets to *Livres de France*, the other quality bookshop in town. It was owned by a voluble Lebanese and her equally opinionated assistant, also Lebanese. Both were representatives of that *Francophonie* that seemed to believe that if you couldn't be French at least you could be the next best thing, or Lebanese. In 1986, just before leaving Cairo, I bought a 1773 French edition of Niebuhr's *Description de l'Arabie*, after a pleasant evening and dinner in the owner's Garden City flat. In Jidda I examined the book more closely and found that three of the twenty-five plates had been carefully cut out and removed. They were probably mounted and sold individually as prints. I had always thought there was a cerain honor among antiquarians, and that you didn't have to examine a book the way you would a horse, looking at its teeth. I learned my lesson.

When I returned in the nineties the owner had suffered a stroke and was a shadow of her former self. The assistant swore she would look into the matter, but too many years had gone by, and I really was interested the text anyway. That was intact. The downstairs at *Livres de France* was full of new books, mainly in French. But upstairs there was a room full of old books in French and English. There was everything from reports of the Egyptian survey department, to the massive tomes on the mosques of Cairo, to twentieth-century histories of Egypt and the Levant. It was always worth a look, although I never bought much there. I once saw a copy of Halevy's *Etudes Sabeennes*, but decided not to buy it that day. When I went back the next day, it was gone. It was an object lesson in patience: *as-saber* was not *gamil*, and when you found a book you wanted, it never paid to think about it.

Finally, there might be a visit to Senouhi on Abdel Khaliq Tharwat Street. It was not really a bookshop, but featured local arts and crafts, prints, and fabrics. However, the owner's husband had a back room full of books, into which he refused to admit customers and hardly went himself. Once in the early 1980s he had disappeared into this inner sanctum and emerged with a well-preserved, two-volume, 1776 edition in French of Niebuhr's *Voyage en Arabie*. I bought it for 600 pounds and it was the beginning of an ongoing, thirty-year pursuit of Niebuhr and the Royal Danish Expedition to Happy Arabia. Carsten Niebuhr was the German cartographer on the expedition, and they had spent the year 1761–62 in Egypt on their way to the Yemen. One of the results of the stay was Niebuhr's map of Cairo, the first detailed map of the city, and following his itineraries was a good way to learn the Fatimid city. The *Voyage en Arabie* was the only book I ever bought at Senouhi.

East of the rough quadrangle of commercial Cairo lay the area of the old Ezbekiyya Gardens. It was so called after the park planted by Mohammed Ali in the 1830s after deciding that the Europeans in the city needed a promenade. Earlier it had been the site of a *birket*, or pond, that was flooded with the opening of the *khalig*, or canal, that formed the western boundary of the medieval city. Originally dug by the Pharaoh Sesostris and leading to Kolzum near present-day Suez, the *khalig* had been repaired successively by the Emperor Trajan and by Amr ibn al-As after the Arab conquest in 641 AD. But shortly afterwards it fell again into disrepair, except in the vicinity of Cairo where, into the eighteenth century, it was still ceremonially opened with the rise of the Nile. It was now Port Sa'id Street, and the tramway.

The area to the west of the medieval city had an interesting history. Outside the walls of the Fatimid city and home to Copts and successive waves of immigrants, including Mongols and followers of the Great Khan of the Golden Horde on the Volga, it occupied a midway position between the city and Bulaq, the port on the Nile. Later it became the gathering place of jugglers, acrobats, animal tamers, and prostitutes. Much later, with the Mamluk urban project, it was the home to summer pavilions and the residences of many prominent beys, as they increasingly built near the *birket*. After the French occupation of 1798–1801, it became the center of European Cairo, and European consulates had lined the streets that bordered the Gardens. The Russian, Portuguese, Austrian, French, Prussian, Swedish, Italian, Dutch, and Greek consulates were all within 750 yards of one another to the north and east of the Esbekiyya. The British Consulate was on the west, near the original Shepheard's Hotel. The old Opera House sat to the south. The Ezbekiyya had always been an area of light industry and there was still a lively commercial neighborhood near the Opera telephone exchange building, sitting to the east of what had been the pond.

The gardens, reduced in the 1980s to miserable tufts of grass, festooned with barbed wire and smelling of stale urine, were undergoing a revival with the building of the Opera metro station. The southwestern corner was now walled off and there were actually gardens again: freshly-planted grass that was a vivid green, a huge banyan in the middle, and palms, eucalyptus, oleanders, and acacias scattered over the site. The bookstalls that were once a feature of the area had been relocated to Sayyida Zaynab and al-Azhar streets. What was left of Opera Square was dominated by the mosque of 'Uthman Katkhuda, sitting at the corner of Gumhuriyya, the street of fabric shops and tailors, and Qasr en-Nil Street. The amir 'Uthman Katkhuda Kasdugli was a prominent bey who established a sprawling commercial and residential complex in the early eighteenth century. The mosque was all that remained.

The word *katkhuda* was Turkish and referred to an Ottoman military title. During the Ottoman period it was assumed by prominent beys in Egypt, among whom Abdel Rahman Katkhuda was the virtual governor of Egypt during Niebuhr's year in the city. The mosque was known today to every taxi driver in Cairo as the mosque of *el-kikhya*, the vulgar form of katkhuda. Across the street was the equestrian statue of Ibrahim Pasha, the son of Muhammed Ali, one of the more enlightened of Egypt's tyrants and author of the Egyptian military renaissance in the mid-nineteenth century. Pointing in the direction of Syria, the scene of his greatest triumphs, Ibrahim was known to Cairenes as *Abu Suba'*, or "the father of the finger." Behind the horse's left flank had been the site of the *Ezbek* mosque, built by the eponymous Mamluk emir in the fifteenth century. It was torn down in 1869.

Beyond the refurbished gardens lay the Sednaoui department store, a reminder of pre-revolutionary days. Shopping at Sednaoui was like shopping must have been before the revolution, with a visit to a counter to select the item—and collect a chit; deliver the chit to another counter where the item would be retrieved; then to the cashier to pay and receive another chit; and finally to the counter where the item would be delivered on surrender of the last chit. Each step along the way required *baksheesh*. Most of the big department stores in the city had been owned by Jews but Sednaoui was a Syrian. That made no difference and it was nationalized along with the others in the Nasser years. Behind Sednaoui was the *Ghayt el-Nubi* where the Nubian *suffragis* lived. The neighborhood was self-contained, with butchers, bakers, little foundries, electrical shops, printers, woodworking shops, hardware stores, shoe stores, vegetable sellers, barbers, and street vendors selling everything from Syrian apricot paste to little packets of tissues.

Beyond and to the north of Sednaoui lay *Shari' al-'Arous*a, leading eventually to the tramway. The street survived the downturns in the area to the west of the *khalig* because it led directly to Bulaq. Today it was narrow but typically crowded with people, tractor-drawn garbage carts, cars, and trucks. Butchers offered the usual fare in these poor neighborhoods, sheep's heads, calves' feet, lungs, intestines, and other organs difficult to identify. Fishmongers offered silvery little things the size of sardines, and odd white fish with tiny mouths. They come from the Red Sea. These were not the fat shrimps they sold in Zamalek. The end of the street, where it intersected *Shari' al-Geish*, had been the site of the *Bab al-Sha'riya*, one of thrity-one gates Niebuhr showed in his map of the city. Nearby was a large covered market of the same name selling vegetables, meat, and fish. Today, nothing remained of the gate.

Cairo was a difficult city to know, if only because it was laid out so irregularly. There was no regular grid like Manhattan or Chicago. That was not only because it was not an American city, but also because it was so old. Actually, it was not the oldest city in the Middle East, or even in Egypt. As a site of human habitation, Damascus was probably older and there were cities in Upper Egypt that predated the original Heliopolis. But in terms of the relatively modern city, dating from Byzantine times, Cairo was still old and had grown up around the needs and propensities of its successive conquerers. Roman (read Greek or Byzantine) Cairo had centered on the fortress of Babylon, south of the present urban sprawl, around what is now called "Old Cairo." Islamic Cairo had grown up around Fustat, or the encampment north of Babylon, chosen by the Muslims when they arrived in 641 AD. The Muslims stayed outside of the city both to avoid contact with the unbelievers and because there were so many of them. Fatimid Cairo, "the city of a thousand minarets," had been built by Shia' conquerers from the west over a period of 200 years, from 969 to the arrival of Salah ad-Din, our Saladin, in 1170. It had originally been a military area as well, and was further north still from Fustat.

Fatimid Cairo was what people generally meant when they referred to Islamic Cairo. But much of what lay within the Fatimid walls had been built by the Mamluks, the caste of military slaves that succeeded the Fatimids and ruled Egypt for the better part of 500 years. The first of the Mamluks, generally considered to be az-Zahir Baybars, arrived in 1260. The early Mamluks were Turks or Central Asians and they were quartered on the island of Rhoda. Hence, they were called *bahri* or reverine, Mamluks. The second wave, beginning in 1382 with az-Zahir Barquq, were from the Caucasus—mainly Circassia although there were a few from Mingrelia and Georgia—and they were called *burgi* since they were quartered in the *burg* or Citadel, built by Salah ed-Din with crusader slave labor. The Mamluks were recruited for their martial qualities and the most ruthless and violent of these men rose to the top, often embroiling themselves and, inevitably the city, in civil strife. When the Ottomans came in 1517, Mamluk rule was theoretically broken. But they lay low for a few years and were soon back on top. It was only with Mohammed Ali in the early nineteenth century that the rule of these outsiders was finally ended, although they remained for the next sixty years as the officer corps in his new European-style army.

Considering themselves descendants of the Hittites, the Circassians came from the northwestern part of the Caucasus and had provided male and female chattels to the great powers for centuries. The Genoese station on the Black Sea, established in the fourteenth century, facilitated the traffic. Circassian women were noted for their beauty and, well into the twentieth century there was hardly a good Turkish family that didn't have a Circassian slave in the household. Light in color, often gray-eyed and said to be brachycephalic (short-headed) in contrast with the dolichocephalic (long-headed) Arabs, the Mamluks in Egypt became a byword for violence and rapaciousness. But a number of them combined their ruthlessness with a passion for munificence, and they left behind them the treasures of Islamic Cairo: *tekiyas* or hospices, *khanaqahs* or Sufi monasteries, *sabils* or public fountains, hospitals, *madrasas*, mosques, and mausoleums where they memorialized themselves.

Under the Mamluks the city expanded with the ambitions of its ruling class, and the areas to the north, south, east, and west of the Fatimid core gradually became populous. First, there was an extension to the south, the first Mamluk urban project, and the area between the southern gates of the city and the ninth-century mosque of Ibn Tulun became dotted with belvederes and country houses. The second expansion took place to the west, around the Ezbekiyya and the pond of the same name. As they died, these former slaves were interred in elaborate tomb complexes that were originally free-standing structures, outside the city core. People moved into the environs and then into the tombs themselves, eventually constituting the southern cemetery and the "City of the Dead." Finally, as the Macedonians and then the Europeans came in the nineteenth and twentieth centuries, the expansion to the north continued and the space between the Fatimid City and the original Heliopolis was filled in with other neighborhoods, including Abbassiyya, the modern Heliopolis, and Nasr City.

All this activity was oriented around the Nile and the cardinal points of the compass. The river ran in a north-south direction and so did the city. For simplicity's sake, it was helpful to think of another rough quadrangle formed by the walls of the Fatimid city and the old *khalig*, lying a mile to the east of the river. To the south were Fustat and Babylon. To the north were Abbassiyya, Heliopolis, and Nasr City. To the east were the cemeteries. To the west was the river and, on the other side, Dokki, Mohandessin, and Imbaba. Further west was the pyramid complex of Giza. It was all very straightforward, at least on paper. But the city had grown like topsy and there was hardly a straight street in all of its environs. That made Cairo on foot a constant adventure.

Even from the twenty-eighth story the city of a thousand minarets was diminished. The minarets, now many fewer than a thousand, competed with the mid-rises and microwave towers of the modern city. But it was still possible to immerse oneself on foot in the spirit of a medieval Muslim metropolis, an open-air museum that was, unfortunately, now falling apart. A constant companion on the walks was the little paperback *Islamic Monuments in Cairo, A Practical Guide*. It had been written by a couple of American diplomats and was the best guide to the Islamic monuments of the city. A morning's walk could just skim the surface, leaving other days and weeks to fill in the details. It began near the mosque of Sayyida Zaynab, to the south and west of the Fatimid city. The mosque had been restored over many centuries and was now one of the most popular sites of pious visitation in Cairo if measured in terms of the attachment of the average Cairene. It was also one of the few mosques in the city to which unbelievers were not admitted.

Beyond, the first intimation of what lay in store was the early fourteenth-century mausoleum-khanaqah of Salar and Sangar al-Gawli. It stood on the right of *Shari' Saliba*, a hundred yards from Sayyida Zaynab. The adjoining jelly-mold domes were supposed to be unique in the city, although the Sultana near the Citadel exhibited the same design. The area was part of the first Mamluk urban expansion, in this case towards the *Birket el-Fil*, the

Pond of the Elephant, so-called after the long, trunk-like extension to the southwest. The *Birket* was long gone. Up the hill and behind Salar and Sangar, friends who chose to be buried together, lay *Qala' al-Kabsh* or Citadel of the Ram, where popular legend has it that Abraham prepared to sacrifice Isaac. Nearby was the madrasa of Qaytbey, where Niebuhr reported a Persian-period or Ptolemaic catafalque that was being used to water animals in 1762. He had made a detailed drawing, and Lane had later reported it as "The Enchanted Trough." Several boys took me up to the roof of a house overlooking *Shari' Saliba* and pointed out what was supposed to be a well in the rubble below. But it wasn't the trough I was looking for. I later found it in the British Museum.

Next on the itinerary was the fourteenth-century madrasa of the amir Sarghatmish. Attached to wall of the mosque of Ibn Tulun, it had been badly damaged in the earthquake of 1992, and steel I-beams now supported the back wall. A crack following the lines of the mortar ran jaggedly from top to bottom and it looked like the wall had buckled outward in places. Alternating courses of masonry appeared in the *ablaq*, or red and white, pattern that was a feature of nineteenth-century Cairo. *Ablaq* was originally Roman, but Mohammed Ali used it to dress up the city and much of the red part was painted. This bit of window dressing probably dated from 1840 and Ibrahim Pasha's victory over the Ottomans in the war of the Morea. The minaret was a transitional piece between the simplicity of Sangar and the standard, more complex Mamluk minaret. Over the centuries that had developed into a square, followed by octagonal, and circular sections, topped by an open pavilion. Some said it came from the design of the lighthouse of Alexandria, not that far-fetched since the lighthouse finally collapsed only in the fourteenth century and Qaytbey had built his fort on the site. Al-Ashraf Qaytbey (1468–98) was the greatest of the Mamluk builders of Cairo and a representation of his mausoleum now appeared on the Egyptian one-pound note.

The ninth-century mosque of Ibn Tulun was the oldest functioning Islamic monument in the city. Ibn Tulun was a Turkish slave of the Abbassid Khalif al-Ma'mun and had been sent as governor to Egypt in 868. He briefly raised the banner of rebellion before the Abbassids restored control early in the tenth century. The mosque was all that remained of the Tulunid city of *al-Qita'i*, plowed under with the restoration. The minaret was in the Mesopotamian ziggurat style and the view from the top, particularly north towards the Fatimid walls, was a glimpse into the past. Inside, the mosque was nearly deserted, five and a-half acres of repose, where the noise and activity of a city of fifteen million people could be temporarily forgotten. Following Niebuhr, I paced off the exterior walls until a pack of dogs emerged from a stand of tamarisks in the rear of the grounds and drove me away.

Outside the walls and back on *Shari' Saliba* lay the fifteenth-century madrasa of 'Ezbak al-Yusufi, the man after whom the Ezbekiyya Gardens may or may not have been called. It had interesting blazons in the facade but even with the description from the book they weren't apparent. It was now nearly noon and men were hurrying into the madrasa to pray. So I retreated to Ibn Tulun and set out from the northeast corner towards the double mosque and *khanaqah* of Shayku on the corner of *Shari' Saliba* and *Shari' Suyufiya*. They lay on opposite sides of the street, then being excavated for a new sewer line. Of all the American projects this seemed to be the most useful if it would free the poor neighborhood from the plague of gray water that periodically covered it to the depth of a foot or more.

Inside, the *khanaqah* was being restored but there remained a few signs of its previous glory, faint remnants of color in the ceiling above the mihrab. The three stories of cloisters were open and the top of the building offered another view of the city, this time to the northwest. Shayku had been a commander to the boy amir, Sultan Hassan. A *khanaqah* was a dervish institution and the derivation of the word was interesting. It was surely from the Persian *khane-gah*, referring to a monastery for Sufis. But the Arabic triliteral *kha-na-qa* meant "to suffocate, stifle, smother, strangle, throttle, choke to death." If anything characterized the Mamluks it was their propensity for violence and many Mamluk pretenders, including Hassan, suffered the above, or a worse, fate.

The Citadel and fourteenth-century madrasa of Sultan Hassan lay another 500 yards ahead. They were a reminder that even in the twentieth century Cairo was still a suspicious city. In my walks I often used the same tools that Niebuhr had used in making his map: a small pocket-compass, my two legs, and five fingers as counters. But even in the last decade of the twentieth century it was the better part of wisdom not to be seen using a compass. This was especially true near the police station below the Citadel, where a group of black-uniformed police in flack-jackets lounged. They looked like a SWAT team. Across the street, the *Bab el-Assab* was still closed for "military reasons," and it was always best to avoid suspicion. Even more difficult was the fact that counting required concentration, and I waved off several salesmen in the Street of the Tentmakers and didn't reply to the little boys who welcomed me to Cairo.

Sultan Hassan had been a puppet in the hands of more powerful amirs. He reigned from the age of thirteen to twenty-eight when he was assassinated. His madrasa was a masterpiece of Bahri Mamluk architecture. The offset portal was an example of how the architects accommodated these monumental structures to the often-irregular plots on which they were built. It was interesting to speculate on how architects operated in the fourteenth century. There probably would have been no working drawings, blueprints to be unrolled if there was a question as to the architect's intentions. Did these buildings exist only in the mind's-eye of their creators, executed by builders who would no more understand a blueprint than the boat builders who still built teak dhows in Sharjah? Inside, beyond the cool and winding—and slightly menacing—vestibule, the familiar cruciform plan of the madrasa revealed itself. David Roberts visited it in October of 1838, making the sketch that would later become the print of the same name. He was not the last to note that "like every other mosque as well as the city itself, it is fast falling into decay." It was boarded up in Niebuhr's time, having been shelled from the Citadel during one of the Mamluks' civil wars. The decoration on the walls around the *mihrab* was beautiful, ornamental *kufic* and fine *thuluth* with alternating bands of floral arabesques. Sultan Hassan was not buried here, only his two sons.

Up the hill towards the back entrance of the Citadel lay the little *Shari' Bab al-Wazir* and in its half-mile length lay more monuments than any street of equal length in Cairo, unless it was *Shari' Mu'izz li-Din Illah* on the other side of the Azhar. There was now almost too much to see and a day's walk could only scratch the surface. The first was the extraordinary fifteenth-century *maristan* of Sultan al-Muayyad. The word *maristan*, a contraction of the Persian *bimaristan*, meant a lunatic asylum or a hospital, and there was almost nothing left of it. But sitting just off the street, the pure lines of its outer shell made it one of the most beautiful of the monuments of Cairo. A hint of Islamic blue remained in a medallion between the arches. Now, its only occupants were the street dogs that rose and moved warily to the back of the structure as a visitor entered.

A hundred yards farther on the right lay the mosque-mausoleum of Khayrbak and the mosque of Aqsunqur. They were actually of different provenance, the first dating from the early sixteenth century and the second the late seventeenth. But they would be forever paired in my mind since they appeared together in the foreground of Roberts' print "Cairo Looking West." I spent several weekends on the mounds to the east of the medieval walls looking for the vantage point from which Roberts made the sketch. They remained two mystery mosques until I finally found them, and then they seemed obvious. But there were reasons why they were not readily apparent today. Then, the *ablaq* masonry was very prominent, at least in some prints, and the red had faded to a barely-noticeable shade of gray. And the minarets had changed over time. Roberts had recorded all four sections of the minaret of Aqsunqur, instead of the three that remained today. Above the third section there had once been the columns with stalactites that Roberts showed in his print. It was still a rare example in Cairo of a completely circular minaret, not the classic square, octagonal, followed by circular pattern. The minaret of Khayrbek was now also truncated, and the top section shown in the Roberts print, composed of columns carrying stalactites with the bulbous finial, was gone. But the dome was still covered with the delicate floral arabesques that Roberts had so carefully rendered.

Kharybek had betrayed the last Mamluk Sultan, Khansu al-Ghuri, at the battle of Marj Dabiq in Syria in 1517, leading to the Ottoman conquest of Egypt. As a reward he was made the first Ottoman viceroy of the country. But forever associated with his name was the opprobrium that attached to a turncoat. The mosque of Aqsunqur was also known as the Blue Mosque because of the Iznik tiles that were applied as a kind of wainscoting in the middle of the seventeenth century. They were a touch of light blue in the otherwise dun-colored field that prevailed in rest of the Fatimid city. Cairo was no Samarkand. The large tree standing in the middle of the congregational area gave the mosque an almost bucolic look.

It took an effort of the will to press on to the few monuments chosen for a brief survey, a conscious decision to resist the temptation that lined both sides of the street. But resistance was necessary if the day's program was to be completed. This was a thriving, outdoor museum and people still lived and worked among the monuments. The *madrasa* of Umm Sha'ban still fulfilled its educational role and today was being used as a girls' school. The sixteenth-century Maridani mosque, once the gathering place of the Turks in the city, still served as the congregational mosque of the neighborhood. Next on the itinerary, as the *Shari' Bab al-Wazir* turned to the northwest and became *Shari' Darb al-Ahmar*, was the fifteenth-century mosque of Qajmas al-Ishaqi. The book called it a "jewel-like structure" from the Burghi Mamluk period. Inside it *was* jewel-like, with the play of multi-colored light altered by its passage through stained-glass windows. A climb through the spider webs of the claustrophobic little minaret yielded a fine view of what had been the medieval city.

Then it was on to the massive eleventh-century *Bab Zuwayla*, the southern entrance to Fatimid Cairo. It had been built by Armenian wazir Badr al-Gamali and named after Berber al-Zuwayla tribe, then quartered in the area. Passage through the gate, undergoing restoration, was into another world, away from the suburban sites favored by the Mamluk latecomers. But even here within the Mamluks had found room to build and the first sight, to the left and now incorporated into the gate structure, was the fifteenth-century mosque of Sultan al-Muayyad. It was notable for its size although the state of repair was ruinous, even for Cairo. Inside, it was another respite from the press of humanity, a characteristic of the mosques of the city, with the exception of those few reserved for believers. I was never made to feel like an intruder, even in the small structures off the beaten path. There was always space for one more soul to sit and read in the cool and quiet. The view from a minaret, a hundred feet above, was even better than that from Qajmas.

Now, it was it became a race to *Shari' al-Azhar* and the midpoint in the tour. "Race" was a relative term since the street narrowed and the crowds thickened, especially on a Friday after the mosques emptied. But this quarter-mile was entirely secular, a teeming area of shops and of the shoppers who patronized them. There weren't the trinkets made of brass, cloth and wood offered in the Khan al-Khalili across the pedestrian footbridge, although you could have a fez made to order at a nearby shop. Instead it was inexpensive clothes, fabrics, shoes, toys, sweets, and spices, the necessities of everyday life. Cars and trucks weren't admitted but horse-drawn wagons were, and there would occasionally be a halt in the flow of humanity as one of the large animals with its tethered burden was turned in the narrow street. It required a great deal of backing and hauling, shouting and cracking of the whip, and the clattering of iron-shod hooves on the pavement. Then the flow would resume, individuals stepping over the fresh manure the animal always left as a result of its exertions.

In the distance was the odd minaret of the Ghuriya, a slender square topped by two smaller squares, each with its own bulbous finial. It was a dramatic departure from the classic Mamluk style, and it seemed that al-Ghuri had foreseen his betrayal and made an architectural pact with the future. A hundred and fifty yards up the *Shari' al-Azhar* were more monuments of our old friend Qaytbey, first the *sabil-kuttab*, or establishment where water was dispensed gratis, and then his *wikala*. The *wikala* was one of few remaining of what had once been hundreds in Cairo. They were caravanserais for merchants, the ground floor consisting of stables for the animals and warehouses for the merchandise, and the upper floors of rooms for their owners. This one now housed craftsmen in brass and copper, pottery, and inlaid wood. They charged an entrance fee.

Al-Azhar Street was always a break. It was roughly the midway point in distance, although not in terms of the sights to be seen. It had been just over a mile and a-half from Ibn Tulun to the Azhar. It would be just over another mile, to the *Bab al-Futuh*, the northern gate of the medieval city. We were about halfway there, if the tour extended to Burckhardt's tomb beyond the walls.

It was also a break from the medieval city and and a time to recharge our batteries. Across the footbridge and on the edge of the Khan al-Khalili was Dahan, a purveyor of kabobs. If the morning was sufficiently advanced and it was not Ramadan, the fires would be lit and the kabobs—cubes of meat, liver, and kidney—along with a specialty of the house, *nifa* or roast goat, would have been prepared. After we had seated ourselves and the last vestiges of the aerosol insecticide had dissipated, the plates would be wiped and the glasses upturned by an officious waiter. *Torshi*—pickled turnips, carrots, and onions—and *tahina* would come first, followed by the meat. The *kababgis* below would first place the skewers over the coals then urge the embers into flame with fans made of ravens' feathers. Their upper bodies were stripped to the minimum in the heat and they handled everything with their bare hands. A quarter-kilo of kabobs cost the equivalent of about four dollars. It was good and filling, although the *baladi* bread was the inferior product of the local bakeries, not the steaming loaves made by the *fellaha* at the Marriott. Not everything new was bad.

After lunch came the highlight of the tour, *Shari' Mu'izz li-Din Illah*, the north-south artery of the Fatimid city. Over the rough mile of its extent, and in the side streets and alleys behind it, lay scores of mosques, *wikalas*, hospitals, *madrasas*, *sabil-khuttabs*, *khanaqahs*, and mausoleums. It was a visual feast and weeks could be spent in exploring the alleys and byways off the street itself. As before, it required resistance to the temptation that lay everywhere. But it was impossible to miss the thirteenth-century hospital complex of Sultan al-Mansur Qalawun. One of the wonders of an early age of attention to public health, it had been the quarantine station in Niebuhr's day. It was said that there had been a hospital on the site since its' founding, although the structure was undergoing restoration in the late twentieth century and medicine was no longer practiced there. The minaret was massive, the square first section inlaid and looking like it belonged in Faz or Rabat.

Next, on the same side of the street, was the fourteenth-century madrasa and mausoleum of al-Nasir Muhammad. One of five sons of Qalawun, his reign supposedly marked the high point of Mamluk culture in Egypt. The Gothic doorway was originally that of a Crusader church in Acre. Inside, it was a warren of gloomy passageways leading to the open square of the madrasa. The light in the mausoleum was filtered through stained glass windows and the tomb itself was undergoing restoration. Next was the late-fourteenth-century madrasa of az-Zahir Barquq, a slave of Qalawun and the first of the *burgi* sultans. His tomb in the northern cemetery would have been in the desert then, well outside the city. Now, it was just another neighborhood in greater Cairo. This was a massive pile, the substantial gray stone asserting the importance of the man and the caste he represented.

If Barquq was massive, the eighteenth-century *sabil-kuttab* of Abd al-Rahman Katkhuda was not. It was light and airy, with delicate horseshoe arches on the ground floor filled with latticework, followed by the pavilions on the second and third stories. It no longer fulfilled its original function of dispensing water gratis to the populace, but the upper stories were still being used as a school. For an Egyptian pound a man in a gallabiya permitted entrance to the structure and to much else besides. The building sat in the middle of the street, parting the flow of traffic. To the left was the main street itself, and to the right a series of mosques and palaces to which, for a small fee, the same man would serve as escort. The *sabil-kuttab* had recently been restored by the Germans, but it soon looked old again. That was probably because the agents that aged it were still at work. The dust, heat, and rising water table had always been there, but added in recent years was the air pollution that came from the millions of vehicles in Cairo. If they didn't appear on the other side of Azhar Street, they did here, and pedestrians competed with passenger cars, little trucks, and horse-drawn wagons. The vehicles always took precedence. It was mainly trucks, little Suzukis and Toyotas, moving raw materials in or finished goods out of the area. This was not like Bokhara or Khiva, where the Soviets had done much valuable work preserving the monuments of Central Asia. The fear there was that the cash-strapped former republics would now allow the monuments to deteriorate.

But Fatimid Cairo was still a living city and *Shari' Mu'izz li-Din Illah* was lined not only with monuments to the past, but also establishments serving the needs of the present. People had to eat to live, and to eat they had to work. There were ironmongers, workers in sheet metal, carpenters, and shops that made the *shishas* or water pipes that were now features in the five-star hotels. All required transportation and that meant vehicular traffic and pollution. The workers had to eat and there were butchers, bakers, and *fool* carts, where a nourishing meal that included vegetable protein and starch could be had for a few piasters. And, for some reason, this area was the *suq* where you bought green olives in season and onions year round. The latter lay in great mounds outside the shops at the end of the street near the *Bab al-Futuh*. If you wanted red onions, or yellow onions, or white onions, they were all there, sometimes packaged in large mesh sacks. The European housewife who wanted little pearl onions for a *coq au vin* would find them near the mosque of the mad Sultan al-Hakim, and only there.

Al-Hakim's eleventh-century mosque had recently been restored and was extensive, white, and immaculate. It lay at the end of *Shari' Mu'izz li-Din Illah* and permitted access to both gates in the northern wall, the *Bab al-Futuh* and, a hundred yards to the east, the *Bab al-Nasr*. Built, like the *Bab Zuwayla* by engineers and masons from Iraq, the two gates marked the northern limits of the Fatimid city. The walls to the east of the gates were worth exploring, revealing the occasional hieroglyphs and pharaonic reliefs in the stones the Mesopotamian builders used in their construction. Arrow slits admitted the only light into the gloomy passageways. Built to protect

Cairo from the Mongols, the walls connected with the Fatimid walls to the north, south and east, although Salah ad-Din's plan for a continuation of the walls to the west was never completed. But the Mongols never made it to Cairo and it was only in the civil wars that the city walls played much of a part. Jabarti describes the pomp as the heads of Ali Bey's victims were ceremonially carried on silver trays through the *Bab al-Nasr* in 1766.

In fact, all the crucial battles in the history of Egypt had taken place outside the city. Saint Louis and the French of the Seventh Crusade had been stopped in the Delta in 1247 and in 1517 the Ottomans defeated the Mamluks in Syria long before they reached Egypt. In 1798 Napoleon slaughtered the Mamluks in the Battle of the Pyramids in Giza to the west. The French squares, consisting of the sweepings of Europe, had decimated the reckless charges of the men who despised firearms as unmanly. In 1882 the British had crushed Orabi's forces at *Tel al-Kabir* to the east. And in 1941, Mussolini had his white charger flown into Derna on the Libyan coast in preparation for the ceremonial entry into Cairo. With his keen sense of history—and the histrionic—he would have been a natural fit, and we can imagine this latter-day Mamluk prancing through the *Bab al-Nasr* to the cheers of millions. But Rommel had been stopped at al-Alamain. It was a near thing though, and the skies over Garden City were gray with ash as the British burned their files.

The final stop on the tour would be the tomb of Johann Ludwig—or Jean Louis or John Lewis—Burckhardt. If there was a name, other than Niebuhr's, that was esteemed in the annals of European travelers in the Near East, it was that of Burckhardt. He had died of dysentery in Cairo in 1817. I knew that he was a Swiss and had called the Swiss embassy, since they had supposedly located the site of his grave. But those who knew—the former Ambassador and pastor of the Protestant church—were now gone. Someone thought it was near the *Bab al-Sharia'*. But that would have been on the western shore of the *khalig*, an unlikely place for a tomb. So I called back and received updated information: the tomb was not near the *Bab al-Sharia'* but close to the *Bab al-Nasr* outside the northern walls, a more likely location. So I walked the length of *Shari' Mu'iz li-Din Illah*, leaving the city by the *Bab-al-Futouh*, and made my way east to the *Bab al-Nasr*.

The area was north of the city but really was not a part of the Northern Cemetery. Niebuhr's map showed no tombs in the area in 1762. But today there were, and the always-helpful poor of Cairo helped me to find them. I said I was looking for the tomb of Sheikh Ibrahim Burckhardt—a *khawaga*—and Sha'baan, a passerby, led me for five minutes through a warren of clapboard huts and little grave markers to a rude *qahwa*, or coffeehouse, run by one Mabrouk. He had the key to the tomb and confirmed that it was Burckhardt's. So we walked to a small plaster building where Mabrouk unlocked the door. Inside lay a very Turkish scene, the catafalque in marble, six feet long by two feet wide and four feet high. At the head was a marble slab surmounted by a turban. On the slab was the following, in Arabic:

> God alone is eternal.
> This is the tomb of the late Sheikh al-Haj Ibrahim al-Mahdi Abdullah Burckhardt of Lausanne (may God in his infinite mercy receive his soul). He was born in Muharram, 1199 AH. He passed away in Egypt in the month of Dhul Higgah, 1232 AH.
> In the name of God, the Merciful the Compassionate.

Afterwards we sat while Mabrouk made tea. The surrounding buildings were poor and dilapidated—badly weathered wood and cracked plaster—but it was quiet and cool under the awning. I offered to pay for the tea for all of us, for Mabrouk and Sha'baan and me and a rogue with a lazy eye and three-day growth of beard who appeared after our tour of the tomb. But Mabrouk wouldn't accept money. Sha'baan and I walked back to the street outside the *Bab al-Nasr*. He also refused payment, one of the more endearing traits of Cairenes uncorrupted by contact with outsiders. There had been a recent piece on the Euro channel about the dangers of walking or driving alone in Johannesburg. But here I was in one of the poorest sections of one of the poorest cities in the world, without the slightest concern about theft. I had probably 500 pounds in my wallet. They wouldn't take it even if offered.

So there it was, Cairo on a particular day. And it had only been an *hors d'oeuvre* of what was on offer. In addition to the Islamic, Fatimid and Mamluk remains, there were pharaonic ruins to the west at Giza and Dahshur and, downtown, remnants of much later phenomena, traces of the European period and even of the cold war flirtation with the Eastern Bloc. The city was a giant open-air museum with a little something for everyone. And for all of their misinformation, the museum's courteous docents—the people of Cairo—were always ready to assist an outsider. It seemed to be a rule that the poorer the neighborhood the readier they were to help. For all of the talk of Islamism, I was never made to feel unwelcome, even in mosques. I sensed hostility only once, in the wretched little neighborhood to the east of the *Bab al-Nasr* where the zealots reportedly ruled. But it was the exception that proved the rule.

How could you not love Cairo.

www.ingramcontent.com/pod-product-compliance
Lightning Source LLC
Chambersburg PA
CBHW050436240426
43661CB00055B/2401